FOREIGN TRADE AND
ECONOMIC CONTROLS IN DEVELOPMENT

A Publication of the Economic Growth Center, Yale University

FOREIGN TRADE AND
ECONOMIC CONTROLS
IN DEVELOPMENT
The Case of United Pakistan

NURUL ISLAM

New Haven and London   Yale University Press

To my children

Designed by Sally Harris
and set in Times Roman type.
Printed in the United States of America by
The Vail-Ballou Press, Binghamton, N.Y.

Library of Congress Cataloging in Publication Data

Islam Nurul.
   Foreign trade and economic controls in development.
   (A Publication of the Economic Growth Center,
Yale University)
   Includes index.
   1. Pakistan—Commercial policy—History.
2. Pakistan—Economic policy. 3. Pakistan—Economic
conditions. I. Title. II. Series: Publication of
the Economic Growth Center, Yale University.
HF1590.5.I84   382′.095491   81-1122
ISBN 0-300-02535-1   AACR2

10 9 8 7 6 5 4 3 2 1

Contents

Tables

Foreword

This volume is one in a series of studies supported by the Economic Growth Center, an activity of the Yale Department of Economics since 1961. The Center is a research organization with worldwide activities and interests. Its purpose is to analyze, both theoretically and empirically, the process of economic growth in the developing nations and the economic relations between the developing and the economically advanced countries. The research program emphasizes the search for regularities in the process of growth and changes in economic structure by means of intercountry and intertemporal studies. Current projects include research on technology choice and transfer, income distribution, employment and unemployment, household behavior and demographic processes, agricultural research and productivity, and international economic relations, including monetary and trade policies, as well as a number of individual country studies. The Center research staff hold professorial appointments, mainly in the Department of Economics, and accordingly have teaching as well as research responsibilities.

The Center administers, jointly with the Department of Economics, the Yale master's degree training program in International and Foreign Economic Administration for economists in foreign central banks, finance ministries, and development agencies. It presents a regular series of seminar and workshop meetings and includes among its publications both book-length studies and journal reprints by staff members, the latter circulated as Center Papers.

Hugh Patrick, Director

Preface

This study of foreign trade and economic controls in relation to the economic development of Pakistan from 1950 to 1970 needs justification on two counts. There have been other studies of the foreign trade regime in Pakistan, such as *Economic Policy and Industrial Growth* (Cambridge, Mass., MIT Press, 1969) and *Pakistan's Industrialization and Trade Policy* (Oxford, England: Oxford University Press, 1970), both by S. R. Lewis. There have also been studies of selected aspects of foreign trade and economic policies in Pakistan. This work may be regarded in some ways as a sequel to the earlier studies. It draws upon earlier findings but supplements, extends, and places them in the wider context of Pakistan's overall development policies and experience.

This study shares many features with the studies undertaken and published by the National Bureau of Economic Research on foreign trade regimes and economic development under the joint editorship of J. N. Bhagwati and A. O. Kruger. It has, however, some special characteristics. First, it emphasizes the analysis of trade and exchange controls in the broader context I have just mentioned. It delves into institutional aspects that have direct or indirect bearing on trade and economic policy issues in relation to economic development. It examines the nature and degree of changes in the intensity of trade and economic controls in Pakistan in response to changing economic circumstances as well as differing perceptions and priorities of policymakers in different periods. It distinguishes two principal periods, the first extending from 1947 to 1958, when economic controls were introduced and strengthened in all their ramifications, with minor fluctuations in their intensity and pattern. The second period, from 1958 to 1970, started with an enthusiastic attempt to dismantle controls and place greater reliance on the price mechanism and private enterprise, but this movement suffered a setback after the 1965 war in India and subsequent changes in economic circumstances, especially a slowing down in the flow of external assistance. The distinction between these periods is necessarily a little arbitrary; the first decade had in fact seen a partial attempt at liberalization in 1955, with a devaluation in the rate of exchange and a modest increase in export-intensive

schemes. Moreover, the relative roles of public and private enterprise changed
and fluctuated over time, with greater emphasis on private enterprise in the
second period, when it acquired some size and economic strength, especially in
West Pakistan, benefiting from substantial government help and assistance in the
earlier period.

Second, the study offers an extended analysis of the employment and income
distributional aspects of economic controls and policymaking in Pakistan. It
deals in some detail with the nature, magnitude, and problems of regional inequality and imbalance in development between East and West Pakistan that
subsequently created economic and political tensions of such magnitude as to
become a major factor in the breakup of United Pakistan. Third, it attempts to
extend the examination of economic controls and policies beyond the static
allocational effects to their impact on savings, capital accumulation, and productivity growth.

The study is divided into three parts. The first examines the principal characteristics of two decades of growth and development in United Pakistan. After a
short introduction to the political and economic setting, part 1 discusses the main
features and priorities of development strategy as well as the institutional aspects
of planning and policymaking machinery. Part 2 discusses in detail the evolution,
structure, and effects of trade and economic controls in Pakistan including an
examination in depth of the institutional aspects of economic controls—a feature
that distinguishes it from the earlier analyses of the subject. It includes an
extensive discussion of export policies and performance and brings together
some hitherto unpublished material. Furthermore, trade and foreign exchange
controls are related to the wider context of domestic policy instruments and
controls. Part 3 extends further the analysis of allocative efficiency and supplements it with an examination of the effects on growth and equity, both interpersonal and interregional.

The experience of United Pakistan has special lessons for both economic
historians and policy analysts. During the 1960s Pakistan was hailed as having
achieved considerable economic progress, in terms of both industrialization and
rapid economic growth. At one stage in the early 1960s its liberalization measures were commended as an example of how policy changes and institutional
reforms can accelerate growth. By the late 1960s economic growth had slowed
down, and policy changes were reversed. Conflict between growth and equity
became acute in a mixed economic system in which the roles of controls and the
price mechanism and of public and private enterprise were changing. The pursuit
of growth objectives without adequate attention to the inequities in distribution
and the lack of widespread participation in the decision-making process had
disastrous political and social consequences.

The study ends in 1970, when the unique features of Pakistan as a country divided between two regions separated by a thousand miles of foreign territory came to an end. Two independent countries emerged from the war in 1971, with very different economic systems, structures, and sociopolitical orientations. Any analysis extending beyond 1970 would have to consist of two books, one on Pakistan (previously called West Pakistan) and one on Bangladesh (previously called East Pakistan).

This book was started in the tumultuous days of 1971, when a war was being waged for the independence of East Pakistan, now Bangladesh. During part of that period I was a fellow at the Economic Growth Center, Yale University. I benefited greatly from suggestions and criticisms from several anonymous reviewers who provided extensive comments for improvement and revision of the manuscript. The revision was undertaken in 1976/77 while I was a fellow at Queen Elizabeth House, Oxford University. The book has taken a long time to complete, and I hope it has benefited from the perspective provided by the lapse of time between 1970 and 1976. During the period covered in the study, I lived through and participated in many of the discussions and controversies related to economic controls and policymaking in Pakistan. I hope that distance in time from the events depicted and analyzed has helped to lend some detachment and objectivity.

I wish to express my gratitude to the Economic Growth Center as well as to Queen Elizabeth House for financial assistance as well as for arrangements for undertaking this study.

PART 1
TWO DECADES OF
GROWTH AND DEVELOPMENT

1

Introduction

"United" Pakistan completed two decades of growth and development in 1970. The first decade was a period of relative stagnation. The second was one of respectable economic performance, judged by standards of similarly placed developing countries. But by the end of two decades the economy developed stresses and strains that were due partly to the pattern of growth itself and partly to the interplay of sociopolitical and economic forces. The interaction of these forces culminated in the breakup of Pakistan in 1971.

Pakistan emerged in August 1947 from the partition of British India. It comprised two geographical areas separated by a thousand miles of Indian territory. East Pakistan was a relatively homogeneous region culturally and linguistically as compared to the more heterogeneous West Pakistan. At independence, Pakistan had a total population of 75 million. It was a major exporter of raw cotton, the world's largest producer of raw jute, and a net exporter of food. Manufacturing capacity was negligible, with the exception of an oil refinery in West Pakistan, a few cotton textile mills, and limited capacity in sugar refining, tea processing, and cement manufacture. The aftermath of partition brought a large influx of refugees to Pakistan and disruption of established trading and financial institutions as well as of the transportation and communication network. The immediate problems of creating a minimum of physical infrastructure and an administrative system drained virtually all its physical and manpower resources. It was only by the early or mid-1950s that attention turned to the problems of development and growth.

There were, however, important changes during the 1950s in the structure of the economy in terms of diversification and industrialization. The rate of growth of the economy quickened during the second decade; progress toward diversification of the economy, away from an almost exclusive dependence on agriculture, continued. Economic policymaking became more sophisticated and administrative experience and skill grew at a rapid pace.

During the 1950s and 1960s the gross national product (GNP), at a 1959/60 factor cost, increased by 3.9 percent per annum, whereas GNP per capita in-

Table 1.1. GNP and Per Capita Income (1959–69 factor cost)

Years	GNP (Rs million)	Population (million)	Growth rate of GNP (%)	Growth rate of population (%)	Per capita income (Rs)	Growth rate of per capita GNP (%)	Current prices GNP per capita (Rs)	Current prices Growth rate of per capita GNP (%)
1949/50	24,466	79			311		253	
			2.6	2.3		0.30		
			2.5 (1949–59)	2.3 (1949–59)		0.2 (1949–59)		2.3 (1949–59)
1954/55	27,908	88			316		318	
			2.4	2.3		0.01		
1959/60	31,439	99			318			
			5.2	2.6		2.6		
1964/65	40,525	112			360			
			5.6 (1959–70)	3.0 (1959–70)		2.65 (1959–70)		
1969/70	54,280	132			410		567	6.0 (1960–70)
			5.7	3.0		2.7		

Sources: Government of Pakistan, Planning Commission, The Third Five Year Plan (May 1965); p. 1; Government of Pakistan, Planning Commission, The Fourth Five Year Plan (July 1970), p. 1; Government of Pakistan, Ministry of Finance, Pakistan Economic Survey, 1969/70, pp. 2–5.

Table 1.2. Structural Change in GNP (Percentage share)

Sector	1949/50	1954/55	1959/60	1964/65	1969/70
Agriculture	60.0	56.1	53.3	49.1	45.0
Manufacturing	5.8	8.0	9.3	11.0	12.0
Large scale	(1.4)	(3.6)	(5.0)	(7.1)	(8.8)
Small scale	(4.4)	(3.4)	(4.3)	(3.9)	(3.2)
Construction	1.0	1.5	2.1	4.4	5.0
Others	32.2	34.4	35.3	35.5	38.0

Sources: The Third Five Year Plan, p. 3; *The Fourth Five Year Plan,* p. 2; J. J. Stern and W. P. Falcon, *Growth and Development in Pakistan, 1955–69,* Harvard University, Center for International Affairs, Occasional Papers no.23 (Apr. 1970), p. 9 (for figures relating to 1954/55 and 1959/60).

creased by about 1.4 percent per annum. The rate of population growth was about 2.5 percent during the entire period. There were significant differences between the first and second decades. During the second decade the growth rates of overall GNP and per capita GNP were, respectively, 5.4 and 2.6 percent, as contrasted with 2.5 and 0.2 percent during the first decade. In terms of absolute per capita income (in 1959/60 prices) there was an increase of barely Rs 7 in the first decade and of Rs 92 during the second decade. In spite of rapid growth during the second decade, Pakistan remained one of the poorest countries in the world. The absolute figures of GNP and rates of growth in different periods are given in table 1.1.

The composition of GNP altered significantly during the two decades, as seen in table 1.2. The most marked changes in the composition of GNP were the growing significance of the manufacturing sector, especially the large-scale industrial sector, construction and services being next in order of importance. Agriculture suffered the expected decline over these years, though it still dominated the economy in 1970. It was valuable as a source of foreign exchange and as a market for the output of the industrial sector. As a source of employment it continued to be critical (see table 1.3).

Pakistan has been a recipient of substantial foreign assistance. Annual average per capita aid was high among the developing countries; its dependence on aid,

Table 1.3. Sources of Employment (In percent)

Sector	1950/51	1954/55	1960/61	1964/65	1969/70
Agriculture	74.8	71.8	68.7	68.3	66.1
Others	25.2	28.2	31.3	31.7	33.9

Source: The Third Five Year Plan, p. 153; Stern and Falcon, *Growth and Development in Pakistan, 1955–69,* p. 161.

expressed as a percentage of imports financed by aid, was even higher. There was a consistent increase in the ratio of external assistance to GNP throughout the period up to 1964/65. The percentage of foreign payments financed by aid, however, continued to rise up to the end of the 1960s.

APPENDIX

Table 1A1. Sectoral Rates of Growth

Sector	1949/50–1959/60	1954/44–1959/60	1959/60–1964/65	1964/65–1969/70
Agriculture	1.3	1.4	3.5	4.5
Manufacturing	7.4	5.3	8.6	6.8
Others	3.5	3.0	6.7	6.9

Sources: The Third Five Year Plan, p. 2; Stern and Falcon, *Growth and Development,* p. 9; *The Fourth Five Year Plan,* p. 21.

Table 1A2. Visible Trade (Annual average in Rs million)

	Exports	Imports	Balance
1950/51–1954/55	1,716.2	1,492.4	+223.8
1955/56–1959/60	1,594.1	1,949.8	−355.8
1960/61–1964/65	2,102.0	3,984.0	−1,882.0
1965/66–1969/70	2,967.9	4,738.0	−1,768.6

Source: Central Statistical Office, *Pakistan Economic Survey 1969/70,* statistical appendix.

Table 1A3. Invisible Trade (Annual average in Rs million)

	Exports	Imports	Balance
1950/51–1954/55	171.9	568.8	−396.9
1955/56–1959/60	292.5	890.6	−598.1
1960/61–1964/65	488.9	1,091.5	−602.6
1965/66–1969/70	792.5	1,896.4	−1,076.9

Source: State Bank of Pakistan, *Balance of Payments of Pakistan,* for individual years.

Table 1A4. Trade Ratios

GNP	1954/55	Yearly average 1954–60	1959/60	Yearly average 1959–65	1964/65	Yearly average 1964–70	1969/70
Exports	8.0	5.8	5.6	5.3	5.9	5.0	4.1
Imports	7.1	7.1	7.5	10.1	11.1	8.0	6.2

Source: Ministry of Finance, *Pakistan Economic Survey 1969/70,* pp. 4–5, 103.

2

Economic Planning and Institutions

Economic planning in Pakistan started in a major way with the First Five Year Plan in 1955. That the discipline of the plan was honored more in its breach than in its observance did not detract from the quality of the exercise or from the fact that it was the first comprehensive statement of the problems of economic development in Pakistan.

The First Plan was primarily concerned with the public sector program, which consisted of a number of large projects, many of which were inherited from the preplan period. The private sector investment program was more in the nature of broad projections. Although the plan did profess multiple objectives such as income growth, employment expansion, and distributive justice, in addition to specific goals in social services and in food production, the basic criterion for the selection of the investment program was its contribution to income and output.

This was also true of the Second Five Year Plan starting in 1959/60 even though it did cover the private sector investment targets in a more systematic manner. The process of planning private industrial investment was systematized in the form of the Industrial Investment Schedule, which indicated the broad industry groups and the quantum of investment therein that the private sector was expected, or was to be persuaded, to invest. The financial institutions and industrial licensing agencies were assigned the task of implementing the industrial plan. These private sector targets were to be pursued mainly by means of indirect controls in the form of fiscal and monetary policies or incentives.

The methodology of planning in both the First and Second Plans consisted of determining the size of investment by a process of trial and error in the framework of a simple Harrod–Domar type of model. The available resources from domestic savings and the expected availability of foreign aid were estimated first; the expected growth of income was thus derived. If the target income growth rate, resulting from the expected savings rate and the rate of capital inflow, was considered too low, in view of the rate of increase of population and

8

popular expectation of the rise in the levels of living, the target was raised upward. The implications in terms of a higher rate of domestic saving or capital inflow were explored. Despite the limitations, the formulation of plans in this manner, stating the objectives of growth and resource requirements, had helped Pakistan to negotiate consistently and effectively for an increasing rate of capital inflow to supplement domestic resources.

Only in a very limited way in the First Plan and to much greater extent in the Second Plan, attempts were made to ensure a certain minimum of intersectoral consistency. In the absence of a comprehensive, multisector input–output framework, the aim was an approximate balance between the supply and demand of the important, key commodities like steel, construction materials, and power. Attempts were made to forecast consumption demand for important industrial and major agricultural commodities on the basis of expected increase in population and a rough estimate of income elasticity of demand. It was only in the course of the preparation of the Third Five Year Plan that a comprehensive input–output framework was used to seek intersectoral consistency. In addition, on the basis of alternative rates of targeted growth rates of income and final demand, the implications in terms of investment as well as of foreign exchange requirements were explored and were matched against the expected saving and export possibilities. Furthermore, the implications of alternative rates of saving and growth of exports as well as agricultural growth rates were explored.

As in many developing countries the rate of domestic saving, especially the rate of public saving, became the major issue at the time of the preparation of each plan. Attention was focused on the size of the public investment program. This was not only the crucial determinant of plan size but also the main means for attracting foreign aid. In this context the tax effort of the government assumed a central role and the debate for and against a big public investment program became a debate between the Ministry of Finance and the Planning Commission, the former urging caution and conservatism and the latter advocating bold, new departures and larger programs. The State Bank of Pakistan (the Central Bank) threw its weight on the side of conservatism, since failure to raise taxes implied deficit financing and militated against the pursuit of monetary discipline.

In terms of achievement or fulfillment of planned targets of investment and output the First Plan was a failure. On the other hand, the Second Plan was more than successful in the sense of overfulfilling targets. The skeptics, however, argued that the targets were too modest. In fact the most significant development in the Second Plan took place in agriculture in directions that were not foreseen in the Plan. The considerable increase in investment in private tube wells, aided by a liberal import policy for their components, made major substantial contributions to increase in gains in agricultural output in West Pakistan. This more than offset the shortfall in planned expansion of public irrigation and permitted the gains from the use of fertilizers to achieve its potential in increasing agricultural production.

The beginnings of the Third Five Year Plan in 1965 were marred by the outbreak of Indo-Pakistan hostilities, a suspension and then a reduction of foreign assistance, two consecutive years of bad harvests, leading to a rise in food imports, and a rise in defense expenditures. The Plan had to be revised downward and intersectoral priorities were changed. There was a greater emphasis on quick yielding projects, on the utilization of existing capacity, and on import-saving industrial investment. The rates of saving and investment fell short not only of the Plan targets but also of the levels reached toward the end of the Second Five Year Plan.

STRATEGIES OF PLANS

The strategy of development in terms of intersectoral priorities raised few controversies in Pakistan, especially during the 1950s. The priority of investment in physical infrastructure was obvious. Pakistan inherited very little large-scale industry at independence. Given large internal market demand and the availability of domestic raw materials such as jute, cotton, sugar cane, hides, skins, and wool, the major lines of advance in the field of industry, based on such raw materials and conforming to its comparative advantage, were easily recognized. Import substitution in these sectors proceeded apace. Policies were geared to give additional stimulus to this pattern of import substitution.

However, it was not until the early 1960s, when Pakistan had already achieved a reasonable rate of progress in the consumer goods industries, that questions were raised regarding the relative emphasis on consumer goods vis-à-vis capital goods industries. It was argued that there was an overexpansion of consumption goods, with the result that the rate of saving was lower than what the Five Year Plan projected.[1] It was suggested that the pressure exercised by those who were involved in investment in the consumer goods industries militated against a significant rise in taxes to mobilize savings. In view of high initial costs and overvaluation of the exchange rate they were unable to compete in the export markets. Any restraint on domestic consumption would have caused excess capacity, low profits, and unemployment in the most important sector of the domestic manufacturing industry and would have had adverse consequences for private enterprise. This argument had some validity, especially in the early

1. A. R. Khan, "Import Substitution, Export Expansion and Consumption Liberalization: A Preliminary Report," *Pakistan Development Review* 3, no. 2 (Summer 1963): 208–31; J. H. Power, "Industrialization in Pakistan: A case of frustrated take-off," *Pakistan Development Review* 3, no. 2 (Summer 1963): 191–207.

period. Yet the question really was whether these consumers' goods industries were not overexpanded in the first place.[2]

The familiar argument that developing countries with bleak prospects for primary exports and rising requirements of capital goods should produce their own investment goods had its adherents in Pakistan. The requirements of capital goods industries in terms of skills, large domestic markets, and considerable resource base were judged surmountable in the context of Pakistan. Examples of countries such as Japan were invoked to demonstrate that it was possible to break the barriers of skill and inadequate natural resources. Further, capital goods were said to have a dynamic world market, which was not available to light consumer goods.[3] With appropriate exchange rates, many of the import substituting industries could export as well.

Intersectoral allocations of investment funds in the industrial sector as well as in the rest of the economy underwent significant changes over the decades. The increasing emphasis on agriculture in later years was evident from the rise in the proportion of investment in agriculture from 7.0 percent in the First Plan to 15 percent in the Third Plan. This was accompanied by a decline in the relative importance of investment allocated to industry, fuels, and minerals. The investment in such basic infrastructure as water, power, and transportation, most of which was related to agriculture, retained its importance throughout the planning period. In the Third Plan, the composition of indusrial investment was also geared to the needs of this sector, as evidenced by greater emphasis on fertilizer and agricultural implements. The allocation to education was low relative to the manpower requirements of the economy. As years went by, implementation of plans faced the crucial bottleneck in trained people. Education claimed barely 3.8 percent of investment resources in the Second Plan and 5.1 percent in the Third. Even the composition of this meager investment was inappropriate, most of it being geared to urban high income groups. The nature of the education system was ill suited to the needs of development. While there was a critical shortage of medium-level technicians there was an abundance of liberal arts and science graduates. Barely 4 percent of the children at the secondary level received technical education. The annual compound growth rate of educational enrollment was 5.8 percent at the primary level, 7 percent at the secondary level, and 12.7 percent at the college and university level. Throughout the entire period of

2. G. Papanek, *Pakistan's Development: Social Goals and Private Incentives* (Cambridge: Harvard University Press, 1967), chaps. 3, 8.

3. Subsequent experience demonstrated that export pessimism in the field of light consumer goods was not totally warranted. In later plans, however, greater emphasis was placed on investment, and intermediate and capital goods industries. Government of Pakistan, Planning Commission, *Heavy Industry in Pakistan* (Karachi, 1962).

planned development the highest allocation to health was of the order of 2 percent. Even though hospital beds increased from 17,000 in 1949–50 to 39,000 in 1969–70, while doctors went from 3,000 to 21,000, there was in 1970 only one doctor for 7,000 people, one hospital for 3,500, and one nurse for 20,000. However, health and education always suffered when a cut in the development program was needed. The intersectoral allocations were governed to a certain extent by such considerations as the initiative and efficiency of the sponsoring and executing departments or agencies of the government in charge of various sectors. The departments or ministries of social sectors were often the weakest. The competent and powerful civil servants habitually gravitated toward economic ministries rather than ministries in charge of social sectors. It was to the former that power and prestige belonged, especially in a regime of licensing and controls. Because competence in project preparation and implementation was a vital factor in determining allocation, the social sectors suffered.

PLANNING MACHINERY

An analysis of the institutional framework, particularly the political and administrative framework, is essential for an understanding of the economic development efforts as well as policymaking in Pakistan. The history of Pakistan's political and administrative development can be conveniently divided into two distinct periods. The first period comprised the decade between 1947 and 1958 and the second one started in 1958 and continued throughout the 1960s. The first decade was characterized by excessive political instability. The governments that were formed on the basis of unstable coalitions among political parties changed frequently, with the result that there was no continuity either in policymaking or in its execution. Commitment to economic development was low. Constitution making was the primary concern of political parties and government alike during most of the 1950s. The fact that a six-year development program was hastily put together in 1950 was more fortuitous than anything else. It consisted mainly of projects and programs, that were approved by the government for the public sector and were not examined in relation to either consistency or efficiency.

A Planning Board was first established in 1954 with the help of foreign technical assistance. The First Five Year Plan was the first comprehensive statement of Pakistan's economic problems and priorities. Its principal achievement was not so much in providing a consistent and an efficient intersectoral balance but rather in analyzing the critical problems of Pakistan's economic development. For the first time the policymakers were presented with the alternatives involved and the range of considerations that should go into the final choice among alternatives. Unfortunately the Planning Board was not given adequate political support. Its role and status were not clearly defined and its leadership did not have political backing. As the Second Plan document puts it, "There were several reasons for the failure (of the First Plan): political instability, absence of sustained endeavours, lack of imaginative approach, organizational problems requiring urgent solutions and nonobservance of the discipline of the Plan. Yet in explanation it must be remembered that the preparation of the First Plan was not completed until near the middle of the five year period which it covered and that it never received formal sanction at the highest levels of the government, with the result that efforts demanded for its implementation were not expended."[4]

The second decade, starting in 1959, saw important changes in all the categories in which the First Five Year Plan displayed shortcomings. The new military government, although suspending all political activity and all popular participation in government, accorded at the same time high priority to economic development efforts. But in its attempt to channel the energies of the people toward the goal of economic development the military government used the civil service as the primary organizational weapon.

The planning machinery was raised in status and was given additional responsibility as a result of the criticisms expressed. Its functions were expanded to cover foreign aid negotiations and annual or short-term economic policymaking. Thus the discipline of the Plan was brought to bear on the annual budgets, which incorporated not only the yearly breakdown of development projects but also short- and long-term fiscal and other economic policies designed to implement the plan. The President himself became chairman of the Planning Commission, which was included in his own secretariat.

The National Economic Council, under the chairmanship of the president, was the supreme decision-making body in matters of economic development and policy. The Planning Commission served as a technical secretariat of the National Economic Council. Strains in the relationship between the planning and finance ministries proved to be manageable.[5] The prestige of the Commission was at least partly derived from its exclusive role in aid negotiations and partly from its role in relation to the National Economic Council, which was presided over by one who was the chief executive of the country as well as of the Planning Commission. The quality of the staff of the Planning Commission and its analytical ability improved considerably over the years with the result that the growing sophistication in the Commission's professional work vis-à-vis other ministries, including finance, provided it with an additional advantage, thereby enhancing its position in the economic decision-making process.

4. Government of Pakistan, Planning Commission, *The Second Five Year Plan (1960–65)* (1960), p. xiii.

5. The finance minister was a strong supporter of the planning process, which diminished the potential for traditional conflict between the planning and finance ministries.

ROLE OF THE CIVIL SERVICE

The government, which provided the political support to the planning machinery, was run by civilian bureaucrats and army officers. Although after 1962 President Mohammad Ayub Kahn did involve the elected representatives to a limited extent, the ultimate power always lay in the hands of the president. A government such as this was not subject to the shifting compromises among different political parties with divergent and often conflicting interests. However, the preeminence of the civil servant in the decision-making process predated the establishment of this authoritarian government. Rapid changes of government and considerable uncertainty regarding political leadership during the 1950s meant that the civil servants were the most permanent element in the system. They provided the necessary continuity in decision making and administration. Over time they arrogated to themselves, almost by default, power and responsibility that belonged to political leadership in a properly functioning democracy. They became a force by themselves. The top echelon of the civil service was a closed group; it did not allow multipoint entry into its fold from other professions. Recruited to the civil service early in life they were groomed to occupy top positions by dint of their membership in this service and by seniority. ''The size and nature of the civil service establishment meant first, that the government had an instrument for the effective execution of policies and programs; second, that government effectiveness was extremely variable, since the civil service was much stronger in some fields; third, that the really able and experienced civil servants were a tiny group, one of the scarcest resources in Pakistan.''[6] In this context economic policy was almost exclusively the result of decisions taken by government officials. Private businessmen and industrialists did not have the social prestige of the civil servants; in fact, they had inherited the lowly status of their predecessors, who were mostly petty traders and small industrialists. The natural assumption of the businessman, officials, and the public, therefore, was that the government should dominate the economy.

During the 1960s the relative positions of the various interest groups in the economy underwent important changes. By that time there were industrialists who wielded significant economic power through concentration of control over industrial and financial enterprises. The previous humility of the petty traders vis-à-vis the government officials began to give way to the arrogance of the emerging industrial bourgeoisie. There was an increasing interlocking of interests among the bureaucracy, the landed interests, and the industrialists largely through mobility of the members from one group to another.[7] It is not only that

6. Papanek, *Pakistan's Development*, p. 179.

7. S. T. Burki, ''Group Interests in a Practorian Society—A Case of Ayub's Pakistan,'' unpublished manuscript, Center for International Affairs, Harvard University, 1970. This paper contains a very good discussion of the role of various interest groups in Pakistan's political development.

the bureaucrats developed interests in business and land through direct investment but also that the landed interests and business classes sent more of the members of their class to the civil service. In fact, intragroup mobility was more in the direction of the children of civil service workers entering industrial and business careers.

Thus increasingly through the 1960s the close interrelationship of interests between those who made economic policy and those whose fortunes were affected by economic policy decisions created new pressures in the field of economic policymaking. Whereas in the 1950s the weak bargaining power of the special interest groups in the economic life of the country gave the bureaucracy a relatively free hand, except in agriculture and matters related to agriculture,[8] during the 1960s it had to accommodate increasingly the interests of the army, who exercised the ultimate political power, as well as those of the business classes and landed oligarchy, with whom the army developed close interrelationships.

There was a dichotomy between East and West Pakistan in terms of the composition of economic interest groups. In the East there was neither a landed gentry nor a large industrial class. The political pressure groups were mainly the rural and urban middle classes. With the imposition of the authoritarian regime in 1958, there was no way for the various interest groups to generate pressure openly. Public issues could not be brought into the open for debate or discussion. The more powerful among the interest groups, in West Pakistan, the landed gentry and businessmen, could directly operate and influence government decision making without the aid of a legislative process. Their pressure was more concentrated and more effective because these interest groups were small and well organized. In contrast the middle classes were diffused and unorganized and needed the institutions of democratic government to make their influence felt. This class division coincided with the regional division. The landed and business interests were mainly concentrated in the West. Thus the bias in policymaking was inevitable.

POLITICAL INSTITUTIONS

Ayub introduced the system of "basic democracy" in 1962. The local governments elected directly by the people were the principal pillars of the system. The members of the local government elected in turn the national parliament, which had very limited financial and legislative powers. This allowed the rural middle classes a role in the governments of local institutions. However, they were still excluded from any direct participation in national affairs. Moreover,

8. During the 1950s the students and the urban middle classes, especially lawyers, undoubtedly had an active political role. However, an unstable political government and as a consequence ineffective legislative processes meant that these groups could not make their influence felt in economic policymaking.

some members of the local governments were nominated by the president of the country to the extent that their autonomy was diluted. Subsequently, the president himself was elected by members of the local government. Urban middle classes were effectively disenfranchised because their role was limited to voting for the "basic democrats," i.e., members of the local government. The basic democrats, who elected the members of the national parliament, were small in number. They were vulnerable to manipulation by the civil servants through the mechanism of economic patronage because the government exercised wide powers of control and regulation of economic activity. The members of the indirectly elected parliament came from the landed aristocracy, business interests, lawyers, and urban professionals in that order of importance. The predominance of the first two groups was most pronounced in West Pakistani members of parliament.

Economic policy, therefore, had to be based on significant compromises with such interest groups as the landed and business oligarchy. Only in East Pakistan was it subject to the pressures of middle classes. The absence of big industrial and landed interests made the urban middle class the most vocal group.

The economic policies of this period encouraged and connived at the concentration of urban economic power. A major consequence of this pattern of development was inadequate attention to investment in social sectors such as education, health, and social welfare, which could have otherwise broadened the participation of the poorer classes in the fruits of economic development. There was increasing disaffection among the poorer classes in the urban and rural areas. The fall of Ayub in 1969 was not only due to the result of agitation by the urban middle classes (lawyers, students, and other professionals) reacting against their political disenfranchisement. It was largely fed by discontent common among the industrial workers and the poorer peasants, who felt that they did not obtain an adequate share in the fruits of economic progress.

The change in the military leadership in 1969 following Ayub's downfall seemed for a while to recognize the weakness of Ayub's political experiment. They held out a promise to meet the demands of the workers, peasants, and students for greater participation in economic and political life. The new regime found this promise increasingly difficult to fulfill in the course of its two-year administration, which lasted until March 1971.

RELATIVE ROLE OF PUBLIC AND PRIVATE SECTORS

The relative role of private and public investment appears to have followed an uneven course during the two decades of Pakistan's economic development. In the early years, before comprehensive development planning started, the private sector accounted for a greater proportion of the total investment in the country.

The Industrial Policy Statement of 1949 laid down the major outlines of policy. Except in the manufacture of ammunitions, hydroelectric power, railway and other communications equipment, the entire industrial field was left to private enterprise. The state, however, could take over an industry vital to its security and well-being or could own new enterprises in any field if private enterprise was not forthcoming.[9]

In 1949–50 about 60 percent of the monetized investment was in the private sector and the proportion increased to 67 percent in 1954/55, just before the First Five Year Plan was initiated. The performance of the private sector was limited by the absence of infrastructure and of the basic services that only the public sector could provide.

The First Five Year Plan in 1955 described the role of private enterprise as follows:

> Private enterprise has to play an important role in implementing the Plan. As an agency for economic development it has large advantages. It permits a high degree of decentralization, with authority placed in close contact with the actual production, so that no long chain of intermediaries is necessary. The management of one's property is apt to be conducted with much better care than the management of publicly owned resources. . . . The public agencies will have large and growing responsibilities of their own and the assignment to them of tasks which can be successfully accomplished by private enterprise will restrict the base of development. The primary social functions of private ownership are the accumulation and productive investment of capital, and the development of new and better methods of providing the goods and services which people need. If these social responsibilities are realised and discharged, it can be said that the private interest in profit and the public interest in economic development are brought together.[10]

The First Five Year Plan elaborated the special circumstances and considerations associated with the role of public enterprise. First, there was the need for a substantial investment on social overhead capital and services; second, there would be industries in untried fields, in which private enterprise would not be interested because of their technical complexity, high capital requirements, or relatively low profitability. Third, most of the foreign loans from abroad were channeled through the government budget that made it necessary for effective utilization for loans.[11] As a result, during the First Five Year Plan there was a

9. J. R. Andrus and A. F. Mohammed, *The Economy of Pakistan* (New York: Oxford University Press, 1958), pp. 159–60.

10. Government of Pakistan, National Planning Board, *The First Five Year Plan (1955–60)* (Dec. 1957), pp. 85–87.

11. But the last argument for public enterprise was not convincing. It is conceivable that, if private

great shift toward public sector investment in basic facilities and by 1959/60 the share of the private sector in the total fixed monetized investment was only 34 percent. This did not indicate any absolute decline of private investment; in fact private investment by the end of the First Plan was about 30 percent higher than the level of 1954/55.

During the Second Five Year Plan the share of the private sector increased again to about 44 percent and during the Third Plan it constituted 45 percent of the total monetized investment.[12] The public sector investment never fell below 55 percent. The key factors were the large-scale investment in physical infrastructure, water, power, transportation, and communications—all of which were in the public sector. In industry there were two factors that, in spite of growing private investment, did not reduce the share of public investment. With changing patterns of industrialization and a greater emphasis on intermediate and capital goods industries, which, because of large capital requirements and technical complexity, did not attract private enterprise, the public sector was assigned the responsibility of developing the more complicated heavy industries. Secondly, there were attempts to redress inequities in the geographical and regional distribution of industries. In East Pakistan, where private capital fell short of targets during all the plan periods, the public sector had to step in to fill up the vacuum. But this recourse was grossly inadequate with respect to the explicit objective of reducing disparity.

In the mid-1960s questions were raised about the performance of the private sector in terms of its efficiency and contribution to economic development. There was a feeling that private enterprise had led to a concentration of income and wealth in a few hands. The increased interlocking of industrial interests, on the one hand, and financial and banking interests, on the other, implied that concentration in one field aided the emergence of centralized control in the other. Such concentration prevented the entry of new enterprises and the development of professional management. The government tried to mitigate the undesirable effects by encouraging small-scale enterprises. The Pakistan Industrial Credit and Investment Corporation (PICIC) and the Industrial Development Bank of Pakistan (IDBP) were established to give more attention to small enterprises or new entrants; attempts were made to orient the import policy toward welcoming new entrants into import trade. There were also various tax incentives, specially designed to induce private enterprise into backward regions in West Pakistan and

---

enterprise were willing to enter a particular field or undertake a particular project, the public sector could channel funds to it through the budget either as loans or as grants. This was indeed done in the subsequent years in Pakistan.

12. Government of Pakistan, Planning Commission, *The Fourth Five Year Plan (1970–75)* (July 1970).

East Pakistan. There were attempts to liberalize import controls and to adopt fiscal devices that would be less discriminatory between the small and big industrial and trading enterprises. These measures were very limited in scope and even then they were adopted only in the second half of the second decade. It was too early to assess their effects and in any case they were not expected to produce significant results.

PART 2

TRADE AND ECONOMIC CONTROLS
IN PAKISTAN:
THEIR EVOLUTION, STRUCTURE, AND EFFECTS

3

Introduction

During the two decades of development in Pakistan, economic controls constituted crucial instruments of economic policy in Pakistan. History, politics, ideol-
ogy, and psychology—all contributed to the introduction of a wide variety of
measures of direct intervention in its economic system. Economic controls had
fluctuated in intensity and variety over the years. Intervention depended on the
changing economic circumstances and the shifting attitudes of the policymakers
toward price mechanism versus controls; there were years of relative liberalization followed by a period of intensification.

The economic considerations that underlay the introduction of controls related
to efficiency and equity. Under a private enterprise system the working of the
price mechanism was thought to create elements of monopoly and to generate
forces of inequality. In Pakistan there was a growing tendency toward concentration of economic power and fortunes in a few hands in the industrial and trading
system. Given the initial unequal distribution of assets and income, a free play of
market forces tended to accentuate them. Unequal ownership of assets provided
unequal access to income, to loan capital and credit facilities, and to information
and education; it cumulatively increased opportunities for earning higher incomes. Access to capital markets was highly skewed. Controls were intended to
allocate resources and income-generating capacity more equitably. These factors
related to the system of both industrial and trade controls.

Controls were also introduced in several instances because it was felt that
adjustment of imbalances, often short term, between supply and demand required
in the short term major or discontinuous changes in prices. Given the unequal
distribution of income, major changes in prices were likely to lead to inequitable
consequences for income distribution and would have imposed intolerable bur-
dens on the poor. Controls were particularly invoked in periods of shortage of
supplies or of excess demand. If shortages were short term or temporary, the
reliance on the price mechanism to equilibrate supply and demand would provide
signals for a degree of adjustment and changes in supply and demand that were
likely to be far in excess of the needs of long-run equilibrium. This would have

created or indeed aggravated instability in prices as well as in supply and demand, especially when there are lags in the process of adjustment of supply and demand. Excessively high prices under the pressure of short-term shortages would depress demand well below the long-run equilibrium level or would stimulate supply in excess of long-run requirements. This would result in a misallocation of resources. Hence there was a strong predilection toward the imposition of controls wherever short-term shortages developed. However, the difficulty was that the distinction between short- and long-term shortages was not clear and it was not readily obvious in all cases that short-term shortages or imbalances were not likely to persist. In other words the policymakers were not always sure in their diagnosis of the nature of disequilibrium between supply and demand, i.e., whether they were short or long term in nature; also they were not certain about price elasticities of demand and supply.

Also, the adjustment of shortages through price changes was not favored because price rises were likely to push the supplies out of the reach of the poor, who would thus be deprived of what was thought to be their equitable share of scarce supplies. The introduction of controls over price and distribution was thus thought to be the only way to ensure an equitable access by the poor. Seldom were there stocks in the hands of the public agencies or private sellers or consumers to tide over short-term disequilibrium by releasing from or accumulating stocks. Usually there was not only insufficiency of stocks, but also lack of any assurance that private stocks would serve a stabilizing or an equilibrating function. No less significant was the impetus to speculative forces that reliance on price mechanism in a period of shortage might provide. The speculators and hoarders tended to aggravate shortage by withdrawing supplies from the market; the consumers tended to store up in anticipation of future shortages. Direct interventions were considered an antidote to such speculative forces. Therefore, the smaller the stocks of goods and services, including foreign exchange resources, the greater the likelihood of resort to controls in periods of imbalances between supply and demand.

Moreover, once introduced in the short run, controls tended to outlast the short-term factors that brought them into being. First, experience with controls on the part of public officials often made them conscious of their power over economic life, and they were reluctant to surrender their newfound power. Second, experience with the administration of controls to deal with short-term shortages encourages them to use controls for long-term aims of correcting market imperfections with a view to achieving equity and efficiency.

There were also divergences between private and social costs and benefits that reliance on the price mechanism could not take into account. Controls were deemed necessary to take external economies into account in allocational decisions governing the alternative uses of resources. This was true not only in the case of the industrial investment decisions but also in agriculture, for example, in respect to allocation of land under alternative crops.

Private enterprise or the decision-making process could underestimate the future, ignore external economies and social benefits, and could be unaware of or neglect national security. For example, self-sufficiency in the domestic production of items of essential need, including food, was often motivated by political and strategic considerations rather than strictly economic ones.

Given the choice between direct and indirect controls, i.e., taxes and subsidies, the preference of the policymakers for the former was partly based upon the fact that the indirect controls worked out their effects slowly, and often their precise impact was uncertain. The results of changes in the instruments of indirect control such as taxes and subsidies were not always predictable or quantifiable in terms of their impact on consumption, production, and trade. Whereas the impact of direct controls on investment, consumption, imports and exports, and so forth was apparent and easily quantifiable, that of indirect controls such as fiscal and monetary policies was uncertain. The latter required time to work out their effects through the forces of the market, through the responses of the individual decision makers to changes in prices, incomes, or assets, which indirect measures may bring about. The precise quantitative magnitude of the response of the buyers or sellers, traders or investors was uncertain.

Historically, Pakistan at birth as a new country in 1947 inherited an elaborate system of controls from the British administration. Many of these controls were introduced by the British administration during World War II. The civil servants of Pakistan who had worked in British India during the war were familiar with the nature and administration of these controls. Also the civil servants believed that controls were both effective and efficient. Controls were thought more efficient not only because the civil servants who enacted them felt that they were better educated and less tradition bound than the private individuals functioning via the market mechanism, but also because they felt that they had a wider horizon and were less obsessed with self-interest than the petty traders and newly emerging industrialists who would work to bend the market forces in their own favor. The private entrepreneurs had inadequate information or had little knowledge or expertise to use the information or to react to interpret the price and market signals. Throughout the 1950s public investment extended to a wide range of economic activities. Public ownership combined a system of direct controls over private enterprise, often considered a natural extension of the role of the government to achieve primary economic or social objectives. To public officials, public ownership signaled abridgement of the functioning of the price mechanism; therefore, it was assumed that for public sector managers, it was not necessary to rely on the price mechanism to guide and determine the allocation of resources.

There was in fact a vicious circle in this system of controls. When some controls were established, it was often found necessary to extend controls over a wider area to make the existing controls effective. One set of controls led to another. Price controls led to distribution controls because otherwise price controls remained ineffective. The controls over distribution or rationing of supplies eventually led to the controls over production or to the allocation of production targets or quotas to the individual production units. The controls over imports or foreign trade led to controls over all dealings in foreign exchange, for both visible and invisible transactions.

Similarly, the controls over output led to the controls over inputs, which were used in the production process. The key inputs, such as cement, steel, iron, and oil, were critical in securing the desired composition of final output. Again, the controls over total supplies eventually extended to the controls over exports and imports because supplies available for domestic consumption were dependent not only on output but also on imports and exports. The controls tended to proliferate because commodities were interrelated as either substitutes or complements of each other on either the side of demand or that of supply; there was, in addition, interrelationship between inputs and outputs so that the controls over one led to the establishment of controls over another.

As experience with the administration of the economic controls accumulated and their effects on the growth, efficiency, or equity were evaluated, there was a recognition that although the price mechanism had its inefficiencies and imperfections, direct controls had their own inefficiencies and limitations, which were often serious. Moreover, unequal ownership of assets and inequity of incomes and opportunities not only created distributional inequities in the operation of the price mechanism but also generated inequities in the administration of controls. Inequality of political power, originating at least partly from inequality of economic power, and interplay of group interests based on regional or occupational interests or on castes or creeds, affected the way in which and objectives for which controls were used. Furthermore, the distribution of the benefits of controls tended to be directed favorably toward those groups that had political power or institutional leverage over the administrators of controls and dispensers of public bounties. The evaluation by the policymakers of the relative costs and benefits of the price mechanism versus controls fluctuated over time, but at no point was there a tendency to abandon controls entirely to the free play of prices and market forces. There was, on the whole, a bias in favor of controls, whatever combination of prices and controls was chosen in a given period.

Part 2 deals with the genesis and operation of the economic controls in terms primarily, but not exclusively, of exchange and trade controls. Chapter 3 deals with the rationale of economic controls in Pakistan. Chapter 4 provides a historical overview of the exchange control system and its evolution through time.

Chapters 5 and 6 deal, respectively, with the operation of the import and export controls and their consequences on foreign trade and the domestic economy. Chapter 7 discusses the attempts at liberalization of exchange controls in the 1960s and their consequences. Chapter 8 treats the domestic policy instruments and controls, which interact in diverse ways with trade controls.

4

The Exchange Control System: A Historical Overview

EMERGENCE OF QUANTITATIVE RESTRICTIONS AND CONTROLS

The first phase in the evolution of exchange rate policy in Pakistan extended from 1947 to 1955. In this early period, two significant external developments molded the exchange control policy. One was the devaluation of a large number of currencies in 1949 following the devaluation of the British pound. The other was the Korean War boom and the following slump of the early 1950s. The overvaluation of the rupee, the liberal import system of 1950–52, and the subsequent imposition of stringent import controls in this period can be best seen against this backdrop.

In 1949 Pakistan decided not to devalue. The nondevaluation decision could have been justified on various grounds. It was believed—not quite correctly as events later demonstrated—that export receipts would remain unaffected partly because export demand was assumed to be inelastic, and partly because returns to principal export crops in terms of domestic prices were deemed adequate to secure increasing supplies. Import demand was also assumed to be inelastic because of Pakistan's heavy dependence on imports of capital goods and manufactured consumer goods, virtually none of which it produced. Devaluation would therefore raise the import bill without an offsetting increase in export earnings. The cost of investment would rise, and the higher prices of imported consumer goods would add fuel to the inflationary process and neutralize the negligible competitive advantage gained by exports. In addition there was perhaps an underlying concern to maintain existing exchange rates.[1]

The relevance of the arguments advanced in favor of Pakistan's decision not to devalue was difficult to test for two reasons. One was the deadlock in trade with India. The other was the Korean War boom, which resulted in an unprecedented increase in export earnings. The deadlock in trade with India was the result of

---

1. A. F. A. Husain, "Pakistan's Commercial Policy in the Recession," *Pakistan Economic Journal* 4, no. 1 (May 1954): 72.

that country's refusal to recognize Pakistan's nondevaluation and of India's devaluation. India's action was prompted by its own needs and by the belief that Pakistan's overwhelming dependence on the Indian market would force Pakistan to reconsider the decision. Pakistan's decision not to devalue meant that India's existing balance of payments deficit with Pakistan would be further aggravated. This it could not afford because a decline in trade between the two would be inevitable.[2]

The surge associated with the Korean War, on the other hand, created an accelerated increase in world demand for raw materials. Export receipts increased phenomenally. This expansion nullified the effects of reduced trade with India and permitted easier access to international markets. In view of Pakistan's urgent need to diversify her imports geographically this was very fortunate. Pakistanis had little or no experience in the conduct of foreign trade. Most trading houses and firms remained in India. A relaxation of controls was a prerequisite to encouraging the growth of indigenous trading classes. Large export receipts permitted such a phase of free import policy. Thus even without devaluation Pakistan was not faced with foreign exchange problems.

However, by 1951 Pakistan's currency had become considerably overvalued with consequent repercussions on the economy. The principal reason was that Pakistan had a higher rate of inflation than the other trading partners. For the large industrial establishments that imported capital goods and raw materials directly without the intermediary of traders, the cost of imports was indeed low. For the consumer, and the rest of the industrial sector, which relied on commercial importers or traders, the overvaluation of the exchange rate was of no help. The domestic prices of imports went up, including substantial scarcity premiums, which were reaped by the importers. However, the cost of the government-account imports on food and defense was kept low. This obviated the need for either an increase in taxation or a decrease in nondevelopment expenditures, both of which would have helped reduce domestic inflationary pressure.

The post-Korean War recession brought into sharp focus the underlying disequilibrium in Pakistan's external economic relations. The crisis in the balance of payments was created by the sharp fall in export earnings. The onset of the post-Korean War slump did not turn the government's attention to exchange rate adjustment. Instead the crisis was met by the adoption of a stringent system of import controls, buttressed by wide-ranging direct controls on prices, production, and distribution and by a set of differential incentives to individual exports.

The import control system was systematized and made increasingly elaborate. The importers and the exporters were required to be registered by the Controller

2. Under the then prevailing payment arrangements between India and Pakistan all deficits in excess of Rs 150 million by either country had to be settled in sterling.

of Exports and Imports. The compulsory registration of traders provided the government with authority to penalize those who violated the trade control regulations by the cancellation of their registration and, therefore, their right to engage in external trade. Importers were divided into two groups: commercial importers and industrial importers. The former were traders who imported for resale whereas the latter were the actual users of the commodities licensed to be imported. Licenses for neither category of importers were transferable to the nonlicensees. During this period the bulk of the revenue from import duties was derived from imported consumers' goods and raw materials. Most capital goods were either duty free or subject to very low rates. Import duties in this period were more a source of revenue than an instrument for regulating imports, except in a few cases, where the Tariff Commission decided to levy protective duties.[3]

The extent of the import restrictions introduced during this time can be gauged from the decline in the ratio of imports to national income as well as from a decline in the volume of imports during this period compared to the period of free imports, known as the period of Open General License (OGL), between July 1950 and December 1952. There were two distinct aspects to the decline in imports of this period, which accompanied an increase in the degree of direct controls over imports. One was the growing relative increase in imports undertaken directly by the government agencies and the other was a reduction in the proportion of imports subject to regulation of the free market mechanism. The ratio of the government account imports to total imports rose from 18.7 percent from the period of OGL to 25.3 percent during the subsequent period. The index of the private account imports, with the average for the OGL period as the base, fell to 52 in 1953/54, and further to 40 in 1954/55.

In an attempt to expand trade during the same period, Pakistan entered into a number of bilateral trade agreements, most of which were of a permissive nature and did not involve purchases or sales of specified quantities at predetermined prices. However, in view of the limited contacts of Pakistani traders with the outside markets and the relative lack of familarity on the part of overseas purchasers with Pakistani products, these agreements helped to introduce Pakistan's products to foreign markets and thus provided a framework for facilitating trade with a number of countries. Because many of the partner countries were operating some kind of controls on exports and imports an important consequence of the bilateral trade agreements was a mutual agreement to remove obstacles by issuing licenses for imports and exports. Therefore the bilateral trade agreements contributed to a speedy diversification of foreign trade.

The adverse balance of payments during this period, which persisted in spite of

3. By 1954, only 13 industries were granted protection by the Tariff Commission. They were mainly consumers goods industries except for steel rerotting, switchboards, and the manufacture of paints and varnishes. Government of Pakistan, Ministry of Economic Affairs, *Report of the Economic Appraisal Committee* (Nov. 1952).

considerable cuts in imports, was met by drawing upon foreign exchange reserves, accumulated during World War II in the form of pound/sterling reserves. The excess aggregate demand in the economy was further aggravated by monetary expansion during this period. Creation of credit in both the public and private sectors during 1950/51 and 1951/52 led to a substantial increase in the money supply. Although the rate of monetary expansion slowed down in 1952/53, it went up again during the next few years, mainly due to expansion of credit in the public sector. These expansionary forces were only partly moderated by a heavy drawing on the foreign exchange reserves.[4]

This period also witnessed the introduction of a set of wide-ranging controls on prices, production, and internal distribution of commodities to counteract the expansionary monetary policy and an overvalued exchange rate. The policymakers in Pakistan, most of whom were civil servants, had a presumption, partly born out of wartime experience, that a situation of scarcity necessarily involved recourse to direct controls over prices and supplies. The Economic Appraisal Committee, which was the first, most authoritive expert body and was appointed by the government in 1952/53 to examine direct controls which were already in operation at that time, favored the continuance of direct controls in various fields.[5] The official wording was: "Control orders in respect of various commodities should be kept ready and a plan for the administrative organization and procedure should be drawn up in advance. The controls should be introduced as soon as a long-term shortage of the particular item threatens to develop."[6] In the same vein the committee endorsed import controls because they were considered "unavoidable in circumstances where exports were inflexible and export prices were not favourable." Exports of food grains and vital materials were also to be controlled in order to avoid domestic scarcity.

Export promotion then became an important facet of policy. An Export Promotion Committee established in 1952 made the following recommendations:

1. The abolition or a considerable reduction of export duties on agricultural exports;
2. Free imports (without quantitative restrictions) of the import components of manufactured and primary exports as long as the value of exports exceeded the value of the import components;
3. A subsidy to the exporters in the form of import entitlements (fixed as a percentage of exports) to be freely sold in the open market, for use by the importers for the imports of a specified list of commodities, mostly essential items.

4. R. Soligo, "Monetary Problems of Pakistan," *Journal of Political Economy* 75, no. 4, pt. 2 (Aug. 1967): 635–50.
   5. Ministry of Economic Affairs, *Report of the Economic Appraisal Committee*, pp. 90–97.
   6. Ibid., p. 36.

The government followed up on the major recommendation. Export duties on primary exports were reduced or eliminated. Wool was exempted from duty starting in 1952 and the export tax on tea was suspended from 1952 to 1955. The export duty on cotton was reduced substantially by 1955/56. Export duty on raw jute and on hides and skins remained virtually unchanged.

Furthermore an export incentive scheme went into operation in 1954/55. This program allowed exporters of a specified list of primary and manufactured goods to receive a uniform import entitlement of 30 percent of their export proceeds. This entitlement could be freely sold and used for a specific list of imports, most of which were inessential consumer goods in scarce supply. The items that were eligible for this export incentive scheme were of relatively minor importance and covered merely 1.7 percent of the total exports in 1954/55. Despite these measures the major exports of Pakistan continued to be sluggish.

The continued stagnation in the volume and the prices of major primary exports aggravated Pakistan's difficulties in export trade. Although the overvaluation of the exchange rate kept down the rupee receipts from the export cash crops such as jute and cotton, their relative price vis-à-vis the prices of the competing alternative crops dropped from an average of 107 during 1951/52–1953/54 to 64 during 1955/56.[7] The adverse movement in the relative prices was greater for cotton than for jute. The domestic prices of other export crops such as tea and wool improved, while the domestic prices of hides and skins maintained the high level reached in 1951/52. Even though domestic prices increased as a result of rising internal demand, the supply response was slow because of a considerable time lag in the production process. Although domestic prices were high, the relative returns from exports did not increase because the ratio of export prices to domestic prices in the case of wool, tea, hides, and skins fell during the period 1952/53–1954/55.

Thus the adverse price ratios of jute and cotton vis-à-vis the competing crops were combined with the adverse ratio of export prices to domestic prices in the case of other primary exports to inhibit exports. Then the government turned its attention to an adjustment of exchange rates and undertook the devaluation of the rupee by 33½ percent in 1955. This was the beginning of the second phase of the exchange control regime in Pakistan.

DEVALUATION IN 1955 AND ITS AFTERMATH

The second phase in the evolution of the exchange control regime in Pakistan occurred between 1955/56 and 1958/59. This period, which combined the basic

7. Richard Mallon, "Export Policy in Pakistan," *Pakistan Development Review* 6, no. 1 (Spring 1966): 57–79.

features of exchange control and import restrictions that had been introduced earlier, differed from the earlier one in three respects. A devaluation in 1955 proved inadequate, compared with the magnitude of disequilibrium in its balance of payments. Secondly, unlike in the earlier period there were no accumulated foreign exchange reserves to draw upon. Thirdly, exports continued to stagnate partly because of increased domestic absorption of industrial raw materials.

A number of justifications were provided in support of devaluation. The first was that Pakistan by now had established a range of manufacturing industries that could enter the export market. Unlike the case of primary exports, elasticity of export demand for such manufactures was considered high. Second, devaluation would not affect the cost of living significantly because imports supplied a smaller proportion of consumer goods than in 1949. Third, by raising the landed cost of imports, it would cut mostly into the profits of imports. Only in rare cases, where the spread between world and domestic prices was small, would prices rise. It was difficult to judge whether the magnitude of devaluation was adequate. What was clear, however, was that Pakistan apparently did not intend to use devaluation to establish an equilibrium exchange rate. This was evident from the continuation of import restrictions and differential export incentives in the postdevaluation period.[8] In fact interventions in exports and imports increased and proliferated.

In the judgment of the authorities in Pakistan the adjustment of the exchange rate in 1955 was more appropriate for its major exports than for the minor ones, in the light of their relative domestic costs and prices vis-à-vis international prices. The earlier measures adopted to adjust the effective exchange rates for various minor exports was apparently based on the differences in the elasticities of supply and demand for individual commodities. The duties on primary exports were readjusted. For example, the export duty on raw jute was raised by 33 percent; that on jute cuttings (i.e., the inferior varieties of jute) was doubled and the export duty on tea, which was suspended during 1952–55, was reintroduced and increased to 0.60 Rs per pound. Thus, in the case of jute and tea the effective rate of exchange was lowered below the new exchange rate. The adjustment of the effective exchange rate for tea was intended primarily to offset the advantage to the export of tea that the new exchange rate might provide and therefore to secure an adequate supply for domestic consumption. Devaluation would have increased the export of tea because of an elastic export demand (Pakistan was a marginal supplier of tea in the world market), thereby raising the domestic price considerably. The duty on jute was raised on the assumption, held throughout the 1950s, that the elasticity of export demand for raw jute was low. In the case of cotton, hides, and skins, an opposite policy was followed. The duty on cotton

8. Government of Pakistan, National Planning Board, *First Five Year Plan.*

was reduced. During 1956/57 and 1958/59 the rate of duty fluctuated between Rs 80 and 50 per bale for desi-cotton against between Rs 100 and 60 per bale from 1951/52 to 1955/56. For the other varieties of cotton the rate of duty stayed at about Rs 115 per bale against Rs 80 and 135 per bale during the earlier period.

The effective exchange rates for the minor primary exports as well as for selected manufactured goods were lowered in terms of foreign currency by an expansion of the export promotion scheme. Whereas in the predevaluation period all the commodities that were eligible for the export promotion scheme were given uniform import entitlement, in the postdevaluation period a differentiation was made between primary commodities and manufactured commodities in terms of the percentage of import entitlement. The subsidy accruing to the exporter from these import entitlement schemes was derived primarily from the high profits and scarcity margins obtained from the domestic sales of imported goods.[9] (Primary exports and manufactured exports were both eligible for 25% import entitlement in the early period, while manufactured exports were eligible for 40% import entitlement in the later period.) The import entitlements of primary exports could be used for the import of any of the items on a special import list so formulated for their exclusive use.[10] The exports of manufactured goods could, however, use their entitlement only for importing raw materials, equipment, and packing materials that were used in their production. Further, the list of primary commodities that were eligible for import entitlement was modified to exclude such items as crushed bone, steel castings, mustard seeds, oil cakes, and grape seeds, which together had accounted for 60 percent of the earnings under the previous incentive scheme. It was felt that additional incentive was no longer necessary for those items and that the new primary commodities should now be included under the scheme. The incentive to any particular primary export was, therefore, considered to be essentially temporary in nature and was to be provided mainly to enable the exporters to undertake the additional costs of entering and establishing themselves in foreign markets. Thus, starting with a uniform import entitlement in 1954, the rate of export incentive was increasingly differentiated for different exports between the years 1954 and 1958, not only in terms of percentages of import entitlements but also in terms of the commodities for which the entitlements could be utilized.[11]

9. The expanded list of the manufactured goods eligible for this scheme by 1956 consisted of 53 items in all (*Pakistan Trade* 6, no. 11 [Nov. 1955]: 45–46).

10. Ibid.

11. At one stage in 1958 a list of new primary goods was introduced that entitled them to 10% of their export proceeds for the import of goods from the import list specially prepared for them or for the import of machinery and equipment required for the production of the items exported. Moreover, the exports of manufactured goods could later use 5% of their exports for the import of items admissible under the import list for primary commodities. Later on a special import entitlement of

Table 4.1.   Export Earning and Export Price (Million dollar and dollar price, index value)

	Earnings		Change	Price
	1954/55	*1955/56*	*(%)*	*1955/56* [a]
Jute	179.6	197.8	+10	88
Cotton	103.7	104.1	+0.4	86
Wool	16.9	18.0	+6	84
Tea	14.8	6.3	−58	81
Hides and skins	9.6	10.2	+6	82
Jute manu- factures	3.4	18.0	+430	—
Cotton manu- factures	—	6.7	—	—
Miscellaneous exports	39.5	42.6	+7	—
Total	367.5	403.7	+10	87

Source: S. A. Meenai, ''Devaluation—An Assessment,'' *Pakistan Economic Journal* 7, no. 1 Mar. 1957): 108–09.

[a]1954/55 = 100.

An additional measure of export subsidy introduced in 1956 was the refund of custom duties paid on the imports of raw materials that were used by the manufacturers in the production of exports. Thus the devaluation of 1955 evolved into a system of multiple exchange rates, which were established by means of such measures as export taxes, refund of import duties in specified cases, and import entitlement schemes. The effect of devaluation, coupled with export promotion measures, was an increase in export earnings of both raw materials and manufactured exports (table 4.1).

The fall in export price was not entirely due to devaluation. There was also a weakening in international demand, as in the case of tea and cotton, and thus the fall in export price was attributable to external circumstances. The increase in the volume of export commodities other than tea and coffee was partly the result of an increase in the volume of world trade.

In spite of devaluation and export incentives, export earnings during the second half of the 1950s did not show a consistent increase. This was caused primarily by stagnation in agricultural exports. The poor performance of agricultural exports was a result of (a) stagnation in agricultural production and (b) an increasing absorption of agricultural raw materials by domestic industries.

The stagnation in agricultural production is indicated by the fact that the index

---

50% for artificial silk fabrics, 25% for cloth, and 10% for iron ore was introduced. *Pakistan Trade* 9, no. 8 (Aug. 1958): 4–6.

Table 4.2.   Growth of Production of the Major Export Crops (In tons)

	Cotton	Jute	Tea
1951/52	248	1,131	21
Annual average for 1952–55	282	951	23
Annual average for 1955–58	299	1,084	44

Source: Government of Pakistan, Ministry of Finance, *Economic Survey, 1959-60 and 1966-67*, appendix, p. 9, table 3.

of production, which was 95 in 1953/54 (1949/50 = 100), fell to 86 in 1955/56 and was no higher than 93 by 1957/58. There was no increase in the production of the principal export crops (jute, cotton, and tea), as seen in table 4.2.

Moreover, increasing domestic absorption of the raw materials by the manufacturing industries, coupled with stagnant production, reduced the ratio of exports to domestic output of the important, primary exports, as seen in table 4.3.

At the same time there was increasing domestic absorption of industrial output with resultant diversion away from the export market. There was an absolute decline in the annual average volume of exports of cotton, cotton manufactures, hides and skins, and leather manufactures, whereas the combined value of jute and jute manufactures and wool and woollen manufactures recorded only a slight increase. The pull of the domestic demand on the import-substituting manufacturing industries, acting as a drag on their exports, is illustrated remarkably well in the case of cotton textiles (table 4.4).[12]

The pressure of excess domestic demand was also felt in the case of tea. While the annual average production of tea dropped slightly from an average of 53 million lb during 1951–55 to 51.5 million lb during 1955–59, the annual average exports of tea dropped by almost one-half between the two periods.[13] In order to prevent a drastic fall in the domestic consumption of tea, the export tax on tea was raised in this period with a view to discouraging exports.

The excess domestic demand was created at least partly by the substantial amount of deficit financing that was undertaken by the government during this period. The increase in money supply during 1954/55–1956/57 was about three times the increase in the previous four years, resulting in a considerable rise in domestic prices in general and of exportables in particular, which were already pushed by the devaluation. The rise in domestic prices during this period was

12. Soligo, "Monetary Problems of Pakistan," p. 647.

13. Parvez Hasan, *Deficit Financing and Capital Formulation: The Pakistan Experience, 1951-59*, (Karachi: Pakistan Institute of Development Economics, Jan. 1962), p. 42.

Table 4.3.   Ratio of Exports to Outputs for Primary Exports

	Cotton	*Jute*	*Tea*	*Wool*	*Hides and skins*	*Fish*
1951/52	0.79	0.77	0.74	0.66	—	0.06
1952/53						
1954/55	0.71	0.97	0.47	0.88	0.73	0.10
1955/56						
1957/58	0.41	0.79	0.29	0.97	0.64	0.07

Source: See table 4.2.

greater than that in the outside world, especially in the countries with which Pakistan had important trade relationships. The impact on prices was partly met by direct controls on distribution and prices. Between 1954/55 and 1958/59 the index of the implicit GNP deflator rose from 75.8 to 93.0 whereas the combined price index of the trading partners rose by no more than from 94 to 100.[14] To a much greater extent than in the partner countries the rise in domestic prices whittled away the effects of devaluation on Pakistan's exports.

The combined result of export stagnation and excess demand was reflected in a deteriorating balance of payments situation.[15] This was accentuated by a decline in the terms of trade in this period (table 4.5). The visible balance of trade recorded an annual deficit of Rs 3.558 billion during 1955/56–1959/60 as contrasted with the average annual surplus of Rs 2.238 billion during the previous five-year period (1950/51–1953/54). The deficit on the invisible account increased from about Rs 400 million to about 600 million.

The value of imports of food grains during all these years exceeded the value of total capital goods imports. The foreign exchange reserves, which were about Rs 941.6 million in December 1950, fell to Rs 631.0 million by December 1954. Gains in reserves in the mid-1950s were lost again by the end of 1958, when they were about Rs 765.9 million in December.

Thus, the exchange rate adjustment that Pakistan undertook in 1955 was merely a delayed reaction to the earlier devaluation undertaken by her trading partners. Its effects were more than overtaken by the rapid rise in costs and prices in the second half of the 1950s. During this period a contraction occurred in the volume of foreign trade in relation to domestic economic activities. The ratio of imports to GNP declined from 7.8 percent in 1950/51 to 5.2 percent in 1954/55 and 5.6 percent in 1958/59. The ratio of exports to GNP fell from 12.3 to 9.7 percent in the corresponding years.[16]

14. N. Alam, "The Experience of an Overvalued Currency: The Case of Pakistan" (Ph.D. diss., Yale University, 1968), table 5.

15. Hasan, *Deficit Financing and Capital Formulation.*

16. Government of Pakistan, Ministry of Finance, *Pakistan Economic Survey, 1969–70* (1970).

Table 4.4.   Domestic Production and Absorption of Cotton Textiles (Million yards)

	Production	Imports	Exports	Domestic absorption
1951/52–1954/55	261.7	107.3	0.5	368.5
1955/56	482.9	69.9	2.8	550.0
1956/57	521.7	13.5	16.7	518.5
1957/58	555.9	3.5	3.2	556.2
1958/59	598.1	1.6	12.8	586.9

Source: Parvez Hasan, *Deficit Financing and Capital Formation: The Pakistan Experience, 1951–9* (Karachi: Pakistan Institute of Development Economics, Jan. 1962), p. 42.

Pakistan's response to foreign exchange shortage, excess domestic demand, and agricultural stagnation was to introduce a system of wide-ranging controls not only on foreign trade and exchange but also on domestic production, distribution, and prices. All commodities imported under the government account, which included such key items as food grains, sugar, coal, and iron and steel, were subject to price and distribution controls. Moreover, government account imports assumed increasing importance during this period, growing from 25 percent of total imports during 1950–54 to 53 percent during 1954–58.

The private sector imports during 1954–63 were reduced further below the lowest level reached during the previous period (1950–54). The value index of the licensed private imports varied between 40 and 45 percent of the level of imports reached earlier during the period of free imports. Besides strict licensing of imports there was a restriction operating through the system of advance deposit requirement for imports. After remaining in abeyance for some years, this measure was reintroduced with 15 percent deposit requirements in 1957/58.[17]

LIBERALIZATION PHASE: 1959–65

The subsequent period in the evolution of the exchange control system coincided with the introduction of the Second Five Year Plan (1960–65) and was marked by attempts to liberalize the system of controls. The spurt in the intensity and coverage of economic controls, especially price and distribution controls following the imposition of martial law in 1958, was short-lived.[18] Authorities soon realized that prices could not be maintained at low levels for long without increasing supplies. Rigid controls on prices and profits were acknowledged to

17. N. Alam, "Experience of an Overvalued Currency."
18. The number of commodities whose prices were to be fixed by the government was reduced from 14 to 13 and the number of commodities whose prices were to be regulated by fixing profit margins was reduced from 87 to 24 (Husain, "Pakistan's Commercial Policy in the Recession," pp. 72–75).

Table 4.5. Terms of Trade

	Export unit value	*Import unit value*	*Index of terms trade*
1954/55	79.0	63.4	124.7
1955/56	93.9	87.4	107.3
1956/57	104.1	108.3	96.1
1957/58	113.3	106.8	106.1
1958/59	101.4	102.3	99.1

Source: Hasan, *Deficit Financing and Capital Formation,* appendix tables.
Note: 1959/60 = 100.

be discouraging production, not only because they bore no close relation to the costs of production but also because they did not generate profits high enough to induce or stimulate entrepreneurial efforts and incentives.

Thus the government's policy entered a new phase during 1959/60 with an official pronouncement that price controls were not intended to be a permanent feature of government policy. At the same time the number of commodities whose prices were directly or indirectly controlled was reduced. The Second Five Year Plan enunciated the principles of the new economic policy as follows:

"The Plan proposes a decisive move towards a more liberal economy, and a bold switch over from direct controls to a policy of regulation of the economy through suitable fiscal and monetary controls." The Plan document emphasized the possibility of

potential conflict of considerable severity between exchange controls and effective private enterprise. . . . If the allocation of foreign exchange is controlled, decisions that can determine the success or failure of a private undertaking are in fact reserved for public authority. The co-ordination of multiplicity of controls affecting the vast multitude of decision making units was cumbersome and inefficient. The information that the price system generated for the individual units was not available or was not used by the control authorities.

The plan, therefore, postulated that controls which were too costly to enforce were to be eliminated and the rest were to be rationalized. Greater use of taxes and subsidies to curtail consumption or to regulate the allocation of resources was advocated. The plan specifically urged an upward revision of interest rates to encourage a more efficient as well as a more equitable allocation between the large privileged borrowers, on the one hand, and small enterprises, on the other.

The first major decontrol of an essential commodity occurred in April 1960, when controls were taken off the movement and price of wheat and its products in West Pakistan.

To build adequate stocks an arrangement was made with the United States government for the import of wheat under the PL 480 aid program spread over a period of two years. In East Pakistan rationing was abolished in 16 out of 19 district towns in 1960, and the system of monopoly procurement of rice by the government was no longer compulsory. Further relaxations of controls occurred when, in the beginning of February 1961, price and distribution controls on yarn and cotton textiles were removed. Shortly afterward the government announced the decontrol of 29 more items out of a total of 44. By 1963 there were controls on the prices of only 15 commodites.

The general atmosphere of liberalization affected foreign trade as well.[19] The initial step in trade liberalization was taken in 1959 by the introduction of the Export Bonus Scheme. Under this scheme the exporter of a ''bonus commodity'' surrendered his foreign-exchange earnings to the Central Bank, i.e., the State Bank of Pakistan, and received, in addition to the rupee (local currency) equivalent, a voucher that entitled its owner to purchase foreign exchange equal in value to a fixed percentage (which varied depending on the commodity exported) of the amount earned. The foreign exchange purchased by the voucher could be used for importing a wide range of goods, for traveling on business, and for purchasing other services abroad. The voucher could be freely bought and sold on the open market; its price was determined by the supply of vouchers, which depended on the export items covered by the scheme, by the percentage of exports available in the form of vouchers, and by the demand for the vouchers, which depended on the items that were permitted to be imported under the scheme. With a few exceptions the imports eligible under the Export Bonus Scheme were not subject to any quantitative restrictions. Importers were free to buy any number of bonus vouchers at the prevailing market rate and to use these vouchers to import any quantity of the eligible items. The volume and composition of imports under the scheme were thus determined by the market forces. However, the liberalization could be considered only marginal because only about 10 percent of the total licensed imports were effected under this scheme.[20]

In early 1961 a second step toward liberalization was taken in the form of a new Open General License system, which brought two changes in the system of import licensing. First there was an attempt to enlarge the number of importers who gained access to import licenses. The import licensing system, as described in detail later on, determined not only what was imported in what quantity but also who was allowed to import. The traders who did not have an import license at the time when the system was introduced in the early 1950s, and who engaged

19. The attempts at liberalization are analyzed in detail in chap. 7.

20. P. S. Thomas, ''Import Licensing and Import Liberalisation in Pakistan,'' in N. Islam, ed., *Studies on Commercial Policy and Economic Growth*, (Karachi: Pakistan Institute of Development Economics, 1970), appendix table A-2, p. 34.

in import trade at a later date, now had access to licenses. This increased the number of eligible importers. When an item was placed in the new OGL list, the importers who were already on the approved list of importers (called category holders) were permitted to continue importing their preexisting quotas, but additional licenses were given to new importers to stimulate competition in the import trade. The second element in liberalization was to allow licenses issued ordinarily for use within a six-month period to be automatically renewed in the next six-month period for an equivalent amount of import. The quantum of license for the next period was therefore not subject to rescrutiny and examination by the import control authority. This system was allowed only for a limited number of imports deemed essential. Under this new system of repeat licensing a limited number of initial licenses was issued at the beginning of the shipping period (six months), but upon showing proof of use of this license, the importers could get another license. For a few items and to some extent the issue of licenses was thus made a little more responsive to the internal demand and supply situation.

By the end of 1963 the imports under the new systems constituted about half all licensed imports.[21] By 1964 a further step was taken to allow a number of items to be imported without the need to obtain a prior import license from the import control authority. During 1964/65 between 50 and 60 items were in this category. These liberalization measures greatly contributed to an increase in the volume of imports (which almost trebled between 1958/59 and 1963/64). Imports under these schemes constituted more than 70 percent of the imports that were administered by the import licensing authority (excluding those imports undertaken directly by government departments and not administered by the import licensing authority). Imports on private account as a percentage of total imports increased from 53 to 72 percent between 1958/59 and 1963/64.[22]

Another significant change in policy that accompanied the import liberalization measures was a greater reliance on fiscal and monetary policies for influencing the quantity and the composition of foreign exchange usage. Between 1959 and 1963, import duties rose by about one-third, with increases ranging from 11 percent on certain processed raw materials to 115 percent on semiluxury consumer goods. In July 1964 a regulatory duty was imposed on the free list imports as described above.

The liberalization efforts need to be viewed in the context of a number of developments in Pakistan's economy during this period. Important among these were an acceleration in the growth rate of output, especially in agriculture, a substantial increase in foreign exchange earnings facilitated by improved terms

21. Ibid., table A-9, p. 40.
22. Ibid., table A-1, p. 33, and table A-10, pp. 41–42.

of trade, and an increased inflow of foreign assistance. In addition greater attention was paid by the government to an anti-inflationary policy, including the mobilization of domestic resources and maintenance of monetary stability. The environment of general affluence in respect to the availability of both internal and external resources provided a greater flexibility in economic policymaking.

The acceleration in the growth rate in agriculture was the result of policy changes associated with increased investment in agriculture and the introduction of new technology, i.e., high yielding varieties of seed, especially for wheat and rice in West Pakistan. First there was a relaxation of controls on prices and acreage; second there was an expanded supply and a subsidization of fertilizer and irrigation pumps. The result was a substantial increase in the profitability of agricultural production that led to the adoption of the new highly productive technology. There was a great spurt in the installation of private tube wells in West Pakistan,[23] which was facilitated by a subsidy on the cost of drilling and installation of tube wells, and by the liberal importation of components of tube wells at a highly overvalued official rate of exchange. The agricultural value added at constant prices increased 50 percent between 1958/59 to 1964/65. The improved agricultural growth stimulated the growth of manufacturing by keeping the prices of wage goods and raw materials low and by expanding the domestic market for manufactured goods.

The acceleration of the agricultural growth rate also had favorable implications for the balance of payments. Combined with an increased flow of food aid under the PL 480 program it reduced the need for food imports and permitted the establishment of domestic buffer stocks. It enhanced the degree of food security, i.e., the ability to meet the impact of fluctuations in domestic output, variations in weather conditions, or an adverse turn in the world market for food. The growth in agriculture helped increase agricultural exports and contributed to the rising export earnings from both raw and processed materials, the latter being especially encouraged by the Export Bonus Scheme. The favorable foreign trade position in this period is shown by table 4.6.

The high rate of growth in export earnings was also facilitated by a favorable movement in the export unit value; the index of export unit value increased from 128 in 1958/59 to 158 in 1964/65. The movement was especially favorable in 1960–62. The import earning capacity of exports also improved, as can be noted from the movement of terms of trade in table 4.6.

The foreign exchange situation was further eased by an increase in the inflow of foreign aid during this period compared to the preceding period. This was

23. The number of private tube wells increased from 3,295 in 1958/59 to 13,646 in 1963/64. See Ghulam Mohammad, "Private Tubewell Development and Cropping Patterns in West Pakistan," *Pakistan Development Review* 5, no. 1 (Spring 1965).

Table 4.6. Foreign Exchange Position in the Early 1960s (Values in million dollars)

	Export earnings	Primary exports		Export unit value[a]	Terms of trade[a]
		Raw cotton	Raw jute		
1958/59	278	42	138	128	80
1959/60	387	43	153	127	80
1960/61	360	32	178	186	110
1961/62	387	32	178	156	97
1962/63	472	84	167	144	85
1963/64	483	77	158	141	89
1964/65	506	67	177	158	112

Source: 25 Years of Pakistan in Statistics (Karachi: Central Statistical Office, 1972).
[a]1954/55 = 100.

partly the result of the setting up of an Aid Consortium for Pakistan in 1960. Whereas the total commitment of foreign aid during the First Plan period (1955–60) was $0.99 million, during the Second Plan (1960–65) the figure rose to $2.37 million.

In addition there was a considerable acceleration in the growth of tax revenues during this period. Total tax revenues increased by 60 percent between 1959/60 and 1964/65, compared to a 30 percent increase in the previous five-year period. The tax/GNP ratio climbed from 6.3 to 8.3 percent in the corresponding years. The increase was mostly from indirect taxes, especially the higher import tariffs imposed during this period.[24]

The first half of the 1960s was a period of comparative price stability. The increase in prices in Pakistan during this period was in line with that in its principal trading partners, as table 4.7 shows.

There was a moderate rise in world prices in this period. Likewise in Pakistan, after a rise of 5 percent between 1959/60 and 1960/61 the price level retained a remarkable stability until 1964/65, when it registered another increase of 5 percent. The stability of prices during this time was undoubtedly aided by an acceleration of the agricultural growth rate. The effects of monetary expansion were cushioned by an elastic supply of food grains in the early 1960s.

The average annual rate of increase in money supply after 1961/62 was Rs 187 million compared to an increase of Rs 400 million annually up to 1961/62.[25] There was undoubtedly an increase in the rate of bank lending in this period compared with the previous period. But the increase in bank lending was offset

24. S. R. Lewis and S. K. Qureshi, "The Structure of Revenue from Indirect Taxes in Pakistan," *Pakistan Development Review* 4, no. 3 (Autumn 1964): 512; N. Islam, "The Tax System of Pakistan," unpublished manuscript, Pakistan Institute of Development Economics, 1970.

25. Soligo, "Monetary Problems of Pakistan," p. 639.

Table 4.7.   Index of Price Movements

	1959	1960	1961	1962	1963	1964
Country weighted price index[a]	102	102	103	103	105	107

	1960/61	1961/62	1962/63	1963/64	1964/65	
Pakistan GNP deflator[b]	105.1	104.1	106.5	105.1	110.9	

Source: N. Alam, ''The Experience of an Overvalued Currency: The Case of Pakistan'' (Ph.D. diss., Yale University, 1968), pp. 50–51.

[a] 1958 = 100.

[b] 1959/60 = 100.

by (a) a large import surplus financed by foreign aid and (b) an appreciable rise in time deposits. The advance in time deposits was partly due to a rise in real income and thus in saving rates and partly due to an increase in the margin requirement for bank advances, especially those against imported commodities. The result was a small net increase in money supply.

An important feature of the composition of bank lending in this period was the predominant role of lending to the private sector contrasted with the predominance of the public sector loans in the earlier period. So long as increases in credit creation were due predominantly to deficit financing by the government, the central bank's effectiveness in controlling the price and quantity of the money supply was limited. Moreover, the commercial banks, unlike in the earlier period, had a lower level of excess reserve and therefore were more dependent on borrowing from the State Bank. This phenomenon increased the effectiveness of the State Bank's control. During this period the State Bank resorted more frequently than before to both general and selective methods of credit control. It raised the bank rate and the reserve requirements of the commercial banks. The bank rate was increased from 3 to 4 percent during 1959 for the first time in the history of Pakistan. In 1963 the reserve requirements were raised uniformly against both time and demand deposits from 2 to 5 percent. At about the same time, there were increases in margin requirements against bank advances for imported manufactures as well as against cotton, yarn, and cotton textiles. The State Bank of Pakistan also introduced a quota system of lending to commercial banks under which it charged progressively higher rates of interest for borrowings in excess of the maximum limit. In 1964 there were 40 percent margin requirements against advances for free list items, and in 1965 advance deposit requirements against all imports were introduced and the cash reserve requirements of the commercial banks were raised from 5 to 7 percent.[26] When an

26. *State Bank of Pakistan, Annual Reports, 1958–66*, Karachi; State Bank of Pakistan, *Banking Statistics of Pakistan, 1964–65, 1969–70*, Karachi. General measures of credit restraint would leave

acceleration in bank credit in 1962/63 to 1964/65 led to increased speculative demand for loans, the State Bank undertook means to curb this by the imposition of a 25 percent margin requirement against the opening of letters of credit for imports. These controls were useful in restraining the domestic demand for exportables so as to divert output from the domestic market to the foreign trade sector. This period thus witnessed an increase in the degree of flexibility in the use of fiscal and monetary policies and in a broadening of the range of economic policy instruments with a relative shift toward indirect and away from direct controls.

SETBACKS IN LIBERALIZATION: 1966–70

During the second half of the 1960s the economic environment deteriorated on several fronts. The Third Five Year Plan, which was formulated after a successful period of planned development during the early 1960s, emphasized its support for a greater reliance on indirect controls. Increased production of essential commodities and improvement of the market mechanism were among the measures advocated for ensuring development with stability. Although planners recognized that by itself the market mechanism did not solve the problem of interregional or interpersonal distribution of incomes, they advocated ameliorative measures not by direct controls but rather by fiscal and monetary policy as well as indirect regulation. However, like the Second Plan, it stated: "The relaxation of direct controls has not been accompanied by an adequate framework of indirect controls through fiscal and monetary policy. The prices of key inputs, notably credit and foreign exchange, have not been adjusted to run an increasingly liberated economy."[27]

This cautious mood of optimism was suddenly disturbed by events beyond control. The consequent decline in economic buoyancy led to setbacks in the process of liberalization. These developments were (a) the outbreak of the Indo–Pakistan War in 1965, (b) consecutive years of bad harvests in 1965/66 and 1966/67, and (c) the slowing down in the rate of external assistance.

The outbreak of hostilities led to a shift in the use of government savings and in the composition of public sector expenditure. The actual decline in development expenditure in the period 1965–70 was not due to a lack of resources. Rather it was due to the substitution of development investment by defense expenditure. The latter increased from about 30 percent of current expenditures and 2.7 percent of GNP during 1960–64 to about 40 percent of current expendi-

---

unaffected agriculture, small-scale industry, and unorganized domestic trade where excess demand might be generated but not be accessible to the manipulation of scheduled bank advances.

27. Government of Pakistan, Planning Commission, *The Third Five Year Plan* (Islamabad, May 1965), p. 123.

tures and 5.4 percent of GNP in 1965/66. The corresponding percentages did fall below 40 and 3.5 percent over the next five years.[28] There was a rise of about 100 percent in excess of current revenues over current nondefense expenditures after the war of 1965, but increased savings were spent on defense. There was little reason to believe that the same growth in savings could not be mobilized in the absence of war for the purpose of development if sufficient motivation existed and efforts were made. Whatever the potential of the economy, it could not come to fruition in this period. The war and its aftermath created conditions of resource stringency that limited development.

At the same time, bad harvests in the context of rising population, increasing urbanization, and considerable credit expansion brought sharp increases in food prices. The fall in output in 1965/66 and stagnation in 1966/67 were at a level below that of 1964/65. This stagnation in production led to a large import of food grains. Part of the increase in food imports in the early 1960s was intended to build up reserves of food, especially of wheat, in order to operate buffer stocks to stabilize the price of wheat.[29] But the large increase in food imports during 1966–67 was primarily to meet domestic shortages.

The third adverse factor was the fall in the rate of capital inflow. Whereas during the Second Plan Period gross assistance was about two and a half times that in the First, the increase in the Third Plan Period was barely 25 percent above that in the Second. Furthermore, the increase in net assistance was even smaller since the debt service payments during the Third Plan were about twice that of the earlier period.

Faced with a stagnant aid flow, Pakistan explored new sources of credit in 1966–70. Average annual flow of suppliers' credit doubled even though it was of shorter maturity and carried higher rates of interest. The stagnation in commodity assistance[30] was especially disturbing because a large part of Pakistan's own foreign exchange earnings had to be diverted to finance defense and food imports and a growing burden of debt service payments. Moreover, an increasing emphasis on agriculture preempted a large amount of commodity assistance for the imports of fertilizers and other current inputs for agriculture. This created particular stringency in the supply of imported raw materials for the industrial sector.

The combination of these adverse developments compelled Pakistan to economize on foreign exchange expenditures and to reorient her development

28. Government of Pakistan, Ministry of Defense, *Budget in Brief, 1969–70*.

29. Moreover, the green revolution in agriculture was confined to West Pakistan, with the result that imports of food were required in East Pakistan in years of bad harvests.

30. The aid givers preferred project aid to commodity assistance. The composition of aid shifted more toward project assistance during the Third Plan; project aid was 56% of the total aid in 1964/65 and went up to 63% during 1965/66–1968/69.

strategy toward activities that were less import intensive or that resulted in an immediate increase in foreign exchange earnings. Agriculture was accorded a high priority in terms of its claim on scarce foreign exchange resources for import of current inputs as well as equipment. Consumer goods and nondevelopment imports were curtailed. But this was not enough. Import controls were tightened in view of the shortage of foreign exchange.

Attempts to liberalize imports initiated in the earlier years thus received a setback. Quantitative restrictions were reintroduced on imports, so that whereas imports doubled between the First and Second Five Year periods, they increased by barely 20 percent between the Second and Third plans. The highest level of imports reached from 1965/66 to 1969/70 was below the highest level reached during the earlier period by about Rs 200 million. Private imports suffered a greater setback than public imports. The highest level of private imports during this period was 20 percent below the highest level attained in the earlier period. The ratio of private to total imports declined from 77.6 percent in 1964/65 to 65.3 percent in 1968/69. During the earlier period (1958/59 to 1964/65) the ratio of exports to GNP rose from 4.7 to 5.3 percent but declined to 4.7 percent in the succeeding period. The import ratio also declined to 7.2 percent. Foreign exchange reserves, after having recorded a steady and significant improvement between 1958 and 1964 to reach the level of Rs 1.176 billion, fell to Rs 864 million in 1968.[31]

There was, however, one redeeming feature in the generally discouraging foreign exchange situation. The external terms of trade did not show any downward trend. While they fluctuated from year to year, the general level of the terms of trade tended to be higher during this period than that in the earlier period, as seen in table 4.8.

Pakistan in these years used a more flexible monetary policy, based mainly on selective credit controls. But toward the end of this period, the State Bank of Pakistan had to introduce a system of credit budgeting that imposed regional, sectoral, and even individual bank ceilings on credit creation. The sectoral allocation was flexible; it was the overall credit ceiling that was the principal concern of the monetary authorities.[32] In the field of fiscal policy and taxation, Pakistan did not fare well. The rate of mobilization of tax resources and public saving slowed down toward the end of the 1960s.

The late 1960s was also a period when there was a growing public consciousness about inequities in income distribution and concentration of economic power. There was considerable political agitation and pressure for mitigating the inequities of the system in terms of not only distribution of income but also

31. Ministry of Finance, *Pakistan Economic Survey, 1969-70*, p. 109, table 51.
32. IBRD, *Current Economic Position and Prospects of Pakistan* (1969), pp. 32–35, 47–50.

Table 4.8.   Terms of Trade

	Export unit values	Import unit values	Terms of trade
1964/65	124.8	89.6	139.2
1965/66	125.3	106.2	118.0
1966/67	147.0	98.0	147.3
1967/68	128.1	101.0	126.7
1968/69	137.3	94.4	145.8

Source: Central Statistical Office, *Monthly Statistical Bulletins.*
Note: 1959/60 = 100.

conditions of the absolute power. The responsibility for inequities was increasingly as critical to the large industrial companies and to their domination in the industrial and financial sectors. At the same time there was disappointment with the results of the "green revolution" because a large share of gains in income and productivity in agriculture aggregated to big and medium landowners to the detriment of small owners and landless laborers.

Authorities held that incentives provided to the private enterprises to save and invest, combined with a relaxation of controls on prices and profits, contributed to this phenomenon. The need to resort to controls and the regulation of large conglomerates, industrial companies, and interlocking financial and trading interests, in view of their rising economic power or market control and in the light of the absolute size of their private economic fortunes, was gaining public support.

5

The Import Control System and Its Impact

There were three components of the trade and payments regime of Pakistan. (1) Licensing of imports and expenditures abroad on invisible services was controlled by import quotas as well as exchange restrictions; the former was administered by the import licensing authority and the latter by the State Bank. (2) Next there was a system of import duties that regulated imports by varying their domestic price; the effectiveness of import duty in a system where quantitative restrictions were effective was not so much in regulating the volume and composition of imports as in siphoning off the windfall profits of the importers. (3) Finally, there was a host of regulations and incentives that affected the volume and composition of exports. An analysis of the anatomy of exchange control requires a separate discussion of all three components. This chapter attempts a detailed analysis of the working and impact of (1) and (2), while an anatomy of (3) is left for the next chapter.

THE WORKING OF IMPORT LICENSING

The import licensing system in Pakistan was closely linked with the exchange control system, which regulated both the inflow and outflow of foreign exchange resources.[1] The exporters were required to surrender their entire foreign exchange earnings to the central bank, i.e., the State Bank of Pakistan, and the foreign exchange expenditures on imports were regulated by an Annual Foreign Exchange Budget. The budget included an estimate of foreign exchange resources, derived from exports and foreign assistance on the one hand and, on the other hand, foreign exchange expenditures, distinguished by broad category as well as between private and public sector expenditures.

1. This discussion of the system of import licensing draws heavily on (a) S. N. H. Naqvi, "Import Licensing in Pakistan," *Pakistan Development Review* 4, no. 1 (Spring 1964): 51–68; (b) Government of Pakistan, Office of the Chief Controller of Imports and Exports, *Manual of Imports and Exports Control* (Karachi, 1964).

The budget was approved by a high-powered interministerial committee.[2] The foreign exchange allocation to the public sector was distributed among the various ministries on the basis of budgets presented by them specifying the allocation between developmental and nondevelopmental imports.[3] The allocation to the private sector was made on the basis of estimates of private sector needs presented to the committee by the Ministry of Commerce. Although there were yearly allocations in the foreign exchange budget, their utilization took place on the basis of each six-month shipping period.

Once the foreign exchange budget was completed and the allocations to the public sector, semipublic development corporations, and the private sector were determined, the actual detailed import decisions were affected by three distinct licensing systems. Import licensing related chiefly to the imports of consumer goods, industrial raw materials, and spare parts and was administered by the Chief Controller of Imports and Exports. Industrial licensing related mostly to the import of capital goods required for industrial expansion, both in the public and private sectors, determined as part of the broader industrial policy of the country. This program was administered by the Chief Controller of Imports and Exports but on the basis of recommendations from the Ministry of Industries. The licensing of imports to be undertaken by the government agencies and public utilities were part of the budgetary process. The administration of actual licensing to the government departments and agencies was undertaken by the Department of Investment Promotion and Supplies in the Ministry of Industries.

In regard to commercial and industrial import licensing the controller had to decide: (1) which particular commodities to import (and which not to import), (2) how much of these commodities to import, and (3) who should import. In view of the overall resource constraints, he had to grade imports in order of "essentiality" in the light of national priorities. With respect to the importers he had to assess their genuineness and financial capacity. He was guided by the deliberations of the Central Ceilings Committee in the Ministry of Commerce, whose job was to specify the commodities to be included or excluded from the import list in each shipping period. The controller was also influenced by the recommendations of the Import Advisory Council[4] in the Ministry of Commerce,

---

2. The committee was composed of seven members, with the finance secretary acting as chairman. The other members were secretaries of the Ministries of Commerce, Industries, Agriculture, Defense, and Foreign Affairs and a representative of the Planning Commission. Separate allocations were made for the public and the so-called semipublic sector, the latter including institutions such as the East and West Pakistan Industrial Development Corporations, the Pakistan Industrial Credit and Investment Corporation, and the Industrial Development Bank of Pakistan.

3. Imports relating to current operations and to developmental or capital expenditure.

4. This committee established by the Ministry of Commerce included as members the representatives from the Chambers of Commerce and Industry and was intended to enable the controller to have

and the Tariff Commission. However, none of these recommendations was binding.

The controller himself assessed market requirements of the recommended commodities by observing price movements as indications of supply and demand, and accordingly imports were either liberalized or tightened within the limits of foreign exchange availabilities. This was done with the help of a price check unit within the controller's office. The controller had the additional task of allocating each import on the import list to eligible importers and fixing their monetary list. The monetary limit for each commodity was fixed to prevent excess imports of any goods and to keep the relative price structure in a desired balance. The limit for each importer was set to prevent an undesirable degree of concentration of import trade in a few hands, or in few regions.

Commercial Licensing

Under the system of commercial licensing the controller distributed import licenses to traders and importers who imported to resell in the market. How did the controller select the "eligible importers" from a large number of potential importers? The problem was solved as early as 1953 by the adoption of a rule of thumb, which defined eligible importers as those who had undertaken imports during the period July 1950–November 1952, when there was essentially complete freedom to import under the OGL system. This was the so-called category system, which constituted the basis of commercial licenses for the next two decades. Under the category system, introduced in January 1952, each importer of the OGL period (1950–52) was given a monetary "category" for each type of goods that he imported, determined by average imports during the five OGL shipping periods.[5] The actual value of each license received by any importer in any subsequent period was expressed as a certain percentage in the monetary value of each category. The variation in this percentage was the main instrument by which the controller enforced a liberal or stringent import policy.

Several importers would join under the leadership of a licensed importer both to secure better prices internationally and to develop a sizable base for domestic business purposes. The largest business volume of the commercial importers was in the resale to cottage industries and small-scale manufacturers who did not have direct access to industrial import licensing; the cottage and small industries were

---

access to a cross section of official and nonofficial opinion on the advisability of making changes in the import list and thus to reduce the element of arbitrariness in such decisions.

5. A category signified that its holder was an eligible importer and was entitled to at least one regular license for one specified commodity in a shipping period. One importer, however, could hold more than one category if he imported several types of goods during the OGL base period.

too small to be recognized and surveyed by the Ministry of Industries for the purposes of industrial import licensing. They also resold to the regular industrial importers as well as to the wholesalers and the retailers.

Industrial Import Licensing

The controller was faced with a more complicated problem in industrial licensing. As in the case of commercial licensing he had to allocate foreign exchange to each category of industrial raw materials and spare parts as well as to each industrial importer in every shipping period. In addition he allocated foreign exchange separately for meeting the current requirements of the existing installed capacity and for the creation of new capacity.

For the first problem the Ministry of Industries had evolved a quota system to routinize the issue of licenses to industrial importers for the import of raw materials and spare parts. Under this system each eligible industrial importer, called a "quota holder," was assigned a quota specifying his requirements for industrial raw materials and spare parts for one shipping period. Most of the existing quotas were created on the basis of industrial surveys, which were undertaken every three years so that new quotas could be created. Thus, unlike categories for commercial licensing, which had not been revised or increased, the creation of quotas was a continuing process. Each quota holder received an assessment certificate that indicated his requirements for raw materials and spare parts to operate on a single-shift basis. The controller then issued industrial licenses called "regular industrial licenses" largely on the basis of these assessment certificates.[6] The entitlement was stated in rupees, not in quantity, which caused hardship to the importers. Because there was no routine prescribed for the revision of entitlement within the three-year period, the real value of an entitlement in terms of imported goods was often seriously eroded by a rise in world prices. Also, the original estimated costs of imports on which the entitlement was based were inevitably subject to errors of estimation.

Insofar as the licensing for the import of capital goods was concerned, the controller acted primarily as an accounting and issuing agency. The allocation of foreign exchange for capital imports was determined under the system of investment targets of the Five Year Plans (this feature is analyzed below). The licenses

6. Assessment certificates or entitlements could be revised if the industrialist was able to show that he had expanded and thus was eligible for a special survey of his requirements, regardless of the three-year cycle. He could appeal against the survey results to the Commerce Ministry and obtain a resurvey. Of course, the possibility of persuading the local survey authority, by extralegal means, could not be ruled out. The one-shift concept that was used could be superseded by an entitlement based on turnover up to a maximum of two-and-a-half shift plant utilization, if past experience warranted such an enlargement of entitlement.

for the import of capital goods were not interchangeable for licenses for the import of raw materials and spare parts.

The import licensing system, which was established in 1953, did undergo modifications in details over the years but the broad outlines presented above remained unchanged. There were at least four major objectives, as indicated by the statements on import policy from time to time, which guided the controller in making his decisions as to how much of which commodities to import and whom to import them from. The objectives were (1) to keep down the prices of essential consumer goods by allowing relatively liberal imports of such goods (and conversely curtailing luxury imports); (2) to ensure the fullest possible use of existing installed industrial capacity and an "orderly" creation of new capacity following priorities laid down in Five Year Plans; (3) to stimulate exports; and finally (4) to attain a better regional distribution of the flow of imports. Over the years, additional considerations crept into the administration of the import licensing system. Moreover, there were changes over time in the relative emphasis placed on various objectives stated above. Greater responsiveness of import supply to demand and export promotion gained in importance. Similarly, in the late 1960s equity between regions and economic groups was a major criterion.

The category system created monopolies in import trade; the established importers who were in business in 1952 were made category holders and given import licenses. Their relative position in the import trade remained exactly as it had been in 1952/53. Entry into import trade was thereby restricted. To offset this concentration, efforts were made subsequently to induct new importers under a so-called newcomers scheme. The purpose was to allow new importers to have access to foreign exchange, especially those from less developed regions of the country where there were no (or few) importers in the 1950–52 base period. Most additional imports were channeled to the newcomers. Furthermore, a wider regional distribution of licenses was promoted by excluding importers located in the main trading centers from the list of those eligible to receive an OGL license.

Another objective of the changes in the system, to make the supply of imports more responsive to demand, was pursued by introducing a system of "automatic licensing."[7] All licenses were issued for six months and errors in estimating initial inventories and market demand were generally not corrected until the following shipping period. The automatic licensing system was essentially an extension of the category system in that it enabled the category holders to get more than one license in one shipping period for the import of the items on the automatic list. This was one aspect of liberalizing the flow of imports. The

---

7. This system entitled an importer to another import license—to the value of 100% of the initial license as soon as he had utilized the first one. To be eligible, one had to furnish a bill of lading equivalent to 75% of the value of the initial license.

number of items placed on this list varied with changing availability of foreign exchange resources. The automatic system permitted flexibility and encouraged speedy use of licenses, especially for those goods for which relative prices and profits were high. Under the system of Open General License the authorities determined or specified the items to be imported, but the decision as to who would import was left to the free play of market forces. When the OGL system was combined with a system of repeat licensing, i.e., in one shipping period an importer could have more than one license, it implied that the quantity of imports was also made responsive to market demands. The system of "automatic or repeat licensing," on the other hand, kept the decision as to who were to be the importers and which commodities were to be imported in the hands of the licensing authorities. Only the amounts of each to be imported were determined by the market. The goal of orienting the supply of imports to demand was also sought in the system of industrial licensing. An attempt was made to move away from the official "assessment of capacity" basis of licensing, which tended to become dated more quickly than it could be reassessed. Basically, selected industries were allowed to request necessary imports of raw materials and spare parts for a twelve-month period. The government then tried to meet one-half of this request each six-month shipping period.

The import licensing system was increasingly used for export promotion. The export industries were selected for more favorable treatment in terms of import entitlements to raw materials and spare parts. A direct link between export performance and import licensing was established in the 1960s in that a few specified industries with adequate export performance to their credit received additional licenses for the import of balancing and modernization equipment, whereas those units without adequate performance were threatened with reduction of import privileges in the future if they failed to expand their export performance. The introduction of the Export Bonus Scheme as described earlier was primarily oriented toward stimulating exports at the same time that it allowed a greater play of market forces for the determination of quantum of imports.[8]

The foregoing discussion amply demonstrates that the system of import licensing was a highly complicated one. The licensing system was distinguished by *types of import control,* i.e., the open general license, automatic licensing, the export bonus scheme, normal import licensing, and export performance licensing, as well as the scheme of cash-cum-bonus import, which was introduced in 1968. The licensing system was also distinguished by *types of importers,* the major distinction being between commercial and industrial imports. There was also a small category of the actual users, who were allowed to import items for their personal or professional use.

8. Discussed below in chap. 7.

The schematic representation of the licensing system given in the appendix to this chapter for four of the selected years (1963, 1964, 1966, and 1968) brings out the complexity of the system. The first year (1963) describes the system before the "free list" attempt at liberalization was introduced; the second year (1964) indicates the change in the licensing system after this liberalization. The third year (1966) represents the effects of the setback in the liberalization efforts in the post-1965 period. The last year (1968) indicates the growing dependence of the import system on the Export Bonus Scheme as well as on the cash-cum-bonus scheme.[9]

Analysis of the licensing system, given in tables 5A1-5A4, confirms that there were frequent changes in the details of the system. The imported commodities were shifted among the various types of control quite frequently; they were moved from one import list (say, the regular, licensed list) to another (say, automatic licensing, the OGL system, or the free list). Sometimes the movement was back and forth. Under the system of industrial licensing the distinction between the established importers and the potential importers was flexible and shifted from one year to the next. For example, during 1963 there were four separate lists of industries for importation of the items on the regular, licensable list, as distinguished from the OGL, the list of automatic licensing, and the bonus list. These four groups of industries were treated differently in terms of more or less liberal access to raw materials. By the end of 1964 the lists of industries were reduced to only two, both of which were entitled without distinction to export performance licensing. During 1966/67, while the two lists were retained, even though the industrial composition of the two lists was changed, not all of them were entitled to export performance licensing. An additional list was established for eligibility to export performance licensing. By 1968 separate lists of industries for the imports of items on the licensable lists were abolished and only one list, expanded and modified, of the industries entitled to export performance licensing was retained. By 1970 export performance licensing was abolished.

IMPORT TARIFF SYSTEM

The level and structure of tariffs in Pakistan were the result of actions taken by two separate agencies with different objectives. Tariffs were imposed both for raising revenue and for providing protection to domestic industries. The Tariff Commission was charged with the responsibility of suggesting the level of protective

---

9. Under the cash-cum-bonus scheme a certain amount of a specific commodity is allowed to be imported under normal licensing at the official rate of exchange, provided an equivalent amount of the same commodity is imported under the bonus scheme at the much higher (bonus) import rate of exchange.

duties. The Ministry of Finance, which imposed duties primarily for the purpose of raising revenue, evaluated the recommendations of the Tariff Commission in terms of their impact on overall revenues as well as on the growth of domestic economic activities. Of course, to the extent that protection was not prohibitive, protective duties yielded revenues while revenue tariffs provided protection.

When examining a claim for tariff protection, the Tariff Commission had to satisfy itself that:

(a) the industry was established on sound lines and conducted with reasonable efficiency;

(b) the industry was likely to be able to dispense with the necessity of protection within a reasonable time period, during which the additional cost to the consumer or government was not excessive;

(c) the protection of the industry was not inconsistent with any treaty obligations undertaken by government.

The commission recommended not only the rate of protective duties but also other forms of assistance to be given to the industry concerned. It could also specify the period for which protective duties and/or other forms of assistance were to be applicable. One may be asked why in spite of strict quantitative restrictions the manufacturing industries sought tariff protection. First, in a few cases of quantitative restrictions the price spread between foreign and domestic price resulting from import restrictions had been insufficient to provide adequate protection for high cost domestic industry. Second, quantitative restrictions had multiple purposes. They were seldom geared to the needs of specific industries but were often oriented to general balance of payment considerations. Their intensity varied in response to changes in the balance of payments and not to the changing competitiveness of domestic industries. Third, even though revenue duties in many cases were sufficiently high to provide protection, they were not fixed according to cost conditions of specific industries. They responded mainly to budgetary considerations.

When screening claims for protection, the Tariff Commission examined a number of aspects of the industry seeking protection. It was not clear how conflicts or trade-offs among the various factors were resolved or what weights were assigned to the multiplicity of objectives. Considerations such as the domestic demand for the products, their prices, their quality, the cost disabilities, and the direct foreign exchange savings all weighed with the Commission.

Since protection was intended to substitute capacity to meet all or most imports, industry had to have sufficient capacity to meet all or most of the domestic demand. Eliminating bottlenecks to production was thus judged important. However, if domestic demand was inadequate, the Commission was reluctant to recommend a tariff. After detailed cost investigation the Commission estimated ex-factory fair price, which was based on the costs of production and a fair rate of return on capital. This gave it a representative firm or group of firms in terms of efficiency.[10] The Commission undertook detailed technical investigations about the quality of products, including inquiries among the users of the product. Frequently it required the adoption of necessary measures for quality improvement, a condition for the grant of protection. This procedure was followed particularly in the case of intermediate goods and investment goods industries.

Specific causes of cost disabilities in a particular industry were important considerations. The limited size of the market and the high costs of labor, materials, overhead, and distribution were studied with respect to their expected movement over time. The Commission compensated only for those disabilities which it thought could be overcome in the course of time. In many cases the size of market proved to be a significant cost-raising factor. The higher cost of skilled labor, the need to hold large inventories due to the uncertainty of imports and administrative delays, and lower labor productivity, all contributed to high domestic costs. The Commission was favorably inclined toward imposing tariffs to overcome these sources of cost disabilities because an improvement in efficiency in these respects over time was a reasonable expectation. It did not rank industries by their relative cost disadvantages and it did not have a predetermined level of disadvantages that it felt should be offset by tariffs. However, the Commission was the final arbiter in matters of protection.

In later years, saving or earning of foreign exchange had become an important criterion in deciding eligibility for protection. In order to merit protection, an industry was expected to have a net foreign exchange saving. However, no particular level of foreign exchange saving was considered necessary in order to qualify for protection. And there was no unmistakable indication that an industry was necessarily preferred, for purposes of protection, if it saved more foreign exchange than another.[11] There was no interindustry comparison of various cost criteria or efficiency criteria to decide on a cut-off point in respect to each criterion before an industry became eligible for protection.

The tariff rates did not have any correlation with the extent of foreign exchange saving because a multiplicity of other considerations affected them. The extent of the differential between import price and domestic cost, the nature of the commodity, i.e., whether it was an essential intermediate good used in the pro-

10. Some industries charged actual prices below the calculated fair price, implying that they earned less than usual profits. These cases were identified as those facing serious competition from abroad.

11. The calculation of foreign exchange saving was based on direct foreign exchange requirements alone. In many cases, however, remittances of dividends and interest on foreign loans and investments were excluded from these calculations, as were royalties, fees for foreign patent rights, and salaries for foreign personnel. And, except in a few cases, neither the foreign exchange cost, nor even annual depreciation of imported capital equipment, was deducted. Accordingly, even the direct foreign exchange requirements were underestimated.

duction of a large number of other commodities, and the degree of other concessions in terms of liberal supply of raw material inputs, a reduction of or rebate on or an exemption from customs duties on imported raw material, among other factors, all affected the final choice of protective tariff rates. The Tariff Commission usually attempted to equalize landed cost (including tariffs) with the ex-factory price. It tried to identify the source of competing imports that provided the maximum competition to indigenous industry in an effort to formulate tariff rates that protected the industry against the cheapest sources of imports but not against obvious or gross inefficiency in domestic production. It often recommended conditional protection if the industry did not charge prices higher than those considered fair. On the whole, the Commission was averse to raising the price of an intermediate product or of capital equipment because of the effect such an increase would have on the cost structure of other industries. In such cases, cost reduction was assisted by the reduction of duties and taxes imposed on raw materials and components.

The Commission in its analyses and recommendations was aware that import duties on the inputs of intermediate products constituted a tax on the finished product, that a duty on the import of finished products was a subsidy, and that the net protective effect on a particular industry was composed of both these elements. In many cases it recommended import duties on finished products and exemption from or rebates on, customs duties on raw materials and components in order to reduce the cost of domestic production, on the one hand, and to raise the price of the imported product in the domestic market, on the other. But the Tariff Commission did not formulate its ideas in a way that enabled it to calculate the rate of effective protection to each industry. The concept of net or effective protection did not appear either in its analyses or in its recommendations.

As explained earlier, the level and structure of import tariffs were only partly a result of recommendations of the Tariff Commission and related to those imports that competed with domestic production and applied to those industries that applied for protective duties. The great bulk of import duties imposed for revenue purposes were not referred to the Tariff Commission but necessarily had both protective and revenue raising functions. Import duties were also imposed to regulate imports in order to save foreign exchange by restricting domestic imports, discouraging luxury imports, encouraging domestic saving, and achieving a structure of composition of imports that would be more equitable for the distribution of income.

IMPORT CONTROLS, STRUCTURE OF IMPORTS, AND IMPORT SUBSTITUTION

Import tariffs and licensing affect the pattern of domestic industrialization by raising the relative prices of imports in a differential manner in the domestic

Table 5.1. Composition of Commercial Licensing (percentage distribution)

Type of commodity	1955	1959	1963
Consumer goods	31.9	15.3	15.5
Raw materials	53.8	65.8	50.4
Capital goods	14.3	18.9	34.1
Total value of commercial licensing (Rs million)	453.3	491.4	738.7

Source: S. N. H. Naqvi, "The Allocative Biases of Pakistan's Commercial Policy," *Pakistan Development Review,* reprinted in Nurul Islam, ed. *Studies on Commercial Policy and Economic Growth* (Karachi: PIDE, 1970), pp. 63-68.

market and thus providing differential incentives to the growth of different industries. But because of the predominance of quantitative controls on imports throughout the period of Pakistan's industrialization, with the implicit tariffs often higher than the actual tariffs, the impact of differential protective tariffs on the emerging pattern of industrialization in Pakistan was very limited. Nonetheless, when fluctuations in the intensity of import control reduced the degree of protection for any industry, tariffs provided the second line of defense.[12]

The change in the structure of import licensing can be gauged by a study of the composition of imports in terms of types of commodity and types of industry.[13] The distribution of commercial and industrial licensing during the 1950s and early 1960s is shown in tables 5.1-5.3.

The structure of import duties over the years can be seen from table 5.2. A few characteristics of the structure and time pattern of import duties may be noted. First, although import restrictions during the period of the First Five Year Plan were more stringent compared with the preplan period, i.e., 1951/52-1954/55, windfall profits earned by the importers were not mobilized for the public sector by means of high import duties. Second, the structure of tariffs was such that machinery and equipment paid the lowest rates of duty, whereas nonessential consumer goods and consumer durables paid the highest rates of duty. Industrial raw materials, intermediate goods, and essential consumer goods paid roughly similar rates of duty, which were higher than those on machinery and equipment

12. P. S. Thomas, "Import Licensing and Import Liberalization in Pakistan," *Pakistan Development Review* 6, no. 4 (Winter 1966): 500-44, and Government of Pakistan, Ministry of Commerce, *Pakistan Customs Tariff, 1968-69* (Islamabad, 1969).

13. The data on the pattern of import licensing by categories of commodities are available for only a few years and they relate only to commercial and industrial licensing, the latter being concerned mainly with distribution of imported raw materials and intermediate inputs among the large-scale domestic industries. The data on industrial distribution of imported capital goods, which was governed by the system of investment licensing, were not available.

Table 5.2.   Average Rate of Import Duties by Commodity Groups

	1955/56 *1959/60*	*1961/* *1962*	*1964/* *1965*	*1965/* *1966*	*1968/* *1969*
Consumption goods					
(a) Essentials	35	55	56	70	70
(b) Others	77	126	131	164	150
Raw materials for					
consumption goods	35	39	48	60	60
Raw materials for					
capital goods	31	34	44	55	66
Capital goods					
(a) Consumer durables	71	85	91	114	115
(b) Machinery and equipment	14	17	22	34	37

Source: (1) P. S. Thomas, "Import Licensing and Import Liberalisation in Pakistan;" (2) Government of Pakistan, *Pakistan Customs Tariff, 1968–69* (Islamabad).

but lower than those on consumer durables and nonessential consumer goods. Over the years there was an increase in the rates of duty on all categories of imports.

Third, insofar as the structure of rates was concerned, the only significant change was the gradual increase in the import duties on capital equipment in relation to those on raw materials, so that by 1968/69 the relative rates on machinery vis-à-vis those on raw materials were higher than they were in the early 1960s. There did not seem to be any significantly greater degree of differentiation in the structure of tariff rates in the late 1960s compared with the late 1950s, at least insofar as it can be discerned in terms of the rate structure of duties on the four categories of imports (see table 5.2).

As is evident from table 5.3, there was a decline in the share of imports of consumer goods between 1957 and 1965 and a rise in the share of capital goods. The imports of raw materials in commercial licensing increased in the 1950s and declined in the early 1960s. Under the system of industrial licensing, while the intermediate and capital goods industries increased their respective shares compared to the 1950s, the consumer goods industries suffered a decline in their share.[14]

The commodity composition of aggregate imports, both public and private as well as under all types of licensing, confirms the conclusions reached on the basis of commercial and industrial licensing (table 5.4). There was a rapid decline in

14. Thomas, "Import Licensing," and Ministry of Commerce, *Pakistan Customs Tariff, 1968–69;* see also S. R. Lewis, *Economic Policy and Industrial Growth* (Cambridge: M.I.T. Press, 1969), p. 104, and *Pakistan: Industrialization and Trade Policies* (Oxford: Oxford University Press, 1970), p. 72.

Table 5.3.   Share of Different Industries in Industrial Import Licensing

Type of industry	1957	1960	1965	1963/64 Direct import coefficients
Consumer goods	60.4	45.6	36.6	10.95
Intermediate goods	28.1	35.5	30.3	12.98
Investment and related goods	11.5	18.9	33.1	22.98
Total value of industrial licensing (Rs million)	304.2	475.9	780.9	—

Sources: See table 5.2.

the proportion of consumer goods imports (excluding food), matched by a rapid increase in the proportion of capital goods imports, especially beginning with the Second Five Year Plan, accompanied by a relatively slow change in the share of intermediate goods and raw materials. In fact there was a fall in its relative share in the First Plan Period compared with the preplan period and a relatively slow rate of recovery during the Second and Third Five Year Plans. The relative share of consumer goods declined over the years, most drastically in the early 1950s. There was a slight recovery in the absolute value of imports of consumer goods in the First Plan Period, followed by persistent decline in the absolute value of their imports during the Second and Third Five Year Plans. As for raw materials, i.e., those used by the capital and consumer goods industries, these imports increased between 1951/52 and 1968/69.

The changing pattern of imports was associated with the changing pattern of domestic industrialization. The absolute decline in the import of consumer goods was both the cause and the effect of the big push toward industrialization in the consumer goods sector. There were important consumer goods such as sugar, edible oils, cotton and other textiles, jute textiles, tobacco manufactures and matches, the import of which registered an absolute decline between 1951/52–1954/55 and 1954/55–1958–60. This provided a considerable stimulus to domestic production in the import-competing industry. The data on commercial licensing to private sector industry confirm the above finding. Lewis has shown that there were declines in commercial licensing for those products that competed with such domestic industries.[15] The progress in import substitution in the consumer goods industry was so substantial that there was an absolute decline in the

15. Lewis, Economic Policy, pp. 147–48. For example, for beverages, tobacco products, cotton, silk and artificial silk textiles, soaps and cosmetics, the amount of import licenses was curtailed progressively throughout the 1950s. These were the very industries in which domestic production was increasing quite rapidly.

Table 5.4.   Composition of Total Imports (Percentage distribution)

Commodity	1951/52– 1954/55	1955/56– 1959/60	1960/61– 1964/65	1965/66– 1968/69
Foodgrains	9.5	16.4	12.8	11.2
Other consumer goods	32.3	25.3	11.4	8.3
Total consumer goods	41.8	41.7	24.2	19.5
Raw materials for consumer goods	19.4	41.7	14.2	20.6
Raw materials for capital goods	11.6	12.5	14.3	11.2
All raw materials	31.0	26.4	28.5	31.8
Capital goods	27.2	31.9	47.3	48.7

Source: Appendix tables in Nurul Islam, *Imports of Pakistan: Growth and Structure: A Statistical Survey,* Pakistan Institute of Development Economics, Statistical Papers no. 3 (Sept. 1967), pp. 1–17.

total value of imports of consumer goods. Of course, some items registered an increase both in domestic production and in imports.

Taking the simplest index of import substitution as the proportion of total supply (domestic production plus imports) accounted for by domestic production, the progress of import substitution, both overall and in terms of groups of industries, can be seen in table 5.5.

The degree of import substitution over the two decades was impressive. In the early 1950s about one-quarter of the total supply of industrial goods was provided by domestic production; by the end of the 1960s, the share of domestic production increased to about 73 percent.[16] The most impressive performance in this regard was in the consumer goods sector.[17] The primary constituent of growth in the consumer goods sector was in fact cotton textiles, sugar, tobacco and matches; in the intermediate goods sector, jute textiles and leather goods had the predominant share. By the early 1960s Pakistan had developed an industrial base, and subsequently the rate of growth slowed down. The impressive performance can also be seen the fact that by 1967/68 Pakistani industries were able to produce 80 percent of their raw material requirements and 45 percent of the capital goods.

The changing contribution of the different industrial groups to the growth of total manufacturing can be evaluated alternatively in terms of the percentage shares of the various industrial groups in the total change in the value added of

16. S. R. Lewis, "Pakistani Industrialisation 1951–1968: Production, Prices and Trade Patterns," unpublished paper, Mar. 1971, table IX. In current prices the relative contributions of different sectors in different time periods were roughly the same.

17. The very high rates of growth in consumer goods in the early 1950s and in the intermediate goods in the late 1950s were partly due to the low base from which these industrial groups started.

Table 5.5.   Rate of Growth of Industry and Share of Production in Total Supply (in 1959/69 Prices)

Growth rate of value added	1951/52–1954/55	1954/55–1959/60	1959/60–1963/64	1963/64–1967/68	
Consumer goods	41	12.4	12.2	4.9	
Intermediate goods	42	20.2	12.9	11.6	
Capital goods	22	22.3	22.7	10.0	
Total	38	15.7	14.4	7.8	
Share of production in total supply	1951/52	1954/55	1959/60	1963/64	1967/68
Consumer goods	24.2	75.1	91.1	97.9	94.2
Intermediate goods	27.9	49.6	59.1	65.9	79.3
Capital goods	23.1	29.6	35.7	34.9	44.5
Total	24.4	58.2	69.7	65.3	73.3

Source: S. R. Lewis, "Pakistani Industrialisation 1951–1968: Production, Prices and Trade Patterns," unpublished paper (Mar. 1971). Total supply is equal to domestic production plus imports.

the entire manufacturing sector in the different periods. Table 5.6 shows this feature to be consistent with the changing growth rates of different industries indicated earlier. The contribution of the consumer goods industry was the largest in the initial period but started to fall earliest as well; the second largest contribution in that period was by the intermediate goods industry, which continued at a higher level than that of the consumer goods industry for a longer period. The smallest contribution was that of the capital goods industry, which picked up in the late 1950s and maintained a high rate of growth for the longest period.

The contribution of the consumer goods sector to the growth in manufacturing value added remains the highest until 1963/64, although declining over the years until mid-1960s. The relative contributions of the other two sectors were not much different; their relative importance was reversed between the two periods in the 1960s, with intermediate goods significantly ahead of the capital goods sector during the later period.

How much was the pattern of import substitution and industrialization affected by the exchange rate and tariff policy? Tariffs and quantitative restrictions were contributory factors in the sense of creating domestic price differentials and hence incentives and differential profitabilities for domestic production in some groups of industries rather than in others. Thus, it is necessary to estimate the degree of protection provided by the exchange rate policies to various groups of industries and to study the relationship between the degree of protection and import substitution.

Because import licensing was the dominant form of protection in Pakistan, tariffs alone did not measure the degree of protection. Nominal implicit protec-

Table 5.6.   Share of Different Groups in Change in Value Added of Manufacturing Sector in Different
Periods (Constant Prices of 1959/60)

	1951/52– *1954/55*	*1954/55–* *1959/60*	*1959/60–* *1963/64*	*1963/64–* *1967/68*
Consumer goods	73.7	54.1	47.3	21.7
Intermediate goods	16.4	24.8	23.4	43.0
Capital goods	9.9	21.1	29.4	35.4
Total	100.0	100.0	100.0	100.0

Source: See table 5.5.

tion, defined as the percentage excess of domestic price over the world price (CIF price) of imported goods, was greater than nominal explicit (tariff) protection. Moreover, the structure of nominal implicit protection was different from that of nominal explicit protection. Therefore, to be meaningful, an analysis of the influence or impact of the exchange rate policy on the pattern of import substitution has to be conducted in terms of an association between the pattern of nominal implicit protection (i.e., differentials between the world and domestic price of imported goods) and the pattern of import substitution. The differences between nominal implicit and explicit protection for broad groups of industries are apparent in table 5.7.

It is evident from table 5.7 that price differentials were far in excess of the tariff rates. Moreover, the increase in implicit protection between the two time periods was greater than the increase in explicit protection. Also, the price differentials in both periods were greater for consumer goods than for either intermediate or capital goods, implying a greater degree of import restriction on the former than on the latter category of imports. If one considers a more detailed breakdown of the tariff rates and price differentials by industry, one finds that in the cases of a few established industries such as cotton and jute textile and leather products, the implicit protection was less than the explicit protection. In other words tariff protection became redundant in those cases. On the basis of a comparison both among three broad groups of industries as well as among individual industries, it appears that the structure of tariff rates (explicit protection) and the structure of price differential (implicit protection) followed a broadly similar pattern; industries with higher rates of tariff protection also had received higher rates of nominal implicit protection by means of more stringent import licensing against their competing imports.

If one looks for an association between import substitution and nominal implicit protection for the three broad groups of industries mentioned above, there was a positive association in the later period but not in the earlier period. In both periods the consumer goods industries with the highest rates of nominal implicit

Table 5.7.   Nominal Explicit and Implicit Protection (In percent)

	Explicit protection (rate of tariffs)		Implicit protection (percentage price differential)	
	1963/64	*1968/69*	*1963/64*	*1966/67*
Consumer goods	94	95	49	317
Intermediate goods	54	46	80	212
Capital goods	47	62	86	150

Source: Nurul Islam, ''Tariff Protection, Comparative Costs and Industrialization in Pakistan,'' Pakistan Institute of Development Economics, Research Report no. 57 (Karachi, Jan. 1967).

Note: Nominal implicit protection is expressed as the percentage of excess of domestic price over world price. The tariff rates and price differentials are a simple average for each industry group.

protection also had the highest proportion of the total supply originating from domestic production. In the later period the intermediate and capital goods sectors received lower rates of nominal implicit protection in that order, and they provided correspondingly smaller proportions of the total supply from domestic production.[18]

When one analyzes the differences in the degree of import substitution among individual industries, instead of among three broad groups of industries, and seeks to relate them to interindustry differences in the degree of explicit or implicit protection, one does not find any conclusive evidence of a close association among them in the two years for which data are available. The lack of relationship can be explained by two principal factors. First, the degree of import substitution achieved in one year is the cumulative effect of the increases in domestic production over the past several years and could logically be expected to be related only to the structure of nominal implicit protection of all those years rather than to one year, unless there was no change in the structure of nominal implicit protection over the years. However, in view of the frequent shifts in import licensing policy and variations in the intensity of control with respect to individual commodities, it is unlikely that the structure of protection did remain unchanged. Second, in many of the industries under consideration for 1967/68, import substitution had already progressed far enough to account for the predominant share of the supply, in some cases approaching self-sufficiency, so that differences among the individual industries in respect to ratio of imports to total supply were not strongly related to variations of their domestic/world price ratios.

18. However, in 1963/64 the intermediate goods sector supplied a higher proportion of the total supply than the capital goods sector although it received a lower rate of nominal implicit protection. Also, the differences between the two groups in terms of nominal implicit protection were greater in the later than in the earlier period.

If the interindustry variations in the degree of import substitution are to be related to the interindustry variations in nominal implicit protection in a given year, one would rather expect that the latter would affect the growth rate of import substitution during the subsequent years. Indeed, interindustry differences in the percentage change in the ratio of domestic production to total supply between 1963/64 and 1967/68 are found to be positively related to variations in the degree of nominal protection in 1963/64. The rank correlation coefficient is 0.55, which is significant at a level of 1 percent. The impact of nominal implicit protection on the pattern of import substitution can also be analyzed by relating the interindustry differences in the growth rate of value added to the interindustry differences in the degree of implicit protection.

The rank correlation coefficient between nominal implicit protection in 1963/64 and the growth rate of value added between 1963/64 and 1967/68 is 0.40 and is significant at a level of 5 percent. There is also a significant correlation between the growth rates between the same periods and the nominal implicit protection in 1968/69. The rank correlation coefficient is 0.49, which is significant at a level of 5 percent.

Another view which can explain the weak relationship is that whereas the generally high level of tariff and quantitative restrictions provided incentives and increased the profitability of investment throughout the manufacturing sector, the differential rates of growth or differential rates of import substitution were in response to other domestic policy measures, i.e., the credit, tax, and investment control policies. Public and private investment first took place in a few industries, encouraged by general import restrictions and domestic policy measures in the 1950s. Subsequently these domestic manufacturers succeeded in getting larger tariffs or stricter import licensing for the competing imports. Therefore, the differential structure of tariffs and quantitative restrictions followed, rather than preceded, the differential rates of import substitution in the different industries. In this situation the industries to be selected were those that any simple analysis of the availability of raw materials, the size of the domestic market, and the requirements of capital and skill in the early years of Pakistan (1947–54) would have led one to choose and emphasize.[19]

As one evaluates the impact of the multiple instruments of economic policy on the pattern of industrialization in Pakistan, it appears difficult, if not impossible, to identify and even more so to quantify the extent to which the exchange rate policy determined the pattern of industrialization or vice versa. Certainly in the early years, when import restrictions led to an absolute decline in the importation

19. The simple consumer goods industries such as textiles, sugar, edible oils, matches, and footwear required little technical know-how, and Pakistan had domestically available raw materials and a market for most of them.

of a number of important consumer goods, there was a direct and immediate impact on the growth of domestic industries, in which both private and public investment played a central role. Thus as investments were made in these industries the manufacturers lobbied for the continuation of import restrictions and in some cases for intensification of restrictions, as well as for the imposition of tariffs. In some cases they pressed for higher tariffs in anticipation that once import restrictions were relaxed due to an improvement in the balance of payments, competitive imports might put their nascent industries into jeopardy. This was indeed the way the Tariff Commission operated in response to requests from the newly developed industries.[20]

In sum, one is inclined to conclude that there were cases in which domestic production occurred in response to general import restrictions and resultant scarcity in the domestic market; these industries in turn sought and received increases in tariffs or in import restrictions to survive and, indeed, to earn excess profit. At the same time, in individual cases investment took place in response to import restrictions, which were stringent enough to provide adequate protection in many cases and redundant protection in a few others.

20. Nurul Islam, *Tariff Protection, Comparative Costs and Industrialization in Pakistan*, Pakistan Institute of Development Economics, Research Report no. 57 (Jan. 1967). Also see chap. 10.

APPENDIX

Table 5A1. Import Licensing System in 1963 (July–December)

Type of import control (by item)	Type of importer Industrial user	Commercial importer	Actual user (consumer)
1. Open General License (50 items)	Industrial importers were not granted OGL license	(1) Established importers (category holders) were allowed OGL license if their imports were below Rs 1,000 per shipping period (2) Newcomers were to be the primary recipients of OGL license (3) Pakistan nationals could become registered importers very easily (4) Initial license was restricted to prescribed limits (5) Repeat licenses were allowed on 75% utilization of initial license	All OGL items were allowed to be imported by actual user on production of satisfactory evidence of personal use and a guarantee of no resale
2. Automatic licensing (12 items)	(1) Initial license at 100% of the entitlement (2) Repeat licenses on 75% utilization of initial license	Same provisions as in the case of industrial user	No
3. Bonus List (174 items)	(a) Every industrial user could import under bonus any raw material to which he was entitled (b) Three industries were to import all their raw material requirements exclusively under bonus (c) The cotton textile industry was to import half its entitlement of textile spare parts under bonus	Registered importers could import unlimited quantities of all bonus items	Any actual user could import bonus items

| 4. Licensed List (175 items) | Four lists of industries were established:

(a) *Ten* export industries were given license on "request" basis. In other words they were given licenses according to their actual requirements. They received whatever they requested, the requirements in the previous shipping period being an indicator of their requirements. Entitlements were based on single-shift capacity requirements. "Request basis" industries could exceed single-shift requirements.

(b) *Thirty-three* industries were granted license of the same *amount* as in the previous shipping period (six month period). In addition they were allowed licenses equal to 100% of the FOB value of exports (export performance license).

(c) *One hundred and one* industries were to get licenses on the basis of their entitlements, the proportions being determined by the Regional Licensing Board (in East and West Pakistan)

(d) *Fifty-one* industries were licensed on automatic basis. Initial licenses were issued at 100% of entitlements, and repeat licenses also were to be given at 100% of entitlements | (1) Only 134 out of 175 items were to be licensed to commercial importers

(2) They were to be licensed on the basis of their category, the percentage of category to be determined by Regional Licensing Board (in East and West Pakistan) | No actual user import for those items was allowed |

Source: Ministry of Commerce, Office of the Chief Controller of Exports and Imports, *Import Policy Statements*, various years, 1963–70.

Note: The individual items given in the Import Trade Classification for the guidance of importers, on the basis of which import "categories" are fixed, are very detailed. The items described above refer to broad category groups or "generic" groups, as the import policy calls them. Within each generic group the detailed listing of individual items is given. There are a large number of individual items within a number of generic groups, such as iron and steel, chemicals, drugs, imports of which were completely banned.

Table 5A2. Import Licensing System in 1964 (July–December) (After the introduction of free list as the first significant step in liberalization)

Type of import control (by item) \ Type of importer	Industrial user	Commercial importer	Actual user
1. Free List (51 items)	(a) Every industrial user could import any item on free list for which he had an entitlement (b) Initial letters of credit could be opened up to 100% of entitlement (c) Letters of credit could be repeated (d) Six out of 51 items were restricted exclusively to the industrial users	(a) Every registered importer could import 45 out of 51 items (b) Initial letters of credit were to be 100% of category entitlement (c) Repeat licenses (d) Non-Pakistani established importers could import 30 out of 51 items only, subject to maximum limits	Actual users could import any free list items
2. Open General License (33 items)	No	(a) All established registered importers with imports of less than Rs 2,000 in one shipping period could be admitted under OGL. Registered importers already admitted under OGL would continue to get licenses (b) Initial licenses were to be restricted to prescribed maximum limits; there were also minimum limits (c) Repeat licenses were to be issued on 75% utilization of initial license (d) Initial license was to be 25% more for those with sizable export performance (not less than twice the	(a) Five items were exclusively limited to actual users. No newcomer during the period would be allowed. Established importers and those already admitted would get licenses for these items

70

		(minimum amount licensed during the last shipping period)	Actual users could import any item
3. Bonus List	(a) Every industrial user can import under bonus any raw material to which he is entitled (b) Five industries (including cotton textiles) were to import all raw materials and spare parts exclusively under bonus, excepting those which have been placed under free list	Registered importers could import any item up to any amount	
4. Licensed List (98 items)	(a) 202 *A* list industries could import non-free list items, to which they were entitled, at 100% of their entitlement with facilities to repeat the initial license (b) 43 *B* industries were to get licenses, on the basis of their entitlements, percentages being fixed by Regional Licensing Boards (c) All industries in both the above lists were to receive export performance licensing up to 50% of FOB value of exports to meet requirements of raw materials and spare parts	(a) Established or registered importers could import only 63 items out of 98 items (b) Percentages of their categories to be determined by Regional Licensing Board (in East and West Pakistan)	No actual user import was allowed

Source: See table 5A1.

Note: N.B. Even though 51 items were on the Free List, these were generic categories. Specific items within each group were not allowed to be imported at all, i.e., banned. There were 12 items within the category of (a) iron and steel; 6 items under (b) nonferrous metals; 21 items under (c) chemicals; 24 items under (d) machineries and maintenance parts; and 5 items under (e) pigments, paints, and colors that were banned. Under the generic heading of drugs and medicines only 36 items were permitted to be imported.

Table 5A3. Import Licensing System in 1966/67

Type of import control (by item)	Industrial user	Commercial importer	Actual user
1. Free List (66 items)	(a) Every industrial user (except jute) could import any item on free list for which he had an entitlement (b) Initial letters of credit were limited to 100% of entitlement (c) Repeat facilities were allowed (d) 26 items were limited exclusively to industrial users	(a) Every registered importer could import 37 of 66 items (b) Initial letters to credit were limited to stated maximum (c) Repeat facilities were allowed (d) Pakistani businessmen could become registered importers quite easily	(a) Three free list items were limited to actual users (such as x-ray equipment for hospitals). (b) Actual users could import any of the other 63 items
2. Bonus List (200 items)	(a) 44 C list industries must import all non-free list raw materials under bonus. (b) Jute industry must meet all import needs under bonus (c) Every industrial user could import under bonus any raw material to which he is en-	(a) Registered importers could import unlimited quantities of all bonus items	(a) Actual users could import any non-free list item (which was not banned)

72

titled ("safety valve" feature when licenses are inadequate)

3. Licensed List

(96 items)

(a) 148 *A* list industries could import non-free list items to which they were entitled at 100% of entitlement, with repeat facilities. (That is, *A* industries could import almost all their entitled materials under Free List conditions)

(b) 110 *B* list industries could get 12-month license; amount determined by Regional Licensing Boards. Only 45% of these licenses could be used in the first 6 months. 35 items were restricted to industrial users only

(c) Selected industries (114 in number) were entitled to export performance licensing at varying percentages up to the maximum of 50% of the FOB value of exports

(a) Importers with categories or former OGL importers could import 57 items

(b) Licenses were to be issued for 12 months, but only 45% could be imported during the 1st six months

(c) Of 57 items, about 25 were to be licensed at flat rate

(a) Four items were restricted to actual users

(b) Actual users of other 92 items could import these under bonus

Source: See table 5A1.

73

Table 5A4. Import Licensing System in 1968 (July–December)

Type of import control (by item) \ Type of importer	Industrial user	Commercial importer	Actual user
1. Free List (14 items) (Almost all the items placed on the free list were industrial raw materials)	(a) Every industrial user can import any item on free list for which he has an entitlement or category (b) Initial letter of credit was limited to 100% of entitlement (c) Repeat facilities were allowed	(a) The registered importers are allowed to import only 7 out of 14 items (b) The amount of imports were subject to maximum and minimum limits prescribed by the licensing authority	Actual users were not allowed. Two items were reserved for import by public sector only
2. Licensable List (31 items)	(a) License issued by the Regional Licensing Board, which determined the percentage of entitlement allowed to be imported by each industrial user	(a) Licenses issued by the Regional Licensing Board, which determined the percentage of category allowed to be imported (b) They were allowed to import only 24 out of 31 items	(a) Eight of these items could be imported by actual users (b) Two items were to be reserved for public sector only
3. Cash-cum-Bonus List (94 items) first introduced in 1967/68	(a) All industrial users could import these items at 100% of their entitlement (b) No repeat facilities	(a) Registered importers could import only 31 items out of 94 items (b) Regional Licensing Boards were to determine the percentage of licensing	(a) Four of these items could be imported by actual users

4. Bonus List (261 items)	(a) All industrial users could import any items up to any amount (b) Moreover, the items permitted to be imported under 3 other lists as above could also be imported under bonus	(a) Same as in the case of industrial users	(a) Same as in the case of commercial and industrial importers
5. Export Performance licensing (52 items)	152 industries were allowed licenses up to varying percentages of FOB exports not exceeding 30% of FOB exports to import raw materials to which they were entitled	Not relevant	Not relevant
6. Trading Corporation of Pakistan (TCP) (10 items)	Starting July 1968, 10 items such as (1) pig iron, (2) steel billets from non-U.S. sources, (3) steel strips, (4) aluminum ingots, (5) copper rods, (6) zinc, (7) sulfur, (8) raw rubber, (9) betel nuts, and (10) artificial silk yarn were to be imported exclusively by the government trading enterprise, i.e., TCP. The private traders would place their order through the TCP. The amount of order would be in accordance with the basis announced by the licensing authority. In other words these items were governed by the same criteria and same basis of licensing as the licensed items except that imports have to be undertaken through the intermediary of the TCP	N.B.: From January 1970 onward the scheme was terminated. A new scheme called Raw Material Replenishment scheme was introduced. 155 industries were allowed to import varying percentages of their FOB value of exports, in terms of raw materials required for the production of their goods under the cash-cum-bonus scheme, which were not provided under cash licensing or under the old scheme of export performance licensing. Maintenance parts were also included among eligible imports. Both traders who exported as well as the export industries were entitled to this privilege	

Source: See table 5A1.

75

6

Export Policies and Export Performances

EXPORT PROMOTION MEASURES

Throughout the two decades, more so in the 1960s than in the 1950s, Pakistan adopted a series of measures to regulate and promote exports. An exporter had to be registered before he could engage in export trade. During the 1950s there were occasional bans or restrictions on the export of items that were in short supply in the home market. There were a few items, the export of which required prior permission of the authorities. More important among the measures inhibiting exports in the 1950s was the system of export duties, mainly on primary commodities, which were, however, progressively reduced in the later years.

The range and variety of incentives used to promote exports in Pakistan proliferated rapidly in the 1960s. The export promotion measures can be usefully categorized in three groups. (1) There were measures linking exports with access to imports. Because access to imports implied extraordinary profits, such a link provided exporters with a subsidy. (2) Fiscal and financial incentives consisting of various tax concessions, rebates, and exemptions, as well as special credit and insurance facilities, formed one set of schemes. (3) Different institutional arrangements for efficient export marketing were another class of measures designed to promote exports.

Linking Exports with Access to Imports

Bilateral and Barter Agreements

Perhaps the earliest means of promoting exports in Pakistan was the use of bilateral trade agreements and barter agreements. Barter agreements usually involved negotiated trade and payments between governments designed to achieve predetermined quantitative relations between respective exports. The commodities and periods of shipment were specified; in most cases import prices for Pakistan were normally predetermined, while the export prices were left to be negotiated in accordance with world market prices. Nonconvertible accounts were often maintained to help guarantee eventual balance between exports and imports. Often large gaps remained between prescribed targets set for trade promotion and actual performance. With the advent of tight import restrictions after 1952, barter trade was increasingly used as a means of obtaining assurances of specific quantities of exports.[1]

Although barter trade was conducted mostly with centrally planned economies (not all trade with socialist countries was by barter),[2] Pakistan also had barter agreements with nonsocialist countries such as Indonesia, Nepal, and India. But the proportion of total exports of major commodities covered by barter trade agreements rarely exceeded 10 percent up to the late 1960s. The proportion of total exports of all commodities covered by barter was much smaller.[3]

The objectives of barter trade agreements, from the point of view of Pakistan, were to expand nontraditional exports into new markets. This was expected to diversify Pakistan's sources of imports, especially for essential consumer goods and industrial raw materials, which were less readily available under foreign assistance.

Pay as You Earn Scheme

A facility for exporters to obtain certain imported capital goods was instituted in 1962 and was called the Pay As You Earn Scheme. This provided a combination of credit[4] and import licensing facilities for prospective exporters operating within the Industrial Investment Schedule[5] as well as public and semipublic sectors.

There were several weaknesses in the scheme, and its function in relation to other export promotion measures was a little unclear. Administratively, the determination of each case on an ad hoc basis slowed down the approval process and created uncertainty about coverage and applicability of the scheme. On the whole the ad hoc nature of determining its applicability did not ensure that investment in export industries would take place according to any consideration of comparative cost advantage.

Export-Based Access to Imports

In June 1954 the first of a series of schemes directly linking import access to export performance was instituted. The Export Incentive Scheme was designed to stimulate certain minor primary and manufactured exports (other than jute,

---

1. J. R. Andrus and A. F. Mohammed, *Trade, Finance and Development in Pakistan* (Karachi: Oxford University Press, 1966), p. 35.

2. United States Agency for International Development (USAID) Mission in Pakistan, *Statistical Fact Book* (Rawalpindi, 1968), tables 8–25, 8–28.

3. Commodities covered are raw cotton, raw jute, rice wool, chrome ore, tanned leather, and jute and cotton manufactures, including cotton yarn, garments, and hosiery (ibid., table 8–26).

4. Credit was repaid out of subsequent export earnings over a period of eight years.

5. For details see chap. 7.

cotton, hides and skins, and tea) by providing import licenses up to a specified percentage (30%) of the value of exports. Restrictions on minimum and maximum sizes of import licenses were specified, as was the list of eligible imports. Although certain minor exports received a boost from this incentive, the scheme covered only approximately 1–2 percent of total exports.

After devaluation in 1955, which itself provided incentives to exports (see chap. 3 above) a new Export Promotion Scheme was adopted to provide a stimulus to new exporters of specified primary and manufactured goods that had not been exported prior to devaluation. While a differential rate was instituted to provide a greater stimulus to manufactured goods,[6] restrictions on the use of the import licenses thus generated were more stringent. Various changes were made from time to time in the rates applicable to exports and in the items eligible for import.

The Export Bonus Scheme, introduced in 1959, was a device used both to subsidize exports and to facilitate imports.[7] Under this scheme the exporters not only received the value of exported goods in local currency converted at the official exchange rate but also obtained bonus vouchers in foreign exchange equivalent to some percentage of their export earnings.[8] This voucher could be used by the exporter to import any item from a list of importables that changed from time to time or could be sold in an organized market at a premium above their face value.[9] Thus the exporter was subsidized because bonus vouchers sold at a premium and the importer received an auctioned import license.

The export performance licensing scheme, which was confined to manufactured exports, fixed percentages of import entitlements according to the import content of individual exports. Even individual export commodities had different rates later. These could be used only for the import of particular items used in the production of the given export commodity.[10] The subsidy implicit in the licenses

6. FOB export rate for primary exports was 15% and for manufactured goods 25–40%.

7. For details see chap. 7.

8. The percentages or rates of bonus were different for different groups of commodities. Primary commodities received different bonus rates from manufactured commodities, which in turn received two or three different rates.

9. These vouchers could be used by exporters or sold in the open market, where the premium would depend on the scarcity premium of imports. This premium would provide a subsidy to exporters.

10. The import licenses granted under performance licensing could not legally be sold or transferred, and the resulting imported commodities could not be traded. However, in the context of an overall stringent licensing situation and a scarcity of foreign exchange there was a great opportunity to engage in illegal black market transactions, which proved very profitable. Although such activity was discouraged by the government, its existence was well established. The announcement of semiannual import policies contained a warning that those caught transferring licenses or commodities were liable to having their licensing privileges taken away.

depended upon (1) the scarcity premium on individual imports in the domestic market and (2) the ratio of imported inputs to total output. So, there were as many rates of export subsidy as there were commodities. There was a change in rate structure in 1964 from a single applicable rate (100% of import content) for all industries covered by the scheme to a series of discretionary rates of up to 50 percent until the middle of 1968 and since then up to 30 percent.[11] The introduction of an indefinite rate structure led to a proliferation of applications to the authorities for decisions on rates and on their revisions. Because each industry's rate had to be determined separately the process was an immense administrative task and took a substantial period of time. Also, special appeals for increases in rates flooded the system with additional work.[12] The coverage of industries eligible for export performance licensing also changed over the years from 35 in 1962 to 90 by the end of 1964 and about 150 from 1967 onward.[13]

As a proportion of total and private imports, performance licensing remained quite small, although it gradually increased toward the end of the 1960s. In terms of private imports under the licensing system, export performance licenses did not cover more than 51 percent even in the late 1960s. The composition of performance licensing imports was weighted more heavily toward spare parts than that of normal industrial licensing.[14] The average share of raw materials was 95.4 percent for normal licensing whereas it was only 80.7 percent for performance licensing. Therefore, performance licensing allowed exporters more ready access to spare parts. To the extent that this licensing permitted a more continuous operation of plant and machinery by avoiding costly or prolonged breakdown, exporters might have found it advantageous to concentrate their importation of spare parts under performance licensing, under which they had guaranteed access to imports.

Fiscal and Financial Incentives

Fiscal Incentives

Since 1961/62 Pakistan had granted relief from income taxation for certain classes of exports manufactured in specified areas. Initially this privilege was extended only to those industries based wholly or mainly on indigenous raw

11. W. E. Hecox, "The Export Performance Licensing Scheme," *Pakistan Development Review* 10, no. 1 (Spring 1970): 30-31. The discussion on export performance draws heavily on this work.

12. The Export Promotion Bureau and the Office of the Chief Controller of Imports and Exports sought detailed information on various aspects of the production process, costs, import components, and sources of supply in order to determine the licensing rates. In a few cases physical inspection of the products and processes of production was undertaken.

13. Hecox, "Export Performance Licensing Scheme," pp. 30-31.

14. Ibid., pp. 35-36.

materials. However, since 1964/65 this privilege was extended to all industries with "appreciable export potential" regardless of the source of raw materials. Industries eligible for this concession were periodically notified. In addition, all units, irrespective of the specific industry they belonged to, that exported at least 30 percent of their output or that used primarily domestic raw materials were eligible. The list of industries that were eligible for the tax holiday included two types: (1) traditional exports of Pakistan, such as carpets, sport goods, cutlery, surgical instruments, leather and leather goods, which faced increased competition from other developing countries, and (2) producer goods, including machinery and equipment, which were import intensive but which required large markets for efficient production.

Furthermore, since 1963 there was an income tax holiday for new manufacturers who had export potential. Certain exports excluding tea, cotton, and jute manufactures received concessions in the calculation of taxable income for income tax purposes. Their taxable income was reduced by a percentage, varying from 10 to 20 percent, depending upon the percentage of output exported.[15]

An exporter was entitled to receive a rebate on that portion of the cost of his exported product which represented payment of the central government sales tax. This program extended to sales tax on the finished product as well as on inputs. Central excise duties were also refunded upon proof of export, a policy that extended to finished products and imports as well. Rebates on custom duties levied on imported inputs used in manufactured exports were also introduced. The rebates applied only to indirect taxes (sales, excise, and customs duties) imposed by the central government and not to those imposed by the provincial government. The manufacturer/exporters, as well as commercial exporters (nonproducing exporters), were eligible for such rebates.

The rebate system suffered from considerable weaknesses. The claims for these rebates were met after long periods of delay, largely due to the fragmentation of the system but also due to multiplicity of rates and the process of verification.[16] Thus the effectiveness of the rebates was reduced. Only toward the end of the 1960s was the system rationalized in terms of standardized rates and centralized administration.[17]

Beginning as early as 1959 reduced freight rates were provided to approximately 30 export commodities for their inland transportation to the shipping point. The examination of a sample of 38 commodities which obtained concessional freight rates in the late 1960s revealed that the reduction in freight rates to the extent of

---

15. Pakistan, Ministry of Commerce, Export Promotion Bureau, *Fiscal Incentives* (Karachi, 1965), and Government of Pakistan, Ministry of Finance, *Economic Survey, 1966–67* (Karachi, 1967).

16. Exporters had to apply at several different places for various rebates.

17. The Export Promotion Bureau in 1967 centralized all the functions for rebate claims.

50 percent or more was obtained in the case of 17 commodities. For 14 others the percentage reduction was between 30 and 45 percent. The rest obtained about 10 to 25 percent.[18]

There was a gradual elimination of export taxes over the entire period. These taxes were temporarily raised during the Korean War boom to absorb some of the difference between prices in producing and consuming countries. Whereas at one time duties were levied on 12 items,[19] the late 1960s witnessed the complete removal of export duties.[20] Until 1967 duties on raw jute and raw cotton acted as a disincentive to producers. The tax adversely affected the volume of exports by reducing the earnings of exporters and growers. The production of competing crops such as rice and sugar cane was stimulated, thereby diverting resources away from the production of exportables to food crops for domestic consumption. Because duties kept domestic prices of raw jute and raw cotton lower than world prices, it provided a subsidy to the domestic textile industries.

Financial Incentives

The more prominent among the financial incentives were the export credit guarantee scheme, liberal financing facilities by commercial banks, and the organization of export market development funds.

The purpose of the Export Credit Guarantee Scheme (ECGS) was to encourage exports by underwriting financial risks in the buyers' country that were beyond the control of exporters and were not covered by normal insurance guarantees. The risks covered by the scheme included insolvency of buyers, inability of the buyer to transfer local funds for payment to a Pakistani exporter, failure of the buyer to fulfill a contract for reasons outside the control of the exporter, and imposition of regulations preventing entry of goods into the buyer's country. The percentage of risks covered was 75 percent for commercial risks and 83 percent for political risks.

Several measures besides the ECGS were introduced to facilitate exporters' access to credit. Commercial banks allowed exporters an interest rebate of 1 percent on advances for exports. The State Bank of Pakistan liberalized its Bill Rediscounting Scheme, under which commercial banks could make advances against bills covering exports or could rediscount the export bills directly with the State Bank.[21] Furthermore, in 1968/69 the State Bank was permitted to discount

18. Government of Pakistan, Ministry of Finance, Central Board of Revenue.

19. A yearly list of these duties is given in G. M. Radhu, ''The Rate Structure of Indirect Taxes in Pakistan,'' *Pakistan Development Review* 4, no. 3 (Autumn 1964), table 1.

20. Export duties on bamboo, cement, and fish were removed in 1950, on raw wool in 1952, jute manufactures in 1953, raw hides and skins and rice in 1955, tea in 1963, and raw jute and raw cotton in 1967.

21. The restrictions imposed by the State Bank on advances, unsecured or secured by a guarantee,

export bills at 1 percent below the bank rate on the condition that the benefit would be passed on to the exporter by commercial banks.[22]

In an attempt to encourage and finance certain aspects of exporting with considerable externalities that were not liable to be financed by any single exporter, an Export Market Development Fund was established in January 1966. The object of the fund was to finance through grants in aid (both partial and comprehensive) projects relating to the exploration of and adjustment to export markets.[23]

Institutional Arrangements

Various standards for exportable goods and commodities were set up from time to time. Toward the end of the 1960s a compulsory standardization of goods offered for export was instituted in gradual stages, widening the coverage of export products. An Export Promotion Bureau was established in the mid-1960s that, in addition to the provision of information, had responsibility for settling trade disputes, providing trade facilities to exporters, motivating quality control, arranging for commodity and market surveys, sponsoring trade delegations and exhibitions, surveying exporters, and advising the government on commercial policy affecting exports. Another promotion measure introduced in the mid-1960s fixed export quotas for manufactured goods. The annual export targets for the manufactured commodities were fixed by the Export Promotion Bureau in consultation with the respresentatives of the specific industry.[24] In the case of industries with organizations or associations of their own, the export targets were distributed among or allocated to individual units or enterprises by their respective organizations. In cases where such organizations did not exist, the Export Promotion Bureau sought to allocate the quotas among producers in consultation with them. An Export Promotion Council, consisting of representatives of trade and industry plus the relevant government departments, was also constituted to advise on policies for meeting export targets and quotas. The export quotas were enforced by means of persuasion and agreement as well as by implicit threats, which related mainly to the withholding of import privileges. In the case of

---

were not applied to advances granted under confirmed letters of credit opened by foreign importers in favor of Pakistani exporters (Pakistan, Ministry of Finance, Economic Adviser, *Economic Survey, 1966–67* [Karachi, 1967], p. 68).

22. Pakistan, Ministry of Finance, *Budget: 1968–69* (Islamabad, June 1968).

23. These included a surveying of foreign markets and dissemination of information obtained, promotion of market research organizations and export marketing institutions, and designing of product to suit export markets as well as consultation services to open offices abroad.

24. Ministry of Commerce, Export Promotion Bureau, *Annual Reports, 1967–69*. Also *Proceedings of Annual Meetings, 1967–69*.

cotton textiles, failure to meet export targets invited penalities, which were administered by the Cotton Textile Association, a representative organ of the cotton textile industry. The proceeds of these penalties went to the Textile Association and were used for the promotion of textile trade. In other areas nonfulfillment of quota could result in the cancellation of import licenses and even in the cancellation of the registration of exporters (i.e., their right to engage in export trade, which was legally conferred by the government only on the registered exporting firms).

The annual export target for an industry was based on the estimate of an exportable surplus, given the expected increases in output and domestic demand. The implicit assumption was that exporters did not face any demand constraint if the exportable surplus was of requisite quality given the prevailing magnitude of export subsidy. The compulsory imposition of an export target on each and every industry was a negation of the logic of comparative advantage. To insist that every firm must participate in the export trade was self-defeating, in view of differences in efficiency. Although not without merit, the argument that participation in export trade would compel individual firms to improve efficiency was incompatible with the use of special incentives to offset high costs. As long as the protected domestic market was guaranteed, compulsory export quotas, to the extent that they reduced the profits of the exporting industry, encouraged the exporters to raise prices in the domestic market. Because foreign and domestic markets were effectively separated and had different elasticities of demand, price discrimination was both possible and profitable.

PERFORMANCE OF EXPORTS

There were important differences in terms of export policy and export performance between the first and second decades of Pakistan's development. The 1950s witnessed stagnation in Pakistan's export earnings while in the 1960s they grew at an average rate of 7.5 percent. The major primary exports declined in the late 1950s and remained at that lower level for the next decade. However, manufactured exports rose consistently throughout the 1950s and 1960s.

Overall Export Performances

The significant features of the export policy of the 1950s were (a) export taxes on the major agricultural exports like jute and cotton, (b) devaluation in 1955, and (c) the introduction of preferential import licensing, i.e., an import entitlement scheme, for a very limited number of primary and manufactured exports. The effective exchange rates that resulted from a combination of these measures during the 1950s are shown in table 6.1.

Table 6.1.   Effective Export Exchange Rates in the 1950s (Nominal or official exchange rate Rs 4.76 per dollar)

A. Agricultural exports

	1952/53 –1954/55	1955/56 –1957/58
Cotton	2.56	3.64
Jute	2.86	4.17
Tea	3.31	4.08
Hides and skins	3.14	4.76
Wool	3.31	4.76
Major primary exports	2.87	4.16
Fish	2.74	4.11
Rice	3.31	4.76
Total minor primary exports	3.12	4.56

B. Manufactured exports

	1952/53 –1954/55	1955/56 –1957/58
All major manufactures in-cluding jute and cotton tex-tiles, leather, and woollen products	3.31	4.76
Selected minor manufactures	3.81 (1954/55)	5.12-5.71

Source: Nurul Islam, *Export Incentives and Responsiveness of Exports in Pakistan: A Quantitative Analysis,* Yale Economic Growth Center, Discussion Paper no. 58m (Oct. 1968).

Although devaluation improved the exchange rates for all exports after 1955, discrimination against major primary exports was maintained. Rates of exchange more favorable than the official rate were accorded to a very limited number of minor primary and manufactured exports. The relative incidence of export subsidy on different commodities implied in the import entitlement scheme was haphazard because it depended upon the relative scarcity of imported raw materials covered by the scheme.[25]

The growth of exports during the 1950s can be seen from table 6.2. During the period 1952/53–1957/58 primary exports fell by 25 percent while manufactured exports rose by about 400 percent.[26] The decline in the value of primary exports in the period following the Korean War boom was associated in some cases with a fall in price. The quantity of exports of jute and cotton, which constituted about 80 percent of total primary exports during this period, recorded an increase. The minor primary exports either increased slightly in value or remained unchanged.

25. W. E. Hecox, *The Use of Import Privileges: As Incentive to Exporters in Pakistan,* Pakistan Institute of Development Economics, Research Report no. 30 (Karachi, 1966).

26. This was partly due to the small base. Manufactured exports were only 2.5% of total exports in 1952/53–1954/55. It rose to about 14.5% in the subsequent three-year period.

Table 6.2. Average Annual Value and Index Numbers of Exports (Value in million dollars)

	Primary			Manufactured			
	Major	*Minor*	*Total*	*Major*	*Minor*	*Total*	*Grand total*
1951/52	567.9	33.7	601.6	0.2	4.3	4.5	606.1
	(157.4)	(98.5)	(152.2)	(5.9)	(105.7)	(57.9)	(150.5)
1952/53–	360.9	34.2	395.1	3.7	4.0	7.7	402.8
1954/55	(100)	(100)	(100)	(100)	(100)	(100)	(100)
1955/56–	271.9	27.6	298.7	31.6	5.5	37.1	335.4
1957/58	(75.1)	(80.7)	(75.6)	(855.6)	(137.6)	(481.7)	(88.3)

Sources: See table 6.1. Also Government of Pakistan, Central Statistical Office, *Foreign Trade Statistics of Pakistan,* 1952–70, Karachi (annual issues).

Note: Figures in brackets are index numbers. The average annual value of exports is shown for periods 1952/53–1954/55 and for 1955/56 and 1957/58.

In the postdevaluation period the dollar value of all the major export items fell.[27] Because in all cases except raw jute Pakistan had a marginal share in world trade, it could have increased the value of exports if it were to produce and supply more to the world market. However, an important factor that militated against the expansion of its exports in this period was the relative stagnation in agricultural production and increasing absorption of exportable raw materials by the domestic manufacturing industries (see chap. 3).[28]

Manufactured exports increased at a rapid rate during the entire period of the 1950s; a spectacular increase took place in the exports of cotton and jute textiles. A decrease in the exports of raw cotton, raw jute, and hides and skins was thus partly compensated for by a rise in the exports of manufactured goods, whose production depended on the use of these domestic raw materials.

The proliferation of the consumer goods industry and the consequent difficulty of formulating a policy of consumption restraint led to increased domestic absorption of exportable raw materials. The question, however, arises as to whether

27. Except rice and wool.

28. In the early 1950s exports were regulated by means of licensing; later all goods and services were made exportable from Pakistan except those placed in the restrictive list of exports, for which specific export authorizations were necessary. Controls over export items were designed mainly to avoid a domestic scarcity of items considered essential for consumption in "reasonable" amounts. Thus, exportation of these items was allowed only when there was a surplus available over and above the needs of the home market. Government of Pakistan, *Report of the Committee on Economic Controls* (July 1965), pp. 41–42. The manufactured exports requiring authorization were (1) cement, (2) sugar, (3) petroleum or petroleum products, (4) mill-made cotton piece goods, and (5) some items of sporting goods. The following primary exports were subject to control: (1) ferrous and nonferrous metal goods, (2) oilseed, (3) juteseed, (4) chilies, ginger, and so on, (5) grain flour, (6) bulbs, potatoes, and so on, (7) beef and mutton, (8) coconuts and copra, and (9) bamboo and timber.

Table 6.3.   Effective Exchange Rate (Rs per dollar)

	Major primary commodities	Minor primary commodities	Major manu- factures	Minor manu- factures
1958/59–1960/61	4.22	5.66	5.54	6.57
1961/62–1963/64	4.34	6.11	5.65	7.63
1964/65–1966/67	4.57	5.33	5.97	6.94
1967/68–1968/69	4.82	5.45	7.35	8.12

Sources: See table 6.2.

manufactured exports could have increased further with a policy of greater re-straint on domestic consumption. It was doubtful that in the very early years the government could have followed a significantly more restrictive policy regarding domestic consumption that would have been politically acceptable, especially in the context of rising expectations of the masses. This does not, however, imply that there was no scope—indeed there was scope—for higher domestic consumption taxes on a few articles coupled with a reduction or an elimination of disin-centives for exports. The need for and efficiency of such a policy were demon-strated subsequently.

By the end of the 1950s Pakistan had indeed adopted a number of new export promotion schemes and had strengthened a few of the existing ones (see ''Export Promotion Measures'' above, in this chapter). The two major methods of export subsidy in the 1960s, as mentioned earlier, were the Export Bonus Scheme and Export Performance Licensing Scheme. The export incentive schemes had dif-ferential impacts on different commodities or groups of commodities. Exemption from duty on imported components, the export performance licensing scheme, and rebate of indirect tax on output were all discriminatory. The system of effective exchange rates which emerged as a result of these numerous and heterogeneous schemes is shown in table 6.3 for the broad categories of exports.

Manufactures had a higher level of exchange rates compared to primary com-modities, and the minor items, both primary and manufactures, had higher rates than the major ones. The effective exchange rates of minor manufactures varied between 6.57 and Rs 8.12 compared to a range of Rs 5.33–6.11 for major commodities.

The growth of various categories of agricultural and manufactured exports during the 1960s is shown in table 6.4. The annual average value of major agricultural exports during 1958/59–1960/61 was lower than for the previous three years. Although exports partially recovered in the mid-1960s primarily due to the growth in the export of raw cotton[29] the value of major agricultural exports did not reach the level that had prevailed in the later part of the 1950s.

29. The export of raw cotton increased from a yearly average of $36.2 million in 1958–61 to $82.8 million in 1967–69.

Table 6.4. Growth of Exports (Millions of dollars)

	Agricultural			Manufactured		
	Major	*Minor*	*Total*	*Major*	*Minor*	*Total*
1958/59–1960/61	224.9	33.2	258.1	77.1	12.1	89.2
1961/62–1963/64	255.3	69.7	325.0	88.10	34.3	122.4
1964/65–1966/67	260.6	72.1	332.7	161.5	75.2	236.7
1967/68–1968/69	248.7	76.9	325.6	227.9	114.6	342.5

Sources: See table 6.2.

However, the miscellaneous primary exports recorded a high rate of increase initially but a lower rate later. More than half the total minor exports were accounted for by rice and fish. Both these commodities enjoyed an increase in the effective exchange rate during the first half of the 1960s but a decline in the latter half. Partly owing to this, the rate of growth slowed down in the second half of the 1960s. Because most of these items were new commodities introduced for the first time in the export market, their export values fluctuated considerably from year to year.

Performance of Important Export Items

Primary Exports

Among the primary exports four items, jute, cotton, rice, and fish, constituted the most important exports and/or provided the main basis for the expansion of export earnings in the 1960s. The problems and the future prospects of these primary exports deserve critical analysis.

Raw jute occupied a unique position insofar as Pakistan was a major supplier in the world market. However, in absolute terms, raw jute exports were still at approximately the same level at the close of the two decades as they had been in the early 1950s, exhibiting no significant growth trend in the intervening years. In fact, raw jute exports declined from 50 percent of total exports to about 30 percent over the two decades.[30] How far was the economic policy in Pakistan responsible for the decline in Pakistan's share in world trade and the production of jute? All analyses until then seemed to point to Pakistan's policy playing an important contributory role in the stagnation of jute exports. Pakistan's attempts to maintain a high export price for raw jute were implemented by means of a number of measures, such as export taxes and maintenance of minimum export

30. The stagnation in exports was associated with a fall in Pakistan's share in the world output of jute from 65% during 1955–60 to about 30% during 1965–69 and the output of raw jute in Pakistan registered only a 10% rise over the early 1950s, whereas the rest of the world had tripled its output of the commodity.

price, as well as controls over acreage and production of raw jute.[31] The export price check created incentives for exporters to engage in illegal transactions in foreign exchange in order to meet the minimum export price. To circumvent this check, a progressive downgrading of the classification of raw jute as well as purposeful mixing of grades of raw jute occurred. The proceeds of high export prices were not passed on to the producers but were siphoned off by export taxes. Neither were these proceeds used directly as subsidies to the producers or indirectly to increase the efficiency of production of raw jute. This adversely affected the competitive pull of jute for land and other resources relative to its principal competing crop, rice. The relative internal jute/rice price ratio that resulted from the policies was not adequate to provide sufficient incentive in terms of price and profitability in order to meet the competition of rice crops. The relative returns of jute to rice were also adversely affected by the fact that subsidized modern inputs had a greater yield and a better relative price ratio in rice than in jute.[32]

The combined effect of the domestic price and production policies, on the one hand, and the exchange rate policy, on the other, was to provide disincentives to an increased production of raw jute within the domestic economy, while at the same time (a) encouraging the production of raw jute and related fibers in competing countries such as Thailand and (b) providing incentives for synthetic substitutes to make inroads into markets for raw jute.[33] The adverse effects of the maintenance of a relatively high export price for raw jute were felt by the jute manufacturing industry located abroad. The jute industry in Pakistan was compensated by the Export Bonus Scheme in the 1960s and was able to reduce the export price of its products. However, owing to tariffs on processed jute goods exported by Pakistan and the high price of raw jute available to the overseas jute manufacturing industry, inroads were made by the synthetics industry in markets

31. The controls over production were abandoned in the 1960s (R. Rapetto, *Optimal Export Taxes in the Short and Long Run: Pakistan's Policies towards Raw Jute Exports* [Cambridge: Harvard University, Development Advisory Service, June 1970]).

32. Ibid., p. 37. Government of East Pakistan, *Long Term Jute Policy and a Programme for Increasing Jute Production in Pakistan* (Dacca, 1968). It was repeatedly pointed out that once the price ratio was corrected there was a possibility of substantially reducing the production costs of jute by the application of modern inputs because the marginal costs were expected to be markedly lower than average costs.

33. For packaging uses, cotton bags, multiwall paper bags, and bulk handling widely replaced jute bags in the developed countries. Up to the 1960s jute consumption in the developed countries might have grown by about 50% more than it actually did, had its use risen as fast as the production of commodities traditionally packed in jute bags. During the 1960s a much more serious threat was the emergence of the new synthetic materials, polypropylene and high density polyethylene. These synthetics underwent rapid price declines in the past decade owing to competition and economies of scale. FAO, Study Group in Jute, Kenaf and Allied Fibres, *Impact of Synthetics on Jute and Allied Fabrics* (Rome, 1969).

abroad. Pakistan could maintain her competitive position in the markets of jute manufacturers only with the help of an appropriate pricing policy for raw jute and jute goods. An improvement in the exchange rate for raw jute was the only effective method of combining the need for low export prices to counter the threat of overseas competition with a relatively profitable domestic price of raw jute, which ensured increased returns so as to encourage investments in modern inputs. Of course an improvement in the efficiency of internal marketing, which would allow the benefits of increased prices to flow from the exporter's level to the grower's level, was a necessary ingredient of policy. It was not necessary for an improvement in the exchange rate for raw jute to be accompanied by a corresponding improvement in that for jute manufacturers, since there was ample scope also for considerable improvement in the efficiency of the jute manufacturing indusry and hence to retain competitiveness in export markets.[34]

Cotton and rice experienced significant increases in exports. This was accompanied by an increase in domestic production of cotton and rice in West Pakistan.[35] The increased growth rate of production of about 6.5 percent was the highest rate of growth among all agricultural crops.[36] The most significant contributory factors to the accelerated growth rates in cotton were the increased use of modern inputs of fertilizer and water, and in rice, modern inputs with new varieties of seed. There was a slight improvement in the effective exchange rate of raw cotton due to the reduction of export duties. Furthermore, a rapid expansion of cotton textile exports increased the demand for raw cotton and improved the price relationship between cotton and the competing crops in the domestic market.

The growth of exports of fine rice was mainly directed toward the specialized markets in the Middle East and Africa, where demand for the particular variety of fragrant rice that Pakistan produced was strong. Fine rice was included in the

34. Since July 1970 the export of raw jute was entitled to a bonus rate of only 10%; however, a 20–25% bonus rate for raw jute and a compensating increase in the bonus rate of about 10% for the jute manufacturers were necessary to meet the threat of competition from synthetics on a long-run basis.

35. Rice production in East Pakistan, primarily coarse rice, did not increase at all during the 1950s and increased only about 2.4% between 1959/60 and 1968/69 (Central Statistical Office, *Twenty Years of Pakistan in Statistics* [Karachi, 1968]). See also J. J. Stern and W. P. Falcon, *Growth and Development in Pakistan,* Harvard University, Center for International Affairs, Occasional Papers no. 23 (Apr. 1970), p. 37.

36. Major crops include cotton, wheat, rice, sugarcane, maize, and oilseeds. The growth rates of the output of cotton and rice in West Pakistan during the 1950s were about 2.3 and 1.9%, respectively. The average growth rate of all the major crops was about 5.4% in this period as against 2.3% during the 1950s.

Export Bonus Scheme, the principal effect being to increase the profits of the rice exporters. But it failed to increase the incomes of the rice farmers, as was hoped, in order to encourage increased production and to lower export price so as to push larger export sales abroad. Given the domestic price at which the exporters obtained their supplies of rice from the domestic market and the prevailing export price, the difference between the two was adequate to provide a reasonable profit margin to the exporters.[37] During the first few years (1959–63) the government procured rice from the farmers at a compulsory price that was substantially lower than both the domestic wholesale price prevailing in the nonprocurement areas and the export price.[38] The actual export price was just about the price that covered the costs of handling and shipment, given the low procurement price, and in addition yielded a reasonable margin of profit for the exporters.

There was one minor primary export, fish, that underwent substantial expansion in the early 1960s under the impact of the bonus scheme. A slowing down in the growth of its export in the late 1960s was partly due to the inelasticity of domestic supply, especially in the case of deep-sea fishing. In the case of export of fish raised in inland waters of East Pakistan, the fall in exports was the result of a deadlock in trade with India following the Indo–Pakistan hostilities in 1965.

Manufactured Exports

As noted earlier, the most significant aspect of Pakistan's export performance in the 1960s was the rapid growth of manufactured exports. Ninety-two percent of the total average increase in overall exports between the first and second half of the 1960s was due to an increase in manufactured exports. By the end of the 1960s they constituted about half of total exports. Cotton and jute textiles constituted 68 percent of total manufactured exports during 1964/65–1966/67, and 66 percent during 1967/68–1968/69.[39] Cotton textiles increased in relative importance, with the exports of cotton yarn growing faster than those of cotton cloth.[40] The relative importance of four important manufactured exports is seen in table 6.5. The dollar value of the total manufactured exports from the mid-1950s up to

37. The external demand for Pakistani cotton was traditionally considered to be elastic; the country produced only 4% of world production. Both the supply and demand for raw cotton were price elastic. The improvement of the price incentives to cotton exports through its inclusion in the bonus scheme was advocated by the Working Group on the Export Bonus Scheme in 1970 and cotton exports were granted a 10% export bonus.

38. The free market wholesale prices of fine rice were 30–85% above the procurement price during this period (S. M. Hussain, "Export Potential of Fine Rice from Pakistan," *Pakistan Development Review* 4, no. 4 [Winter 1964]: 687–88).

39. The proportion of jute and cotton textiles was much higher in the late 1950s, constituting 86.4% of total manufactured exports.

40. Yarn constituted about half the total cotton textile exports toward the end of the 1960s.

Table 6.5. Average Annual Value of Exports (Millions of dollars)

	Cotton yarn	*Cotton fabrics*	*Jute goods*	*Leather manufactures*
1958/59–1960/61	20.4	7.8	48.9	2.6
1961/62–1963/64	9.1	11.9	67.1	6.2
1964/65–1966/67	25.4	30.9	105.4	22.0
1967/68–1968/69	45.3	46.7	135.9	40.5

Sources: See table 6.2.

the end of the 1960s increased about 22 percent whereas those of jute manufactures increased by 15 percent, cotton yarn by 10 percent, and cotton cloth by 37 percent. The exports of cotton yarn and cloth increased at a rate higher than their world exports.[41]

The three most important manufactured exports, cotton textiles, jute textiles, and leather manufactures, were produced from domestic, exportable raw materials. In the 1950s, there was in many cases an absolute fall in the value of exports of primary raw materials, while exports of manufactured goods incorporating these materials expanded. It is relevant, therefore, to examine how the combined exports of raw materials and manufactured goods based on them behaved during the 1960s. In other words, was there a net expansion? This was indeed so, as can be seen from table 6.6. It may be mentioned here that the growth rate of manufactured exports during the 1960s was higher than that of the output of the large-scale manufacturing industry as a whole.[42]

The fastest growing manufactured exports, cotton and jute textiles, had received effective export rates that were higher than the average for all major manufactured exports, as table 6.7 shows. The effective exchange rates were in fact higher than those indicated in the table because incentive schemes other than the Export Bonus Scheme were not included in the estimation of the exchange rates. If the effect of the second most important export incentive scheme, i.e., export performance licensing, was taken into account, the range of the highest exchange rates toward the end of the 1960s varied between Rs 8.73 and 9.09 per dollar for the miscellaneous manufactured exports. The average rate of effective exchange during the 1960s, including all incentive schemes, varied between Rs 6.6 and 7.9 per dollar for manufactured exports as a whole and between Rs 8.1 and 9.9 per dollar for all except cotton and jute textiles.

41. N. Islam, *The Manufactured Exports of Pakistan: Factor Intensity and Related Economic Characteristics* (Karachi: Pakistan Institute of Development Economics, June 1969).

42. S. R. Lewis, "Pakistan's Industrialisation 1951–1968: Production, Prices and Trade Patterns," unpublished paper, Mar. 1971, table VIII, p. 11.

Table 6.6.   Combined Exports of Principal Raw Materials and Finished Manufactures (Rs million)

	Cotton and cotton manufactures	Jute and jute manufactures	Hides and skins and leather manufactures
1958/59–1960/61	64.4	205.2	15.3
	(77)	(110)	(174)
1961/62–1963/64	79.1	235	17.8
	(95)	(126)	(202.9)
1964/65–1966/67	116.1	288	26.9
	(139)	(154)	(308)
1967/68–1968/69	164.7	292.4	41.7
	(185)	(155)	(495)

Sources: See table 6.2.

Note: The figures in parentheses are indices of exports of each category with 1955/56–1958/59 = 100.

Net Foreign Exchange Earnings

Although there was a remarkably high rate of growth of the manufactured exports in Pakistan, the question may be asked as to how much the growth in gross export earnings represented a net gain in foreign exchange earnings. This was often discussed in the context of evaluating the efficiency of export promotion measures.[43] Furthermore, among the important criteria for the determination of investment priorities in the field of industry was the foreign exchange saving or earning capacity of a particular industrial project. Therefore, it was important to quantify the contributions to net foreign exchange earnings made by the exports of different manufactured goods.

The net foreign exchange earning of an export item j (V_j) is the difference between the price paid by the foreign importer (E_j) and the total cost (M), direct as well as indirect, of imports embodied in one unit of final demand. That is,

$$V_j = E_j - M_j$$
$$M_j = \sum_{i=1}^{n} a_{ij}m_i,$$

where a_{ij} is the amount by which output of industry i must be increased for the production of one unit of final demand of commodity j, and m_i is the value of direct imports per rupee of output of commodity i.

43. R. Soligo and J. J. Stern, "Some Comments on the Export Bonus, Export Promotion and Investment Criteria," *Pakistan Development Review* 6, no. 1 (Spring 1966): 38–56, and N. Islam, "Commodity Exports, Net Exchange Earnings and Investment Criteria," *Pakistan Development Review* 8, no. 4 (Winter 1968): 582–605, reprinted in Islam, ed., *Studies on Commercial Policy and Economic Growth*, Karachi: Pakistan Institute of Development Economics, 1970), pp. 359–77, 421–37.

Table 6.7.   Effective Exchange Rates for Manufactured Exports (Rs per dollar)

	Cotton yarn	*Cotton cloth*	*Jute manufactures*
1958/59–1960/61	5.24	5.66	6.57
1961/62–1963/64	5.31	6.41	7.63
1964/65–1966/67	6.20	6.93	6.94
1967/68–1968/69	7.28	8.11	8.12

Source: See table 6.2; see also W. E. Hecox, *The Use of Import Privileges: As Incentive to Exporters in Pakistan,* Research Report no. 30 (Karachi: Pakistan Institute of Development Economics, 1966), and Government of Pakistan, Central Statistical Office, *Twenty Years of Pakistan, 1947-67* (Karachi, 1967).

The estimation of the net foreign exchange earning is, however, problematic because of the absence of direct evidence on E_j, Soligo and Stern,[44] who made the first systematic attempt to estimate the net foreign exchange earnings of the individual manufacturing industries, derived the estimate of E_j from domestic price (D_j) in the following way:

$$E_j = D_j \; \frac{(1 - t_j)}{(1 + pb_j)} = \frac{(1 - t_j)}{(1 + pb_j)} \; ,$$

where t_j is the indirect tax on the domestic sales of the unit of commodity (which is exempted if the unit is sold abroad), p is the premium on the bonus voucher, and b_j is the percentage of the export allowed as a bonus for commodity j.[45] This derivation assumes that the receipt per unit of sale is the same in both the domestic and export markets and that the entire difference between the foreign and the domestic price is accounted for by the subsidy originated from the export bonus and the exemption of indirect taxes on output. The method ignores the effect of the additional export incentive schemes such as (a) export performance licensing, (b) exemption from the indirect taxes on the domestic inputs, (c) exemption from the indirect taxes on the imported inputs, and (d) rebate on the income tax attributable to the exports.

Even if the effect of the additional measures is taken into account, the difference between the FOB export price and the domestic price may in many cases be still more than is accounted for by the combined subsidy originating from all the export promotion measures because of two important factors. First, price discrimination between the home and foreign markets was profitable and possible. The two markets were effectively separated because of quantitative restrictions on foreign trade. The manufacturer-cum-exporter faced a highly elastic demand in the export market and a relatively inelastic demand in the domestic

44. Soligo and Stern, "Some Comments."
45. D_j = domestic price (inclusive of indirect tax); this is assumed to be one.

market, which was not only protected from competition from without but also was characterized by monopolistic market imperfections from within. The consequence of the price discrimination and the imperfections in the domestic market was that the average receipts per unit of export, including subsidy, were lower in the export market than the average receipts in the domestic market. Second, the exporter might be willing to accept a lower rate of profit on the foreign sales, which was not compensated by a higher rate of profit in the domestic market; in other words, the exporter may not be maximizing profit. The sacrifice of the short-run profits might have been worthwhile since a good export performance had become the hallmark of efficiency in the eyes of the government. Toward the late 1960s export quotas were laid down for different industries and for individual enterprises within each industry, nonfulfillment of which was a sufficient ground for incurring the displeasure of the government. At the time of introducing a commodity for the first time in the export market, the exporter sometimes had to charge a price somewhat lower than the prevailing world price in order to offset the consumers' preference for the established brand names and historical trade connections.

So Soligo and Stern estimates would have an upward bias whenever the differential between the domestic and foreign price exceeded the amount of subsidy originating from (a) the bonus scheme and (b) the exemption from the indirect taxes on output. The direct evidence provided by Lewis and Guisinger on the difference between domestic and world price confirms that this was generally the case.[46] To reduce the bias, E has been defined here as $D/(1 + p)$,[47] where D is the value of one unit of final demand in domestic market prices, and p is the percentage excess of domestic market price over the world price multiplied by 1.05. The data on world prices are in most cases based on the CIF import price, and FOB export price is usually less than the CIF price. So the FOB export price for the purpose of the present inquiry was obtained by deflating the world price to the extent of 5 percent to allow for freight and insurance.

The average net foreign exchange earnings per rupee of exports is shown in table 6.8. The net foreign exchange earnings per rupee of exports varied between Rs 0.25 for capital goods and Rs 0.43 for intermediate goods if simple averages were compared. If the group averages were weighted by the proportion of exports of each industry in each group in the total manufactured exports, the net earnings per rupee of exports varied between Rs 0.22 for capital goods and Rs 0.60 for intermediate goods, as seen in table 6.8.

46. S. R. Lewis and S. E. Guisinger, *Measuring Protection in a Developing Country: The Case of Pakistan,* Williams College, Center of Development Economics, Memorandum no. 6 (1966).

47. It may be noted here that the domestic prices used here are the market prices and hence include the indirect taxes on the output, and p accordingly includes the indirect taxes. But the domestic price deflated by $(1 + p)$ yields the estimates of export price excluding indirect taxes.

Table 6.8.   Average Net Foreign Exchange Earnings (For one dollar's worth of exports)

Consumer goods	Simple	Weighted
A. Consumer goods	0.3608	—
(1) excluding cotton textiles and printing and publishing	0.3123	0.4667
(2) excluding printing and publishing	0.3340	0.5312
B. Intermediate foods	0.4331	0.5938
(1) excluding jute textiles	0.4202	0.3800
C. Capital goods	0.2492	0.2180

Source: N. Islam, "Commodity Exports, Net Foreign Exchange Earnings and Investment Criteria, *Pakistan Development Review* (Winter 1968), reprinted in N. Islam, ed., *Studies on Commercial Policy and Economic Growth* (Karachi: Pakistan Institute of Development Economics, 1970), p. 426.

The simple average net earnings were highest for intermediate goods; this was also true if the earnings were estimated exclusively of the cotton and jute textiles, which were the most important components of the consumer goods and intermediate goods, respectively. If the weighted net earnings for the three groups, including jute and cotton textiles in their respective groups, were considered, the relative position of the three groups remained unchanged. But once the jute and cotton textiles were excluded from their respective groups, the weighted average earnings were highest for consumer goods; those for intermediate goods were less than for consumer goods but more than those for capital goods. Thus the capital goods industries ranked lowest in terms of net foreign exchange earnings. Consumer goods ranked higher than the intermediate goods in terms of weighted average earnings. But a number of industries in both groups were based on the exportable domestic agricultural raw materials, the domestic consumption of which in lieu of export involved a loss of foreign exchange that was to be set against their gross earnings.

The net foreign exchange earnings of four sectors, cotton, jute, woollen textile, and leather industries, which were the heavy direct and indirect consumers of the exportable domestic materials, are shown in table 6.9. The average of the two industry groups, i.e., consumer and intermediate goods, declines when the net foreign exchange earnings are estimated, exclusive of the loss of foreign exchange due to the domestic consumption of exportable raw materials. Although the consumer goods still retain the leading position as the net foreign exchange earner, the difference between the two is narrowed, as shown in table 6.10.

It is pertinent to emphasize the important intraindustry differences that existed within each of the broad industry groups in terms of net foreign exchange earn-

Table 6.9. Net Foreign Exchange Earnings of
Agro-Based Exports ($U.S. per one dollar's worth of
exports)

	(A)	(B)
Jute textiles	0.2677	0.2632
Cotton textiles	0.2628	0.2499
Woollen textiles	0.2959	0.2833
Tanning and finishing of leather	0.2014	0.1778

Source: Islam, "Commodity Exports," p. 428.
Note: Column A excludes only direct domestic consumption of exportable raw materials and column B excludes both direct and indirect domestic consumption
of exportable raw materials.

ings. The estimates of net foreign exchange earnings are available for only a few
industries and these estimates do not take into account the indirect import requirements of export. As table 6.11 reveals, there were wide differences between
individual industries or between commodities within each industry group such as
metal products, chemicals, and basic metals in terms of the net foreign exchange
earnings. Within the chemicals group, for example, the net foreign exchange
earnings per unit of export worth one domestic rupee varied from 0.87 to 0.18.
In the pharmaceuticals industry it ranged from 0.96 to 0.03 but in the case
of a few products net earnings were negative. Similarly, in the case of electrical
machinery it ranged from 0.51 to 0.02, while in the case of metal products it
ranged from 0.83 to 0.10.

There was no significant correlation between the net foreign exchange earnings of a manufactured export and its rate of growth over time or its relative
ranking or importance among the manufactured exports of Pakistan, defined as
the proportion of the total manufactured exports earned by the specific industry.
The rank correlation coefficient between the net foreign exchange earnings and
the growth rate of exports during the period 1960–67 was negative (−0.29) but it
was not significant at the 5 percent level. The rank correlation coefficient between the net foreign exchange earnings and the ratio of particular exports to the
total manufactured exports of Pakistan during the period 1961–69 was 0.36 but

Table 6.10. Net Foreign Exchange Earnings ($U.S. per one dollar's worth of exports)

	Simple	*Weighted*
Consumer goods (excluding printing and publishing)	0.3082	0.3145
Intermediate goods	0.3680	0.2709

Source: See table 6.9.

Table 6.11.   Intraindustry Differences (Per one dollar's worth of exports in $U.S.)

Industry group	Range of net foreign exchange earnings	Average of the industry group
Basic metals (3 cases)	0.74–0.67	0.31
Chemicals and pharmaceuticals Chemicals (7 cases)	0.87–0.18	—
Pharmaceuticals (24 cases)	0.96–0.03	—
Pharmaceuticals (7 cases)	(−) 0.03– (−) 0.21	—
Metal products (10 cases)	0.83–0.10	—
Nonelectrical machinery (1 case)	0.63	0.43
Electrical machinery (6 cases)	0.51–0.02	0.35
Nonmetallic minerals (3 cases)	0.47–0.18	0.45
Transport equipment (1 case)	0.31	0.16
Rubber and rubber products (2 cases)	0.54–0.52	0.20

Source: N. Islam, "Commodity Exports, Net Foreign Exchange Earnings and Investment Criteria," *Pakistan Development Review* (Winter 1968), reprinted in N. Islam, eds., *Studies on Commercial Policy and Economic Growth* (Karachi: Pakistan Institute of Development Economics, 1970), p. 430.

was significant only at the 10 percent level. Thus, there was little evidence that exports with higher net foreign exchange earnings per unit were growing faster or that they provided a higher proportion of the total exports of Pakistan.

EXPORT INCENTIVE SCHEMES, CHANGES IN EFFECTIVE EXCHANGE RATES, AND
RESPONSIVENESS OF EXPORTS

What was the effect of export incentives on the growth of exports? A simple way of looking at it is to compare the growth rates of the bonus and the nonbonus exports. Over the entire period from 1959/60 to 1968/69 the exports eligible for the bonus scheme grew at a compound rate of about 12 percent as against the average growth rate of less than 4 percent attained by the nonbonus exports. The bonus exports increased their share of the total exports from 22 to 57 percent during the period. Moreover, compared with the prebonus period the growth rate of bonus exports was considerably accelerated during the period following the introduction of the Export Bonus Scheme, and the difference in growth rates between the two periods was statistically significant. Furthermore, on a rough aggregative basis, a supplementary test of the impact of changes in effective exchange rates on foreign exchange earnings is provided by a positive correlation between the rankings of the four different categories of exports by effective exchange rates and the compound rates of growth, as table 6.12 shows.[48]

Besides the increase in the effective exchange rates, there were a number of favorable factors that contributed to the growth of manufactured exports during the 1960s. The acceleration in the growth rate of agriculture, as already pointed out, had a favorable impact on the agricultural exports such as cotton and rice. The increase in food production in the mid-1960s and the large imports of PL 480 food grains throughout the period, undertaken to offset the effects of domestic shortage, had helped Pakistan achieve a reasonable degree of price stability in this period. The three-year moving average of price indexes of manufactured goods did not indicate a rise of more than 10 percent over the decade of the 1960s. The stability of food prices had kept industrial wages down and hence had strengthened the effects of the improvement in the exchange rates by increasing the relative profitability of export sales compared with sales in the domestic market. Moreover, the beginnings of inflationary pressure in the late 1960s were met by an increase in export incentives and a consequential rise in the rupee returns per unit of export. The index of real effective exchange rate, i.e., the effective exchange rate deflated by the price index of manufactured exports, increased from 100 during the late 1950s to 113 during the late 1960s for all the manufactured exports taken together and to 126 for the minor manufactured exports only.[49]

More detailed, statistical investigations into the responsiveness of exports to changes in effective exchange rates by means of multiple regression analysis was carried out on the basis of a time series for 15 to 20 years.[50]

The analysis was conducted in terms of a few broad categories of exports. The effective exchange rates included the effects of the following: (a) Export Bonus Scheme, (b) export performance licensing, (c) exemption from indirect taxes on imported inputs, (d) exemption from indirect taxes on domestic inputs, and (e) exemption from indirect taxes on output. The study did not include the effects of

48. Government of Pakistan, Planning Commission, International Economic Section, *A Background Note on Bonus Exports during the Third Plan* (Rawalpindi, Sept. 1969).

49. The increase in real effective exchange rates was greater than indicated above, because those figures include only the effects of the Export Bonus Scheme and exclude those of the other export incentive schemes, including export performance licensing.

50. The following discussion is based on Nurul Islam, *Export Incentives and Responsiveness of Exports in Pakistan: A Quantitative Analysis,* Yale Economic Growth Center, Discussion Paper no. 58m (Oct. 1968).

Table 6.12. Ranking of Growth Rates and Exchange Rates (1965/66–1968/69)

	Growth rates (%)	*1963/64*	*Effective exchange rates (Rs per dollar)* *1968/69*
Home remittances	29.3	6.94	8.23
Other manufactures	22.7	6.64	8.05
Cotton manufactures	22.2	6.36	7.60
Jute manufactures	17.4	5.67	7.36

Sources: R. Soligo and J. J. Stern, "Some Comments on the Export Bonus, Export Promotion and Investment Criteria," *Pakistan Development Review* 6, no. 1 (Spring 1966): 38–56, and N. Islam, "Commodity Experts, Net Exchange Earnings and Investment Criteria," *Pakistan Development Review* 8, no. 4 (Winter 1968): 582–605, reprinted in Islam, ed., *Studies on Commercial Policy and Economic Growth* (Karachi: Pakistan Institute of Development Economics, 1970), pp. 359–77, 421–37.

rebates of income taxes on exports, concessions on freight rates, liberal treatment in terms of credit facilities, and numerous other favors that the government with substantial power of patronage in many directions could bestow upon a successful exporter.[51]

The results of regression analysis for all manufactured exports are presented in table 6.13. The results of a few relevant equations for each category of exports are given in tables 6.14 and 6.15.

The results show a high positive elasticity of export earnings to the export incentive schemes as measured by the effective exchange rates. There was no significant difference in the results whether effective exchange rates included the effect of only the bonus scheme or the effect of other minor incentive schemes as well; this was because manufactured exports were dominated by jute and cotton textiles and none of these was eligible for the additional export incentive schemes. The equations confirm the positive effect of domestic output on export

51. The estimation of the quantitative impact of export performance licensing on effective exchange rates posed a special problem. The industrial classification, which was used to estimate the effects of various indirect tax exemptions and the bonus scheme, was available only in terms of broad industry groups. The manufactured exports that were entitled to export performance licensing were much more narrowly defined. They referred to specific products or branches of an industry. In order to solve this problem in the case of an industry, a specific branch or product of which was eligible for export performance licensing, two rates of exchange were estimated: one in the absence of export performance licensing and the other on the assumption that the export performance license applied to the entire industry. The average of the two rates was then taken as the rate relevant for the entire industry. This method of estimating had an upward bias insofar as the particular branch enjoying export performance licensing contributed a small fraction of the total export of the industry, which was true in most cases.

Table 6.13.   Elasticities of Exports to Effective Exchange Rates: All Manufacturers

Dependent variable	Regression coeffients of		Estimated values of		
	$Log \dfrac{E_b}{P_d}$	$Log\ O$	T	R^2	DW
Log M	2.68	—	0.18	0.98	0.93
	(0.40)		(0.02)		
Log M	2.30	1.41	—	0.98	1.00
	(0.48)	(0.17)			

Definitions: M = export earnings for manufacturers, E_b = effective exchange rates when only Export Bonus Scheme is considered, P_d = domestic price level, O = supply of output, and T = time trend.

Note: Figures within parentheses are standard errors of estimate.

supply; P_d represents the combined effect of both supply and demand factors in the domestic economy, whereas O represents only the supply of output.

It might well be suggested that the period covered by the statistical analysis was marked by a growth in world trade in manufactured exports and that, therefore, if the domestic supply was available, exportation would have taken place anyway due to an increasing world demand. It must be mentioned, however, that world exports of commodities that constituted the major share of Pakistan exports, such as cotton and jute textiles, were not growing rapidly; they were indeed among the slowest growing items in world manufactures trade. The equations relating exports of cotton and jute textiles to their respective exchange rates also indicate high elasticity of export supply, as table 6.14 shows.

Pakistan's share in the world trade of cotton yarn was highly sensitive to the variations in exchange rates. The bonus rate on cotton yarn was changed frequently and the exports reacted sharply, responding to variations in the bonus rates.

The high elasticity of export demand for jute goods was also corroborated by an independent study of the elasticity of substitution between competing sources, i.e., imports of jute bags in the United Kingdom market from Pakistan against those from other countries.[52] The elasticity of substitution in response to changes in relative prices was estimated to be -13.24.[53]

52. N. Alam, "The Experience of an Overvalued Economy: The Case of Pakistan, Chapter II" (Ph.D. diss., Yale University, 1968).

53. UNCTAD, *Study of the Origins and Operation of International Agreements Relating to Cotton Textiles,* TD/20/Suppl. 3, Geneva (Oct. 12, 1967), pp. 26–27, 33–37.

When analyzing the growth of cotton textile exports from Pakistan it is important to remember that there were quota restrictions on its exports to the developed countries under the Long-Term International Textiles Agreement, which was further modified and supplemented by means of bilateral trade agreements with a number of developed countries. Pakistan's exports to some countries tended to fall

Table 6.14. Elasticities of Exports to Effective Exchange Rates: Cotton and Jute Textiles

Dependent variables	Regression coefficient of $\frac{E_b}{P_d}$	Value of R^2	Value of DW
Log CY	5.44 (1.44)	0.59	2.93
Log $\frac{CY_q}{TW}$	6.89 (1.75)	0.66	1.27
Log CF	4.67 (0.90)	0.73	1.46
Log $\frac{CF_q}{TW}$	4.30 (0.91)	0.79	2.58
Log J	7.07 (1.90)	0.50	0.65
Log $\frac{J_q}{TW}$	7.70 (1.41)	0.71	1.38

Definitions: CY = dollar value of exports of cotton yarn, CF = dollar value of exports of cotton cloth, J = dollar value of exports of jute textiles, CY_q = quantity of exports of cotton yarn, CF_q = quantity of exports of cotton cloth, J_q = quantity of exports of jute textiles, and TW = the volume of world trade in the respective commodities.

Note: The figures within parentheses are standard errors of estimate.

During the 1960s Pakistan expanded a wide variety of manufactured exports, apart from jute, cotton, and leather manufactures. They consisted of a very large number of items, broadly distributed over the entire range of manufacturing industries, each of which was worth only a relatively small amount. They were consistent recipients of numerous export incentive schemes, including higher rates of export bonus. These miscellaneous exports constituted a small proportion of their domestic output as well as a miniscule share of the world trade in these

---

short of the quotas allotted, partly owing to the cumbersome licensing procedure adopted by these nations, including delays in issuance of licenses. In the case of jute, Pakistan's share of world trade in jute manufactures was obtained primarily at the expense of India because of a favorable exchange rate. There was no price war or aggressive competition in offsetting each other's export incentives for a share of the world market for jute during this period. India had suffered no absolute decline in her total jute manufactured exports. It was the increase in world trade in sacking and jute bags, two varieties of jute manufactures that had gone to Pakistan. This was because in order to capture a larger share of the export market in those items India would have been required to increase its domestic production of raw jute to an extent that would have greatly added to its cost of production by extension of cultivation into marginal lands. This would have made India's exports noncompetitive. Therefore, India moved steadily into hessian (jute cotton fabrics, capable of numerous uses besides packing) and specialized jute products.

Table 6.15.   Elasticities of Exports to Effective Exchange Rates: Minor Exports

Dependent variables	Regressive coefficients of					Values of	
	$Log \dfrac{E_b}{P_d}$	$Log \dfrac{E}{P_d}$	T	Y_w	D	R^2	DW
$Log\ M_m$	2.02 (0.36)	—	—	—	1.66 (0.24)	0.91	1.37
$Log\ M_m$	—	1.51 (0.60)	—	—	1.31 (0.31)	0.88	1.53
$Log\ A_m$	—	1.71 (0.90)	—	0.07 (0.03)	—	0.55	0.84
$Log\ A_m$	—	1.64 (0.70)	—	—	1.20 (0.20)	0.58	0.88

Definitions: M_m = dollar value of exports of minor manufacturers; A_m = dollar value of exports of minor primary products; Y_w = the weighted index of GNP of principal importing countries, the weights being the proportion of Pakistani exports to the respective countries; T = time trend; and D = the dummy variable representing export incentive schemes that could not be included in E_b or E.
Note: The figures within parentheses are standard errors of estimate.

commodities. They were only 23 percent of the total manufactured exports and 78 percent of them each had an annual value less than Rs 15 million. Often from one year to the next, there was a large variation in the amount of exports of these minor items. The equations relating the growth of miscellaneous manufactured exports to the variations in the effective exchange rate yielded elasticities of response between 1.51 and 2.02, as indicated in table 6.15.[54] The elasticity of response of minor agricultural exports that were eligible for export bonus was between 1.71 and 1.64, as shown in table 6.15.

The minor primary exports exclude jute, cotton, tea, wool, and hides and skins. The independent studies of the elasticity of substitution between exports from competing sources, of such raw materials as wool and hides and skins, indicate their responsiveness to price changes. The elasticity of substitution in the case of wool and hides and skins was estimated to be −17.13 and −2.60, respectively, as estimated on the basis of imports from competing sources in the

54. The important difference between these equations and those explaining the behavior of all manufactured exports taken together is the significance of the variable D. D is a dummy variable that stands for those export incentive schemes which could not be included in either E_B or E. When D is used in an equation incorporating E_B it includes the effects of all incentive measures except the Export Bonus Scheme. When it is used along with E, it includes the effects of those factors that are excluded from E. Although E includes other export promotion measures in addition to the Export Bonus Scheme, it still leaves out a few measures, such as rebates of taxes on income earned through exportation, export quotas, and the like, which assumed significance in the period after 1963/64.

major markets of the world.[55] The most conservative estimate of elasticity of export demand for fine rice put it at -3.14.[56]

CONCLUDING REMARKS

The above analysis confirms a considerable degree of response elasticity of the export supply to export incentive schemes. The analysis incorporated the impact of a number of variables on exports, such as domestic demand and supply conditions and changes or growth in world trade. The latter was used as an index of external demand for Pakistan's exports. The domestic price level, i.e., the domestic wholesale prices of the agricultural or manufactured goods, appeared to be an important variable, along with the effective exchange rate, in determining the elasticity of response of the export supply. Changes in the domestic price level represented the combined effect of changes in the domestic demand and supply positions, which critically determined the exportable surplus and hence the elasticity of response of exports to the stimulus of higher returns per unit of export. In commodities such as cotton textiles, jute textiles, and leather textiles, for which exports constituted a significant proportion of total output, exports were actually dependent on the domestic supply and demand situation. The export incentive schemes had the effect of reducing domestic sales whenever domestic supply was not elastic or was not increasing. The response of exports to the change in exchange rate was greater the more elastic the supply and the smaller the rise in the domestic price level caused by the combined pull of domestic and external demand.

The foregoing statistical analysis distinguishes between broad categories of exports, i.e., manufactured and primary exports; within each category it also makes a distinction between major and minor exports. Export incentive schemes, as stated earlier, introduced substantial differentiation or discrimination between individual commodities within the broad categories of both manufactured and primary exports. The extent of differentiation can be seen in the appendix to this chapter (tables 6A1–6A3). The pattern of discrimination between individual commodities in terms of differential exchange rates sometimes changed between individual years and within a short span of time. It is doubtful that the policymakers realized the full impact of the multiplicity of the incentive schemes and frequent changes therein, which resulted in a bewildering variety and range of exchange rates. An analysis of the impact of these policies seldom provided the basis of their decision making.

55. N. Alam, "Experience of an Overvalued Economy."
56. M. Hussein, "Export Potential of Fine Rice for Pakistan," *Pakistan Development Review* 4, no. 4 (Winter 1964): 679.

The question that might be raised is whether such an extensive degree of differentiation or discrimination between individual manufactured exports was necessary. Although all the manufactured exports responded to a high effective exchange rate, did such a degree of industry or commodity discrimination increase the growth rate of the manufactured exports beyond that which a uniform but high rate of effective change for all the manufactured exports would have accomplished? The ranking of manufactured products by effective rates of exchange either in 1963/64 or in 1965/66 was weakly correlated with the ranking by their rates of growth (1960–67). The rank correlation coefficient is low and statistically insignificant. Moreover, it was found that the effective exchange rates in 1963/64 were negatively correlated with the relative importance of the individual manufactured exports, i.e., proportions of individual exports in the total manufactured exports, in 1961/62–1963/64. In other words, relatively insignificant earners of foreign exchange were the recipients of the higher rates of foreign exchange. There was also an inverse relationship between effective rates of exchange in 1964/65 and the relative importance of individual exports during 1964/65–1966/67.

To explain the rationale of extensive discrimination among the individual manufactured exports in terms of the effective exchange rates by reference to their differential elasticities of demand is hardly defensible. Detailed information on the elasticities of demand of individual manufactured exports was not available to justify the degree of discrimination that was in fact practiced. To discriminate between jute and cotton textiles, on the one hand, and the other manufactured exports, on the other, solely on the basis of differential elasticities of demand and, further, to argue that the differential elasticities justify the amount of discrimination actually practiced—but no more or no less—would be difficult to justify. Although it is true that in view of Pakistan's small share in world trade one might argue that the elasticity of export demand for miscellaneous manufactures was greater than that for jute and cotton textiles, this presumption was not necessarily true when one takes cognizance of the market imperfections in international trade. Consumer preference for established brand names, product differentiation and salesmanship, the difficulty of getting access to established trade channels, and other factors did reduce the price elasticity of demand for Pakistan's new, miscellaneous manufactured exports. On the other hand, statistical evidence discussed earlier revealed a very high degree of elasticity of cotton and jute textile exports to variations in the effective exchange rates.

In this context one could, however, argue the case for differentiation of exchange rates between the textiles exports, on the one hand, and the minor miscellaneous manufactured exports, on the other, on the basis of differential "infancies" of these two groups of industries. The miscellaneous exports were the newest exports with high initial costs; in addition, selling in the export markets was a new undertaking and involved a process of learning by doing.

Was the structure of the effective exchange rates related to the costs of earning or saving foreign exchange? Did Pakistan design a structure of export subsidies in such a way that higher subsidies were provided to the lower cost exports, i.e., exports that cost less in terms of the scarce domestic resources? If the infant industry argument for export subsidies was accepted, the higher subsidies to exports that had low cost and discrimination against those with initial high costs but with an expected decline in costs in the long run were not necessarily an efficient use of scarce resources. But then with a uniform and effective exchange rate the lowest cost exports would have expanded at the fastest rate. A higher rate for higher cost exports was justified if they were identified as infant export industries.

The correlation between the ranking of the manufactured exports by effective exchange rates and by the direct and indirect cost of earning foreign exchange was low and insignificant. Pakistan had not achieved the expansion of exports by greater inducement to those that cost less in terms of domestic resource cost. In fact, there was no systematic pattern in the structure of effective exchange rates from this point of view. Was the structure of export incentives related to the factor intensity of exports? In other words, did the labor intensive exports receive a higher subsidy or vice versa?[57] The rank correlation between interindustry differences in the value added per employee and in the effective exchange rates was small and positive, ranging from 0.35 and 0.42. The correlations between the wage value added and effective exchange rates was higher (0.36 and 0.43) than between nonwage value added and effective exchange rates (0.22 and 0.29). The existence of a positive correlation implies that the more capital intensive exports (implied by the higher value added per employee as well as higher nonwage value added per employee) received higher rates of export subsidies and consequently higher effective rates of exchange. Labor intensive industry, according to this analysis, received lower rates of exchange.

In conclusion it may be stated that Pakistan in the 1960s did achieve an acceleration in the growth rate of exports, especially manufactured exports. Among primary exports, cotton, rice, and fish were important successes and so also were the minor agricultural exports. Export performance was highly correlated with improvement in effective exchange rates, which was the result of various export incentive schemes, primarily the Export Bonus Scheme and ex-

---

57. Labor intensity is measured by value added for employee. See H. B. Lary, *Imports of Manufactures from Less Developed Countries* (New York: National Bureau of Economic Research, 1966), pp. 1–50.

port performance licensing. However, the system of export incentives was haphazard, often changing and highly differentiated in terms of groups of commodities. Such a high degree of differentiation among individual export items, especially manufactured exports, was not necessary; this differentiation was not related to variations in their rates of growth or to their relative cost differences or efficiencies. Often, higher cost exports were given higher export incentives without any examination of whether these were genuine infant industry cases with the promise of an increased efficiency in the long run. The export incentives were not differentiated either according to the criterion of factor intensity, however measured, or to net foreign exchange saving. The complicated schemes did not permit one to determine easily the effective exchange rates resulting from the multiplicity of export incentive schemes. A simple structure of incentive schemes, for example, the Export Bonus Scheme, differentiating between major primary and traditional manufactures such as jute and cotton textiles, on the one hand, and newer manufactures, on the other, would have been more efficient as a method of export promotion.

The nature, characteristics, and structure of the export policies, including the export incentive and bonus schemes, have been discussed in chapters 6 and 7. The current chapter analyzes their effects on the performance of exports. The preceding paragraph summarizes the nature of the export incentive schemes in relation to export performance. Taken together, the preceding analyses seem to provide Pakistan with the following lessons of experience.

Starting in the late 1950s and early 1960s the intensification of export promotion measures resulting in an improvement of the effective exchange rate for exports led to a narrowing of the differential between the effective exchange rate for exports and for imports. This helped to encourage increased production of the export commodities as well as their diversion to export markets. The relative attractiveness of the domestic markets, protected as the latter were by quantitative controls, compared to export markets was partly counterbalanced. The export supply was found to be highly responsive to the higher effective exchange rates for exports. The latter helped to offset the effects of domestic inflation and hence of rising costs, rendering export sales profitable. However, the movements in exchange rates did not fully compensate for the rise in domestic costs and prices in relation to world prices.

Second, it was not only the export supply but also the export demand that responded to price incentives. The effects of the Export Bonus Scheme, combined with other incentive schemes, were to enable the exporters to offer competitive prices in export markets. The hypothesis of elasticity pessimism was not borne out by whatever empirical evidence could be marshaled. This was true of both the manufactured and primary exports, including the minor primary exports. This was true not only of commodities in which Pakistan's world market share was small as in the case of tea; it was also true of raw jute and jute goods in which she faced duopolistic or oligopolistic market structure. Of course, Pakistan had the advantage of producing high quality output due to natural advantages the country enjoyed in the production of raw jute. But quality is a substitute for price only up to a point, and Pakistan did learn this lesson over the years.

Third, the response of supply to export incentives or high export exchange rates was not only a function of price obtainable on the export markets; controls, direct as well as indirect, in allocating inputs, both domestic and imported, into the production of the export commodities had a significant impact on export performance. Relevant also were the institutional factors affecting investment, marketing, and distribution. As long as the import control measures were used in making an interindustry allocation of the imported inputs, it was important that the export industries be allowed liberal access to the imported inputs so that they could expand output to respond to the stimulus of the export incentives.

High effective exchange rates for exports in Pakistan were combined with a partial liberalization, during some years, of the quantitative controls on selected imports and exports. Export bonus vouchers, for example, were freely usable for the purchase of the imported inputs for domestic industry.

But it was not true of all imported inputs; what is more important, the degree of restriction on the imported inputs, in respect to its stringency and coverage, fluctuated over time. It created a sense of uncertainty among the exporters and inhibited at least partly their willingness to respond to the export incentives. The import/exchange control regime, owing to the way it was administered, was inherently unpredictable because of frequent changes, which aggravated the uncertainty in export markets, i.e., prices and demand, subject to fluctuations in world trade and to economic changes in the importing countries. This contributed to the unpredictability of future costs and returns involved in exports, which detracted from the efficiency and the long-run beneficial effects of the export incentive measures.

Lastly, there was the question of discrimination among the individual commodity exports in terms of the effective exchange rates. The inefficiencies, as evidenced in a wide dispersion of domestic resource costs among individual exports, were inherent in such a system.

The relative success of the Export Bonus Scheme in the early 1960s was due partly to the fact that they were sustained for quite some time. Assurances were given from time to time about the continuance of the Export Bonus Scheme, even though in the context of frequent changes in its contents such assurances did not always fully achieve the intended results.

Again, during the early 1960s, the agricultural sector performed rather well; its beneficial effects on export performance were felt in many ways, i.e., through expanded supplies of primary exports as well as of raw material inputs to the domestic manufacturing industries, including export industries. Reduced food imports released foreign exchange resources for the purchase of imported inputs for the export industries. At the same time, the export promotion policies were strengthened by supportive fiscal and monetary policies, which helped to restrain inflationary forces, thus contributing to the competitiveness and greater availability of exports.

The reversal of these favorable supportive policies, combined with adverse developments in the agricultural sector in the late 1960s, weakened the effectiveness of the exchange rate policy. The favorable exchange rates for exports were eroded and this was not compensated by additional export incentives or devaluation. There was no clear recognition in Pakistan's export policy that export incentives needed to be sustained in order to produce substantial and long-run effects. There was an inevitable time lag before the beneficial effects of exchange rate adjustment were fully felt. The organization of production and marketing for exports needed time, especially when for a long time the orientation of economic activities had been predominantly toward the domestic market. Short-run inelasticity and setbacks were not to be allowed to reverse the policy of export promotion.

Pakistan's experience seems to suggest that, given the commodity structure of its exports, a system of dual exchange rates would have been appropriate during the 1960s. Moreover, the system of dual exchange rates should have been variable in response to changes in demand and supply for eligible exports and imports. A depreciated exchange rate for all exports other than jute and for all imports other than essential imports such as food, combined with higher exchange rates for raw jute exports, on the one hand, and essential imports, on the other, would have been more effective than the complicated system of multiple exchange rates that did not have a logical structure and rationale.

Also, Pakistan's exchange rate policy did not include a clear recognition of its impact on returns from jute production and export, its predominant export commodity, in relation to the price of rice and returns from its production, its most important crop and essential import. Rice and jute competed keenly for the use of land and other resources. An appropriate policy was to ensure that, given the elasticity of world demand and even the export price of jute in relation to the import price of rice, social costs and returns from the production of the two crops were not out of line with each other.

APPENDIX

Table 6A1. Multiplicity of Exchange Rates for Jute
and Cotton Manufactures (Rs per dollar)

Commodities/bonus rates	1967/68	1968/69
Cotton manufactures		
Bonus rates		
10%	5.60	—
20%	6.44	—
30%	7.17	7.36
40%	7.94	8.23
Weighted average for all cotton manufactures	7.18	7.60
Jute manufactures		
Bonus rates		
20% (10% stamped)	6.09	—
20% (regular)	6.34	6.41
30% (20% stamped)	6.58	—
30% (regular)	7.13	7.32
Weighted average	6.52	7.36

Source: Government of Pakistan, Planning Commission, International Economics Section, *A Background Note on Bonus Exports during the Third Plan* (Sept. 12, 1969), tables I–IV.

Table 6A2. Effective Exchange Rates for Individual Manufacturing
Exports

Industry	1963/64	1965/66
Canning of fruits, vegetables	9.85	8.33
Bakery production and confections	7.85	7.71
Sugar	8.38	7.57
Edible oils, fats	8.09	7.28
Alcoholic beverages	11.85	11.42
Tobacco products	10.47	10.23
Cotton textiles	8.57	7.71
Wool textiles	9.28	7.81
Jute textiles	6.00	6.00
Silk, art, silk textiles	9.42	9.23
Knitting	7.76	7.09
Threadball	9.47	8.00
Manufacture and repair of footwear	9.47	7.85
Wearing apparel	10.38	8.81
Manufacture of cork, wood products	9.19	7.47
Manufacture of paper, paper products	8.85	8.00
Articles, paper, paperboard	8.76	7.90

(*continued*)

Table 6A2. (*Continued*)

Industry	1963/64	1965/66
Printing, publishing, allied industries	8.04	7.28
Tanning, leather finishing	7.85	7.19
Manufacture of rubber	9.52	7.81
Manufacture of fertilizers	7.76	7.04
Paint and varnishes	10.66	8.47
Perfumes, cosmetics, soap	12.23	10.38
Matches	10.23	9.85
Chemical products, n.e.s.	9.37	7.71
Coal, petroleum products	13.61	12.28
Manufacture of nonmetallic minerals	10.52	8.81
Basic metal industries (1 + 2)	8.00	7.24
Manufacture of metal products	9.14	7.47
Machinery except electrical (1)	9.23	7.76
Machinery except electrical (2)	7.95	8.43
Electrical machinery (1)	10.19	8.57
Electrical machinery (2)	—	9.33
Transport equipment	8.14	7.95
Photographic, optical goods	9.62	7.81
Plastic products	8.38	8.85
Sports, athletic goods	7.66	7.14
Pens, pencils, related products	9.38	7.95

Source: N. Islam, *Nature and Impact of Export Incentives and Effective Export Subsidy,* Pakistan Institute of Development Economics, Research Report no. 86 (1968).

Notes: The effective exchange rate for each individual industry group covers only those products within each group that were eligible for export performance licensing. It excludes those products in each group that were not entitled to export performance licensing.

Table 6A3.   Effective Exchange Rates for Manufacturing Exports

Industry	1963/64	1965/66
Canning of fruits, vegetables	8.52	7.66
	11.19	9.00
Cotton textiles	7.24	7.47
	9.95	7.90
Wool textiles	8.00	7.24
	10.52	8.38
Knitting	6.52	6.47
	9.00	7.71
Alcoholic beverages	11.85	10.71
		12.19

(*continued*)

Table 6A3. (*Continued*)

Industry	1963/64	1965/66
Bakery products and confections	7.85	7.09
		8.33
Tobacco products	10.47	9.42
		11.09
Art, silk, textiles	9.42	8.52
		9.95
Threadball	8.14	7.39
	10.71	8.66
Manufacture and repair of footwear	8.19	7.38
	10.76	8.33
Wearing apparel	9.00	8.09
	11.76	9.47
Manufacture of cork, wood products	7.95	7.19
	10.42	7.81
Manufacture of rubber	8.19	7.38
	10.85	8.19
Paints and varnishes	9.23	8.33
	12.09	8.62
Leather, tanning	—	7.04
		7.43
Perfumes, cosmetics, soap	10.57	9.52
	13.85	6.43
Chemical products, n.e.s.	8.09	7.33
	10.61	8.09
Manufacture of nonmetallic mineral	9.09	8.23
products (1)	11.95	9.42
Manufacture of nometallic mineral	9.09	8.23
products (2)	11.95	9.42
Manufacture of metal products	7.90	7.09
	10.33	7.85
Machinery except electrical (1)	7.95	7.19
	10.47	8.28
Electrical machinery (1)	8.81	7.95
	11.57	9.19
Manufacture of transport equipment	8.14	8.62
Photographic, optical goods	8.33	7.52
	10.90	8.09
Pens, pencils, related goods	8.09	7.33
	10.61	8.57

Source: N. Islam, *Nature and Impact of Export Incentives and Effective Export Subsidy,* Research Report 86 (Karachi: Pakistan Institute of Development Economics, 1969).

7

Liberalization of Exchange Control: An Export Bonus Scheme and a Free List

INTRODUCTION

Toward the beginning of the 1960s the weaknesses of the exchange control system were seriously debated. The deficiencies included, besides allocational and growth effects, delays, large inventories, absence of competition, inflexibility, and endemic shortage of imported materials for the small-scale and unorganized sector.[1] No less important were the temptation to and prevalence of graft and corruption among importers and civil servants, resulting in a distribution of licenses that was at variance with the professed criteria of the government. There were therefore those who favored the immediate dismantling of the licensing system, compared to others who supported a slow and gradual lifting of controls on imports by extending a few of the "liberalizing" steps already in operation (such as the OGL and the automatic licensing system). Weaknesses in the system of licensing were evident.

Import liberalization in Pakistan has been used in different contexts and has implied more than one meaning. It implied not only relaxation of restrictions as to (a) what to be imported, (b) how much to be imported, and (c) who is to import, but also the introduction of a greater degree of competition in the import trade.[2] However, both the introduction of a greater competition in import trade and the relaxation of quantitative restrictions are more easily accomplished under circumstances of a larger inflow of imports, prompted either by an expansion of exports or by a larger flow of foreign assistance.

The introduction of a larger number of importers to handle the same volume of imports was, therefore, a liberalization in the sense that total profits on the given volume of imports was shared by many. It distributed scarcity premiums among a larger number of importers. An increase in the total volume of imports, with an

---

1. Discussed in chap. 5.

2. P. S. Thomas, "Import Licensing and Import Liberalization in Pakistan," *Pakistan Development Review* 6, no. 4 (Winter 1966): 500–44.

unchanged system of licensing and quantitative controls, reduced the scarcity premiums per unit of imports but did not restore the market mechanism in the determination of the flow of imports and its composition. Despite a large volume of imports, inefficiencies of the allocation mechanism continued. The restoration of a price mechanism for the determination of the quantum and composition could take place with an unchanged volume of imports, if the prices of imports were allowed to rise and balance demand with supply. Dismantling of quantitative restrictions in these circumstances would require exchange depreciation or a combination of import duties and export subsidies. This would reduce the divergence between effective rates of exchange of imports and exports.

The relaxation of quantitative controls could also be achieved by reducing total domestic demand for imports. This could be done either by direct controls or by fiscal and monetary policy. Total expenditure could be reduced and the composition of demand altered toward decreased import intensiveness, thereby lowering total expenditure on imports. The demand for imports could be indirectly reduced by restricting credit for the financing of imports or for the holding of inventories by traders and industrialists. However, the policymakers in Pakistan were unwilling to use price mechanisms for the adjustment of supply and demand for imports. They preferred to relax restrictions only if the excess demand for foreign exchange was matched by an increased inflow of imports through an increase in foreign assistance, for example.

Pakistan's experimentation with relaxation of quantitative restrictions was limited to two principal methods. They were (1) the Export Bonus Scheme and (2) the introduction of a free list of imports. The Export Bonus Scheme[3] was a method of export promotion that allowed the exporters access to marketable foreign exchange, equivalent to varying percentages of their export earnings. This could be brought by the importers for import, without any restriction, except that the types of imports were specified. Suffice it to mention here that this relaxation was associated with a rise in the effective rate of exchange for imports to an extent determined by the supply and demand of marketable import entitlements received by exporters, i.e., bonus vouchers.

During the early 1960s prior to the introduction of the free list, Pakistan introduced the system of Open General License, the main purpose of which was to introduce new entrants to import trade. The new traders were allowed mostly for items on which licensing authorities had permitted an increase in imports in response to domestic demand. This reduced the profits of established importers. A larger volume of imports implied a lower profit per unit and hence a decline in total profits because lower price was not offset by the expansion in volume distributed among the old traders.

---

3. The details of this mechanism are discussed later in this chapter.

The immediate reason for the introduction of free lists, a list of importables that could be imported without any ceiling or limit on the quantity of each item of imports, was the major concern of the government regarding the shortage of imported raw materials. Although the import of capital goods increased by 50 percent during the three years from 1960/61 to 1962/63, the imports of raw materials were essentially constant.[4] This led to a thriving black market in imported raw materials. Some firms had excessive licenses for particular items, others had few or none; this was mostly due to the use of inadequate and outdated surveys, which were the basis of the import licensing of raw materials. Even though the black market transactions improved the allocation of raw materials, the licensing-cum-black market mechanism was considered inefficient by the authorities. Precisely at this moment the suppliers of foreign aid became seriously concerned with the shortage of imported raw materials and the inefficiencies of the allocation system that affected industrial output. The increased flow of commodity aid for the imports of raw materials was made conditional upon the use of the market mechanism for its allocation. There was, in this respect, an increasing convergence of opinion among the dominant groups in policymaking circles and the suppliers of aid.[5]

Just as foreign aid was instrumental in the adoption of the liberalization program, experience with liberalization and the associated spurt in economic activity brought an additional flow of foreign assistance.[6] When the consortium met for a pledging session, Pakistan had already put more than 50 items on the free list and was arguing that the disbursement rate of project aid was slower compared with nonproject aid. The need for nonproject aid was deliberately presented as the cost of implementing the liberalization program and the consortium agreed to foot the bill. The liberalization program was cited as a successful example of the aid relationship.[7] There were three reasons for this success. First, the liberalization program was a limited operation with a specific objective that was quantitatively defined and whose success could be easily measured. Second, economic policies of which liberalization was a natural by-product had already proved to be a moderate success, (i.e., the active role and performance of the private sector were already evident). Third, the operation was one in which the separate

4. Thomas, "Import Licensing," p. 18.

5. J. White, *Pledged to Development* (London: Overseas Development Institute, 1967), pp. 59–84.

6. "The consortium met at the end of May 1964, just when the liberalization program was beginning to show results. The consortium's next step was obvious. In its opening statement, the World Bank advocated a further dose of liberalisation and pointed out that this would require larger amounts of programme aid" (ibid., p. 80).

7. "The nature of that success is indicated by the fact that credit for getting the liberalisation programme started has at various times been separately claimed by officials in the government of Pakistan, in the USAID, and in the World Bank" (ibid., p. 83).

functions of the participants were easily discernible. The link between the abolition of import controls and nonproject aid was simple.

THE FREE LIST

Although many viewed the free list as a compromise because of exceptions and qualifications, it must be ranked as the most important step toward liberalization since the imposition of detailed licensing in 1953. Initially the free list, in January–June 1964, was financed by U.S. aid and limited to imports of steel from the United States. For imports other than steel, Pakistan continued its previous licensing policies, with increased emphasis on the new OGL, the import bonus, and automatic licensing. Imports under these three schemes increased from Rs 432.3 million in July–December 1963 to Rs 665.0 million in January–June 1964, a rise of over 50 percent. Including free list imports of Rs 354.8 million, import-liberalization policies of different degrees encompassed over two-thirds of private imports regulated by the licensing authority.

With the import policy of July–December 1964 the nature of the government's interpretation of and commitment to the free list became much clearer. First, the list of importable items was expanded by 50 items. Second, although the major part of the free list continued to be financed by foreign aid, Pakistan committed part of its own foreign exchange earnings to finance 22 of these items, including one of the larger ones—maintenance spares—which encompassed about 3 percent of free list imports. Iron, steel, and chemicals were the most important items on the free list.

Fiscal and monetary policies were adjusted to help regulate foreign exchange usage by indirect means, replacing to some degree the licensing controls that were being removed. Marginal changes in tax and credit occurred. Between 1959 and 1963 import duties rose by about one-third, with increases ranging from 11 percent on certain processed raw materials to 115 percent on semiluxury consumer goods. Then early in July 1964 a regulatory duty was introduced on free list imports ranging from 5 to 20 percent ad valorem. Because the sales tax was levied on a base including import duties, the increase in cost to importers was somewhat higher than the rise in duties, averaging about 13 percent. In June 1965 duties on capital machinery imports were increased from 12.5 to 25 percent in West Pakistan and from 7.5 to 20 percent in East Pakistan. In November 1965 a defense surcharge of 25 percent sales taxes was introduced. Thus, the effective tax rate on imports rose approximately another one-third after the advent of the free list.

Supplementing the tax increases, credit controls were also tightened somewhat. Upon opening a letter of credit to initiate payment for goods, an importer was required to make a 25 percent advance deposit, and 15 percent of their value on arrival. Thus government credit was restricted to 60 percent of the import value.

In order to be able to evaluate the implications of the introduction of the free list as a crucial step in liberalization efforts, it is necessary to assess the extent to which free list items were in fact freed from quantitative restrictions. The free list items were not completely free from all restrictions. When the restrictions surrounding the free list were first introduced in 1964, they related to (a) who could import them, (b) geographical regions into which the items could be imported, (c) the country from which they could be imported, and (d) the amount in which they could be imported. Not all free list items could be imported by commercial importers; the latter could import only specific items. Whereas in 1964 the commercial importers could import 45 out of the 51 free list items, in 1966 they could import only 37 out of the 66 items. The rest were to be imported by industrial importers who imported for direct use in their own enterprises. There was a limit to the initial letter of credit opened by any importer, even though all importers were allowed the convenience of repeated letters of credit. One reason for this restriction was to help the smaller importer by slowing down the rate of utilization by the big firms. In the case of a few items the established importers were subjected to restrictions on the number of imports. Twenty-three of the 66 free list items could be imported only from certain specified sources. The commercial importers were restricted to sources of tied aid or barter countries in several cases. However, iron and steel importers were permitted to import from the cheapest sources.

In 1967 the term *free list* was abolished and thus the import figures under this category should be read with caution. Technically, there were 10 items during 1967/68 (financed essentially by aid and barter) that could be imported without the cover of a license but the restrictions surrounding this privilege were considerable. Two items were allowed only for the public sector. The import of the remaining 8 items was limited in different ways. One was that private importers were given a quota equal to their average six-monthly imports under the free list from 1964 to 1967. Second was a limit on the number of items that each firm could import. Any firm that had been importing these items on the free list during the period 1964–67 could choose only one of these items to import during this shipping period (July–Dec. 1967). In addition those firms with categories who continued to import under the free list, when the old categories had ceased to become operational, could select one of their category items to import. Third, there were restrictions relating to tied aid, sources of imports as well as predetermined ceilings on import from specific sources.

The quantitative significance of the free list in liberalization efforts can best be evaluated by considering the distribution of total imports under different lists, bonus, free, and licensable lists. When evaluating the magnitutude of liberalization, it is important to note that it refers only to private and not public sector imports. Of course within the private sector, imports of capital goods for the creation of new or expansion of old industrial capacity was not directly subject to the control of the import licensing authority. During 1963/64 about 62.5 percent of private sector imports were subject to licensing regulation directly by the Chief Controller of Imports and Exports; by 1968/69 the percentage had fallen to 53.6 percent. In light of the above, it is to be remembered that efforts to liberalize import controls related only to about half the total private imports, and total private imports comprised only 65 percent of total imports.

The value of free list imports increased rapidly between the first quarter of 1963 and the third quarter of 1965. In 1963/64 free list imports constituted about 15 percent of the imports regulated by the licensing authority and in 1964/65 the proportion reached the high figure of 50.5 percent. That was the highest percentage ever reached by the free list items. In the following years there was a decline in the proportion of free list imports. It dropped to the low figure of 27.2 percent by 1968/69.

The impact of the introduction of the free list was felt in several ways. It increased substantially the import of industrial raw materials financed by foreign assistance; this in turn increased the rate of use of installed industrial capacity. This effect was confirmed by the U.S. Aid Survey of 65 industrial plants in both regions of the country, which used raw materials on the free list and which imported 90 percent of their raw material requirements. The study was specially designed to cover plants of this nature. The improvement in the rate of utilization of capacity is seen in table 7.1

Even though the iron and steel imports under the free list were financed by U.S. aid and tied to U.S. sources of purchase, which charged higher than competitive world prices, the industries could get regular, more abundant, and assured supplies of raw materials to plan in a more rational fashion and thus avoid frequent shutdowns.

Second, the introduction of free lists changed relative prices of imported goods by reducing the domestic prices of imported free list goods. The weighted aver-

Table 7.1. Percentage of Single-Shift Capacity Utilized

	West Pakistan	*East Pakistan*	*Both*
June–Dec. 1963	53	54	53
Jan.–June 1964	61	63	62
July–Dec. 1964	76	77	76
Feb.–Mar. 1965	80	85	82

Source: U.S. Agency for International Development, Pakistan, *A Case Study of Import Liberalisation in Pakistan* (Karachi, Apr. 2, 1965).

age prices of the free list items registered a fall of 7 percent in Karachi and 6 percent in Chittagong between 1964 and 1965. This changed the structure of nominal as well as of effective protection. The nominal protection for the domestic industries competing with the free list imports was reduced. The effective protection for industries using cheaper, free list imports as inputs was increased.

One of the side effects of the introduction of the free list was the tendency to build up stocks through overimporting. This was due to a lack of confidence about future import policy and due to a fear, based on past experience, that periods of increased supply were often followed by periods of stringency. The fears of the importers were justified by subsequent events. The effect of import liberalization on building up of stocks in 1964/65 can be seen in table 7.2. There was an accumulation of stocks during 1964/65 and a depletion of stocks during 1965/66, when the scope of the free list was limited. The accumulation of stocks and their subsequent depletion were most noticeable in the case of free list commodities, as table 7.3 shows.

A survey of imports on the free list revealed that speculative hoarding by the big importers was a very common practice. Most credit mechanisms such as maximum limits to letters of credit did not succeed in reducing the speculative activity in import trade. Because credit from banks could be the only effective limit on the import of a free list item, (except for items financed by foreign assistance) and because banks favored the more credit-worthy substantial importers, control of the import trade became concentrated. This might partly explain the persistence of the scarcity premium on free list items.[8]

Insofar as the imports of raw materials by the domestic industries were concerned, there was a tendency toward an efficient allocation of the free list imports among the competing firms or industries. The more efficient firms were not limited by the size of their entitlement. Insofar as commercial importers were concerned, the big importers received larger imports. It was not clear whether the distribution of imports among the individual firms and industries was governed more by access to finance or size of establishment rather than by the relative returns on imported inputs for different uses.

The experience with the free list imports seemed to indicate that if there were several scarce inputs, the restoration of the market mechanism in the allocation of one of them did not necessarily lead to an efficient allocation of the free input. This was especially true if other inputs not subject to the market mechanism were either complementary to free input (as in the case of domestic or imported capital equipment) or necessary to obtain access to the free input (such as finance or bank credit). The introduction of the free list for raw materials (which was the

8. M. Alamgir, "The Domestic Prices of Imported Commodities in Pakistan: A Further Study," *Pakistan Development Review* 8, no. 1 (Spring 1968): 35–73.

Table 7.2.   Changes in Stocks of Imported Intermediate Goods in 1964/65 and 1965/66 (Rs million)

Sector of destination	1964/65	1965/66
Consumer goods industries	+120	+20
Intermediate goods industries	+10	−157
Investment goods industries	+49	−147
Construction	+84	−188
Transport and communications	+10	−25
Other services	+7	−5
	+280	−502

Source: Planning Commission, *Import Projections and Commodity Aid Requirements,* June 10, 1966, pp. 9–10.

preponderant group of imports affected by the free list) lowered the price of imported raw materials in relation to imported capital components; in the context of Pakistan, this was an improvement in allocative efficiency because imported capital equipment had been specially favored in terms of availability and price. This particular distortion in relative prices, which was not warranted by relative demand for the imported capital equipment and raw materials, was corrected, at least partially, by the introduction of the free list. At the same time, however, in the absence of any exchange rate adjustment, the prices of both imported capital equipment and raw materials were below what their valuation at the scarcity price of foreign exchange would have implied.

The high scarcity premiums on raw materials and capital goods, which were revealed in several surveys of domestic prices of imported goods, have to be treated with proper caution. The imports of raw materials and capital goods were licensed directly to the industrial establishments. Therefore, they did not pay the high scarcity premium on the raw materials and capital equipment that they

Table 7.3.   Changes in Stocks of Free-List and Non-Free-List Items (Rs million)

(1) *Free-list items*	1964/65	1965/66
Iron and steel	+156	−322
Chemicals	+34	−45
Spares and parts	−10	—
Other items	+27	−88
Total free-list items	+207	−454
(2) Non-free-list items	+73	−48

Source: See table 7.2.

imported directly, and their direct imports constituted the preponderant share of their total import requirements. Most of the raw materials and capital equipment, imported by traders for resale, went to the small-scale industry or the unregistered or unlicensed industrial establishments that did not have import licensing privileges. Moreover, there was some illegal trading or black marketing in the imported raw materials and capital equipment, which the industrial establishments were legally prohibited from reselling.

The scarcity premium on the imported raw materials and capital goods implied that the import license itself provided a security to the banks for financing imports by the small traders; import licenses improved the credit worthiness of the small-importer-cum-traders. The importers without the license had encountered difficulty in obtaining credit.[9] The question has been asked whether the introduction of free lists adversely affected importers in East Pakistan, who had smaller financial resources than their counterparts in West Pakistan and who had lower credit standings with the banks. The answer can be seen in two ways. First, within East Pakistan there were importers of both East and West Pakistan origin. Those of West Pakistan origin were more substantial traders, had resources of their own, and had also good banking connections. They, therefore, had easier access to the banking system for the financing of import trade, even without the benefit of an import license. Thus, the absence of licensing could contribute to the loss of the market share for East Pakistani importers due to the imperfections of the capital market system.

The second aspect of the impact of liberalization on East Pakistan was the possibility of a fall in the share of imports for East Pakistan. This might have happened if the fall in the share for the importers of East Pakistani origin was not offset by an increase in the share of the importers of West Pakistani origin located in East Pakistan. Owing to the lack of allocation of imports between East and West Pakistan under a liberalized import system, the importers located in West Pakistan were likely to obtain a larger share of imports because of their greater financial resources and also because of a stronger demand for imports in West Pakistan due to a higher level of income and growth rate. Under a system of licensing there was a predetermined regional share of imports; in fact some imports could fetch different prices in the two wings more so than is warranted by transport costs because of the restrictions on the interregional movement of imported goods. This happened whenever differences in terms of allocation of imports were not in conformity with differences in relative demands. In fact the share of East Pakistan in the free list imports did not decline below its share of licensed imports; this was partly due to the fact that the free list, as was seen earlier, was not free from restrictions, i.e., it was not completely a system of

9. Thomas, "Import Licensing."

fully liberalized imports. Partly it was due to the reservations of certain free list imports such as cement to East Pakistan only. Moreover, the government and semigovernment productive enterprises were eligible for free list imports in addition to their share in the allocation of imports for the public sector; this helped maintain East Pakistan's share of free list imports because the share of public industrial investment in East Pakistan was considerably greater than in West Pakistan. That East Pakistan's share of free list imports was on the average higher than its average share of all imports was easily explained by these two factors. This was not inconsistent with the hypothesis that East Pakistan's share of free list imports would have suffered if free list imports were really free and if public sector imports did not have a share of free list imports.

Intermediate and capital goods were most affected by the policy of liberalization. Among the free list items the share of intermediate goods was substantially greater than that of capital goods. A comparison of the levels of markup between the two periods, i.e., the period immediately after the introduction of free list 1964/65 and the period after the restrictions were tightened on free list imports in 1966/67, reveals that the increase in markups in the second period was the highest in the case of intermediate goods, among the category of free list items. There was an increase of about 150 percent from a markup of 25.6 percent in the first period to a markup of about 67 percent in the second period. The markup in the case of free list consumption goods went down; these were mostly very essential consumption goods on which very minor restrictions, if any at all, were applied. The decline in markup on the landed cost of the licensed consumption goods was due to a rise in the rates of tariffs, which had cut into the profit margins of these importers.

THE EXPORT BONUS SCHEME

The Export Bonus Scheme adopted in January 1959 was the culmination of a number of steps undertaken in the 1950s that were designed to promote exports by linking them with access to import privileges. But it was also an important step in the liberalization of imports from quantitative restrictions. There were three distinct features of the bonus scheme that distinguished it from the earlier schemes and that characterized this significant measure for liberalizing imports from quantitative restrictions. First, import entitlements earned by both primary and manufactured exports were for the first time freely transferable and also could be used for importing any items on an extended list of eligible imports. The exporters who earned the import entitlements in the first place were not obliged to use them for importing the required raw materials for use in their own enterprise or activity. The export industry earning entitlement to foreign exchange could use it directly for imports; similarly any other importer, commercial or industrial, could freely purchase bonus vouchers or import entitlements and could import any amount from among the permissible list of imports. Therefore, the magnititude of subsidy received by the different exporters was not related to the scarcity of the imported inputs that are specific to their particular industry but was related to the scarcity of a wide range of commodities in common use by a large number of industries and users. Second, the coverage of the scheme was considerably wider than the earlier import entitlement schemes; all exports, both primary and manufactured, except for the major primary exports such as tea, cotton, jute, wool, hides and skins, were entitled to the bonus scheme. However, with a 20 percent export bonus for the primary commodities and 40 percent for the manufactured goods, this scheme provided a higher level of assistance for the majority of the export commodities compared to the previous incentive schemes. Third, services such as shipping, ship and aircraft repairs, and hotels were, for the first time, entitled to the bonus scheme.

Instead of specifying and narrowly defining the commodities that were entitled to the Export Bonus Scheme, as was the case under the earlier import entitlement schemes in the 1950s, the new policy indicated the commodities excluded from the scheme so that it extended the benefit of the scheme to all the new commodities that could potentially enter the export market, even though they were not currently exported.

The exclusion of the major agricultural exports from the preview of the Export Bonus Scheme was based on a number of assumptions regarding their supply and demand elasticity. First, it was assumed that their export demand elasticity was low. In the case of Pakistan's exports of tea and cotton, which constituted a very small share of world trade in these commodities, the assumption was not very realistic even though the price elasticity of world demand for tea and cotton in the importing countries was low. Second, it was assumed that the supply elasticity of the major agricultural commodities was low. This was because the divergence between international prices and domestic costs was greater for manufactures than for traditional primary exports. The degree of the exchange rate adjustment necessary to bring the domestic costs and prices of the manufactured goods in line with their international prices was greater—in some cases much greater— than that which would have been necessary in the case of the primary exports.

A uniform exchange rate adjustment for both agricultural and manufactured exports was not considered feasible. An exchange rate adjustment enough to compensate for the higher costs of the domestic manufactures would have increased the local currency receipts and money income from the agricultural export sector, which because of its predominance in exports would have exerted inflationary pressure on the rest of the economy. Moreover, to the extent that exports of primary cash crops expanded, resources would have been diverted away from food crops and there would have been a rise in food prices and in the cost of living of urban wage earners. This in turn would have raised the costs of manufactures and adversely affected their competitiveness in the export market. Thus a uniform exchange rate policy would on the one hand increase the pull of the domestic market, owing to inflationary development in the export sector, and on the other would raise domestic costs and prices, thus counteracting the favorable effects of devaluation.

The Export Bonus Scheme was conceived primarily as an export promotion measure. The amount of subsidy that the exporter received under the scheme was a function of the rate of bonus and the premium on bonus vouchers, determined by the supply and demand for bonus vouchers. As a result of the relaxation of quantitative restrictions on imports that were financed by bonus vouchers, it was also expected that the scheme would introduce greater flexibility in the available amount and composition of raw materials and equipment to enable a speedier adjustment of production to meet the requirements of the export market. Who will import and how much were not subject to control by the licensing authority, provided imports were included in the permissible list of imports, which was a very wide and diversified list. Instead of waiting for each six-monthly import policy to determine the amount and composition of licenses for raw materials, spare parts, and equipment, an export industry could proceed to adjust the quantity and composition of its output in response to changes in demand, especially external demand. To the extent that the scheme succeeded in stimulating exports, which would have increased the supply of bonus vouchers, imports could increasingly be liberalized or at least increased in quantity, with a beneficial and stimulating effect on output and utilitzation of capacity by domestic industry.

There was considerable ambivalence in policymaking circles about the performance of the Export Bonus Scheme. Was it a measure designed to offset the overvaluation of the rupee? Or was it seen as a temporary subsidy to nascent export industries to overcome the high initial costs of production and of entry into imperfect world markets? In all probability it was both. The first demanded a continuance of the scheme until exchange rates were directly changed or until domestic prices were again in line with world prices at existing exchange rates; the second by its very nature was deemed to be of brief duration. The scheme continued by fits and starts. The effect of this uncertainty about its continuance[10] was that investments in the export sector were slow to occur.

Initially the scheme was announced to be a temporary measure designed to last for two years. However, in 1961 it was extended until 1965, once more with the caveat that it was temporary. Yet again in 1964 a working group from the

---

10. In fact not before ten years of its existence, i.e., 1969, was it officially declared that the Export Bonus Scheme would be continued indefinitely.

Ministry of Finance reviewing the scheme observed: "While the scheme must of necessity be regarded as of a temporary nature, it has got somewhat interwoven into the fabric of the economy and it is difficult to contemplate its complete abolition for some time to come. It is important, however, that steps be taken to ensure that the scope of the scheme is drastically reduced within a reasonable time so that the dependence of the economy on this prop is gradually minimized."[11] Two shortcomings were specifically pointed out by the committee. First, the industries dependent on the scheme got used to their high cost structure with the result that withdrawal of the scheme at any stage would make the task of readjustment in the export market difficult. Second, this scheme induced in exporters a sense of complacency and an indifference to the maintenance of proper standards of quality, so that they were content to sell low quality goods at low prices. The committee considered it essential that the premium on bonus vouchers should not be allowed to go too high because this would oversubsidize exports and jeopardize the long-run objective of developing an efficient, cost conscious, competitive export industry.

To offset this possibility, the committee made recommendations for reducing costs by subsidizing the price of high cost inputs such as freight and power charges for the export industries. The Export Bonus Scheme was thus to be retained unchanged until 1965, and thereafter the rates of bonus were to be reduced in stages so that at the end of five years the two rates of 10 and 20 percent, respectively, should be established in place of 20–30–40 percent. In 1964 the government reduced the bonus rates in one single step to 20 and 30 percent, respectively, and guaranteed the continuation of the scheme for only another five years. Uncertainty about the continuance of the scheme was not ended until 1969, when the permanence of the scheme was finally conceded at an official level. It is interesting to quote the Report on the Future of the Export Bonus Scheme.

> The bonus premium is now taken into account in the cost structure to enable a manufacturer to make a competitive offer to foreign buyers. Therefore, it is now treated by and large as a compensation for overvalued currency. Besides there is no possibility of ever realising the original object of bonus incentive for manufactures, i.e., after having penetrated into foreign markets through cost advantage, the manufacturing sector would so improve efficiency and productivity through greater utilization of capacity and installation of balancing and modernization of machinery that it could ultimately discard the crutches of bonus subsidy.[12]

11. Ministry of Finance, "Report of the Working Group on the Export Bonus Scheme," unpublished (Rawalpindi, 1964), pp. 20–21.

12. Ibid., p. 29.

The bonus scheme was initiated at the following rates: 20 percent for all primary products for jute and cotton manufacturers and for the service industries such as ship and aircraft repairs, and 40 percent for the rest of the manufactured exports.[13] Between 1959 and 1964 a number of changes took place. First, some items of exports were eligible for a bonus in 1959 but were withdrawn from the bonus scheme in the following years; some were reintroduced and a few were not. Second, some items that started out without a bonus became eligible for a bonus at varying rates during the following years. Third, a new bonus rate of 30 percent, in addition to the original 20 and 40 percent bonus rates, was introduced. The bonus rates referred to the percentage of exports that were obtained by the exporters in the form of entitlements to foreign exchange or bonus vouchers.

A major change in the structure of bonus rates took place in 1964. By the beginning of 1964 the number of bonus rates admissible under the scheme had increased to six; 5, 10, 15, 20, 30, and 40 percent. This expanded the number of effective exchange rates. But what was more serious, it encouraged even more appeals for special treatment. In fact, once the proliferation of the bonus rates started, pressure was built up by individual exporting industries asking higher rates of subsidy to compensate for high costs either of production or of market entry overseas.[14] To end the complexity of the scheme, in 1964 the government announced a rationalization of the scheme.[15] Eventually two rates emerged, 20 and 30 percent, and again pressure began to build for increasing the number of rates, i.e., to grant higher rates to individual commodities on the grounds of differential cost advantage or the special difficulties of penetrating the export market.

The most interesting cases of frequent changes in the bonus rates involved rice and various categories of cotton manufactures. Very fine distinctions were made among the various categories of cotton manufactures in terms of the bonus rates. The bonus rate relating to cotton waste yarn was subject to a similar pattern of changes. Fine rice, which did not receive any bonus in January 1959, became eligible for a 20 percent bonus in December, which was reduced to 10 percent in

13. Except raw jute, raw cotton, raw wool, hides and skins, tea, and some varieties of rice.

14. In fact, an individual industry bent on increasing its export bonus rate could build up considerable pressure for an increase in the bonus rate by reducing or slowing down its exports at the existing rate. In fact, for a period in the early 1960s, poor performance in the export market or the high cost of production tended to be used indiscriminately as a rationale for raising the rates of bonus. This was the counterpart of the protectionist policy regarding the import substituting industries, according to which the higher the level of costs, the higher was the rate of protection that was justified.

15. All rates higher than 30% were reduced to 30%. All the newer manufacturers that had enjoyed a 40% bonus rate between 1959 and 1964 were eligible from now on for the lower rate of 30%. Moreover, all exports which received rates higher than 20% now received 30%. All commodities receiving bonus rates up to and including 20% received only 20%.

1965 and was abolished in 1966. The frequent changes in bonus rates for fine rice and cotton textiles were in response to a shortage in the domestic market consequent on larger exports induced by the bonus scheme.

All through this period the jute manufacturing industry was discriminated against; it had been subject not only to a lower bonus rate than new manufacturers but also to a special restricted category of bonus vouchers called stamped bonus vouchers, which fetched a lower rate of premium than the ordinary bonus vouchers. The jute manufacturers were granted a bonus rate of 20 percent and their vouchers were stamped, which made it imperative to use half their bonus vouchers for their own import needs, while the other half was allowed to be freely sold in the market.[16] The rationale behind a lower rate of export subsidy for jute manufactures was that whereas the elasticity of demand for jute manufactures was higher than that for raw jute, it was lower than that for the other manufactures because of the oligopolistic nature of the world market for jute manufactures. The discrimination that the authorities wanted to exercise against jute manufactures could easily have been accomplished by merely assigning them lower bonus rates rather than by using a combination of lower bonus rates and the restricted category of vouchers.

Thus the rates of export bonus changed over the years in response to a multiplicity of considerations. They were changed according to variations in Pakistan's competitive strength in the overseas markets caused by such external factors as devaluation of the currencies of the partner countries, alterations in the domestic supply position of the individual export commodities, shortages in the domestic market with inflationary consequences in the economy, and changes in the level of domestic costs and prices in relation to the level of world prices. All these factors weighed with the authorities in their decisions on the changes in the bonus rates.

A major change occurred in the Export Bonus Scheme in the second half of 1967: the cash-cum-bonus scheme. Importers of cash-cum-bonus items were to purchase a portion of their foreign exchange with bonus vouchers, but when they did so, they were entitled to purchase their remaining foreign exchange requirements at the official rate. Under this arrangement the total amount of foreign exchange, of which an importer was obliged to purchase 50 percent with the help of the bonus vouchers, allowed to each importer was determined by category in

---

16. The premium on the stamped bonus vouchers, i.e., bonus vouchers earned by exporters of jute manufactures varied between 40 and 50% at a time when the premium on the regular bonus vouchers ranged between 145 and 155%. The Indian devaluation in 1966 adversely affected the competitive strength of the Pakistani exports of jute manufactures. In January 1967 the list of imports that could be financed by stamped vouchers was expanded. This had the effect of raising the premium on the stamped bonus vouchers from about 50% prior to 1967 to about 110% after the expansion in the list of eligible imports.

the case of the commercial importers and quotas or entitlements in the case of the industrial importers. In 1967, 73 items could be imported under the cash-cum-bonus scheme; by 1970, 115 items were placed on the list. This scheme had the effect of increasing the demand for bonus vouchers and consequently exercising an upward pressure on the prices or on the premium on bonus vouchers.

The supply of bonus vouchers in the bonus market was altered from time to time by varying both the coverage of the bonus scheme and the rates of bonus. The demand for bonus vouchers was regulated by varying the composition of eligible imports. The main objective of varying the list of importable items under the bonus scheme was to maintain a certain rate of premium on the bonus vouchers, which determined the amount of export subsidy, on the one hand, and the cost of imports on the other. The demand for the bonus vouchers was regulated first by changing the composition of items eligible for import under the bonus scheme, and second by taking particular industries off normal industrial licensing, either wholly or partially, and requiring them to finance their import needs for raw materials exclusively by bonus vouchers. It was only in the late 1960s that any significant use of the second method, i.e., placing the imports of raw materials by industrial establishments on the bonus list, either wholly or partly, was made. No more than six industries were required to import all their raw materials under the bonus scheme by 1964, which was five years after the introduction of the Export Bonus Scheme. The largest number of industries placed on the bonus list for meeting their import requirements was reached in 1966 after the Indo–Pakistan War and consequent stringency of foreign exchange resources. In subsequent years the list of industries required to import exclusively under the bonus scheme was substantially reduced. Such a strong demand for bonus vouchers greatly increased their premium and significantly raised the cost of imports.

The more important of the two methods for regulating the demand for bonus vouchers was changing the composition of the bonus list of imports. The changes in this list have often been very frequent; between the two consecutive six-monthly shipping periods new items were often added to the list and some of the existing items deleted. To illustrate, 25 percent of the items on the bonus list of the previous shipping period were dropped and new items equivalent to 23 percent of the previous list were added in 1961. The corresponding figures in 1964 were 50 percent for both and in 1966, 33 and 40 percent, respectively. However, it must be mentioned that the claims on bonus vouchers of the various items of imports were not equal; they differed significantly in terms of quantity of imports and, therefore, of the impact on the price of bonus vouchers.

Why was the import list so frequently changed? One reason was the need for experimentation, i.e., to find out the sensitivity of the level of premium to the changes in the import list. There was always an implicit understanding about the level of premium in the minds of the authorities as reflected in various policy

Table 7.4. Changes in List of Imports under Export Bonus Scheme

	Jan. June 1959	July Dec. 1959	Jan. June 1960	July Dec. 1960	Jan. June 1961	July Dec. 1961	Jan. June 1962	July Dec. 1962	Jan. June 1963	July Dec. 1963	Jan. June 1964	July Dec. 1964	Jan. June 1965	July Dec. 1965	Jan. June 1966	July Dec. 1966
Number of items covered	166	146	144	132	137	134	150	136	135	129	125	128	110	108	121	116
Number of items covered in previous period that were dropped	—	26	18	24	19	31	13	29	19	20	18	61	20	11	31	11
Number of items covered in previous period that were continued	—	140	128	120	113	106	121	121	117	115	111	64	108	99	77	110
Number of items not covered in previous period that were added	—	6	16	12	24	28	29	15	18	14	14	64	2	9	44	6

Source: Government of Pakistan, Rawalpindi, Office of the Chief Controller of Imports and Exports.

pronouncements or discussions on the Export Bonus Scheme. In 1963/64 the appropriate level of premium was considered to be 125–130. In 1968–69 the appropriate level was nearer 150–180.[17] During 1960–61 a premium below 100 was considered undesirable. In June 1961 it reached the low level of 100 for the first time. The inclusion of 31 new items on the bonus import list in the second half of 1961 was considered to be an attempt to halve a further decline of the premium. When this proved insufficient to halt the decline a highly restricted nonessential item, artificial silk yarn, was added in August 1961. When the market faltered again, import of sugar for general consumption was added to the list.[18] The second important reason that there were frequent changes in the bonus list was to regulate the prices of selected import items. To what extent and how the price of an individual item would be affected if it was included in the bonus list would depend upon whether the bonus premium was greater or smaller than the scarcity premium on the imported goods under the licensing system.[19] If the bonus premium was higher than the scarcity premium for a given item of import under licensing, placing the item on the bonus list would increase its prices and reduce its total import.

Although the bonus scheme involved considerable relaxation of quantitative restrictions on imports, the determination of commodity composition by the market was limited to the list of eligible items. Several factors regulated the composition of imports under the bonus scheme. In the initial years the bonus list contained mainly consumer goods and raw materials for consumer industries, which had limited provisions for import under normal licensing. Also, initially, commodities on the bonus list were not included under normal licensing. This restricted the operation of the market insofar as the excess demand for items imported under license could not be satisfied by bonus imports. Later among the industrial importers there were (a) some who were required to import all their requirements of raw materials under the bonus scheme and (b) others who were allowed to import any item included in their categories or entitlements under the bonus scheme, in addition to their licensed imports. From 1969/70 all importers, both industrial and commercial, could import under the bonus scheme freely all items, regardless of whether they were included in the free list, the licensible list, or the cash-cum-bonus list, and regardless of whether these items were included in the categories and entitlements of the importers. The measure markedly increased the degree of flexibility in the composition of the bonus imports. This scheme recognized the fact that the composition of the quotas and entitlement did

17. Ministry of Finance, "Report of the Working Group," 1964, p. 29, and "Report of the Working Group on Export Bonus Scheme," unpublished mimeographed report (1970), p. 26.

18. Andrus and Mohammed, *Trade, Finance and Development in Pakistan*, p. 80.

19. The scarcity premium expressed as a percentage of the CIF price rather than of the landed cost of imports.

not accurately reflect the actual requirements of the economy because periodic surveys contained inadequate and outdated information on the needs of various industries. Finally, the composition of bonus imports was also influenced by the existence of a special category of stamped voucher, which covered a restricted number of eligible imports.

Although the composition of bonus imports was to an extent regulated by the authorities, there was generally speaking no quantitative limit to the amount of any bonus item that could be imported.[20] Two reasons were adduced for imposing quantitative restrictions on the bonus imports. First, it was feared that the demand for some of the items on the bonus list was inelastic and that, if demand for them was allowed to impinge on the bonus market without restriction, this was likely to push up the premium on the bonus vouchers and hence the prices of commodities that were importable under the bonus list. Second, it was argued that unrestricted imports under bonus, even at a higher price, could threaten domestic industry that was producing competing products. Faced with the immediate need to restrict import demand, the authorities preferred to turn to restrictions, such as by raising import duties, rather than to the price mechanism, despite considerable experience by now with the regulation of imports by means of the price mechanism. Similarly, ceilings were placed on the bonus limits of luxury items. The alternative method of restricting import demand for luxury items through the imposition of higher duties was deemed inefficient. It was argued that the higher the level of duties, the higher the temptation and the greater the gain from the avoidance of taxes. It was somehow believed that the avoidance of quota restrictions by smuggling was less effective than the avoidance of customs duties. It seemed plausible that for bulky items such as automobiles, smuggling to any significant extent was probably less likely than the avoidance of high import duties.

The wide variety of factors discussed above affected the composition of bonus imports, which changed over the years, as table 7.5 shows. The relative importance of different categories fluctuated over the years. This is in view of frequent changes in Pakistan's permissible list of bonus imports and variations in the relative amounts of different categories allowed to be imported under the licensing system. The latter determined the extent to which bonus imports acted as a safety valve. Raw materials appeared to constitute the predominant group of bonus imports. This is in conformity with regular increases in the range of raw

20. However, this freedom was restricted in 1967/68. During this year a number of items on the bonus list could be imported according to the basis of licensing to be announced by the Chief Controller of Exports and Imports. For example, the quota on the import of automobiles and radios was restricted to 50% of a firm's six-month average imports under bonus in 1966/67. In most cases the quantity of imports during the earlier shipping period set the limit to the quantity of permissible imports during 1967/68.

Table 7.5. Composition of Bonus Imports (Percentage distribution)

Commodities	1959/60	1964/65	1965/66	1967/68
Consumer goods	22	38	28	27
Raw materials	40	34	40	44
Capital goods	38	28	32	29

Sources: Ministry of Finance, "Report of the Working Group on the Export Bonus Scheme," (unpublished) (Rawalpindi, 1964), p. 10; Planning Commission, "Report of the Working Group on the Export Bonus Scheme," unpublished data; World Bank, *Current Economic Position and Prospects of Pakistan* (Washington, D.C., 1969), appendix table 5.

materials that were progressively put on the bonus list. The manufacturing industries continued to supplement their requirements with bonus imports. However, the proportion of consumer goods, although lower than the raw materials category, was higher in comparison to its proportion in total private imports. A comparison of the composition of the bonus imports with that of all private sector imports in the late 1960s indicated that the excess demand left unsatisfied by normal licensing was met by bonus imports. This was especially true of imports of consumer goods because their imports were severely restricted under normal licensing.[21] In the late 1960s less than 20 percent of total imports of capital goods in the private sector were financed by bonus vouchers, while about 18 percent were so financed in the case of raw materials.

An important issue that has often been raised in this connection is the extent to which resort to liberalization caused an increase in the impact of luxury goods. It is to be noted that the automobile and parts constituted 9.72 and 11.26 percent of total bonus imports in these two years and, together with wire reception sets and parts, they constituted about 13 and 14 percent of total bonus imports. At the same time artificial silk and nylon yarn respectively constituted between about 5 and 3 percent of the total bonus imports in these years.

One way of evaluating whether the liberalization of imports had unduly or disporportionately increased the flow of luxury imports is to compare the imports of key luxury items under both the bonus and normal licensing systems. The proportion of luxury items, as defined above, in total bonus imports is higher than their proportion in total imports, which were five times the total amount of bonus imports toward the end of 1960s. But if we compare separately the total imports of individual luxury items under all the licensing systems together with those imported under the bonus scheme, it appears that for some licensing items

21. Government of Pakistan, *Report of Working Group on Rupee Resource Projections* (Islamabad: Government of Pakistan, 1970), and Planning Commission, *Memorandum on Import Policy 1967/68: Some Suggestions* (Islamabad, 1967). About 64% of the total imports of consumer goods in the private sector (excluding food) were financed by bonus vouchers in the late 1960s.

the value of imports under the licensing system was considerably higher than their value under the bonus scheme (table 7.6).

It appears from table 7.6 that in the case of half the number of items, such as automobiles and motorcycles, silk and nylon yarn, and clocks and watches, 80–90 percent of the total imports were financed by the bonus vouchers, whereas in the case of the other three items, the imports under normal licensing were considerably more than under the bonus scheme; the bonus imports of some items, such as cosmetics and cutlery, constituted only one-seventh or one-eighth of their total imports.

It was argued that the bonus system, which relied on the market mechanism for the selection of imports in order to maintain a reasonable degree of subsidy for exports, ended up promoting freer access to luxury imports. Two objectives were involved. First it was not necessary to allow the liberal import of luxury goods under bonus to maintain a high rate of premium; broadening the bonus list to raw materials was adequate for that, as shown in 1967. The import of consumer goods, especially those that were considered luxury items, could have been restrained by high import tariffs. The fact that there was a higher proportion of luxury consumer goods under the bonus scheme was primarily due to the inability of internal fiscal and other policies to restrain the consumption level of high income groups and to bring about a less unequal distribution of income.

The range of fluctuations was much greater in the case of the bonus rate than in the case of the premium on the bonus vouchers. The bonus rates fluctuated from zero to a positive percentage and back again to zero when export items were put on and taken off the scheme from year to year. Most of the time the bonus rates fluctuated from 10 to 20 percent as well as between 25–30 and 40 percent. Thus the range of percentage fluctuations varied between 30 and 100 percent in most cases.

Whereas the range of fluctuations in the bonus rate was directly decided on and implemented by the authorities, the range of fluctuations in the premium on the bonus vouchers was only indirectly influenced by them.[22] Moreover, the supply of bonus vouchers was itself partly a function of the export bonus rate and partly a function of the growth or changes in the value of exports under the bonus scheme. To the extent that the magnitude of the bonus rate had an impact on the supply of bonus exports, it also affected the supply of the bonus vouchers and hence the premium on the bonus vouchers. Fluctuations in the demand for bonus vouchers were also affected by speculation in the bonus market. During the mid-1960s, the period for which the bonus vouchers remained valid was reduced

22. This was done, as noted earlier, through variations in the list of importables under the bonus scheme as well as the amount of licenses issued under regular licensing for the same or similar (supplementary or competitive) items of imports.

Table 7.6. Imports of Specific Luxury Items under Bonus and Their Total Imports (Rs million)

	1967/68		1968/69	
	Bonus	*Total*	*Bonus*	*Total*
Refrigerators and air conditioners	2.87	10.00	3.47	16.10
Cutlery and household equipment of base metals	0.34	2.20	0.33	2.20
Perfumery and cosmetics	0.03	4.10	0.04	5.90
Artificial silk and nylon yarn	29.90	35.10	14.30	32.50
Cars, motorcycles, and scooters	31.74	37.80	41.89	54.80
Clocks and watches	4.30	4.10	4.81	4.70

Sources: Ministry of Finance, "Working Group"; P. S. Thomas, "An Analysis of Pakistan's Current Import Policy" (unpublished) (Islamabad: USAID, 1967).

from 90 to 30 days with a view of discouraging speculative activity in the bonus market. Table 7.7 indicates the fluctuations in premium.

Three characteristics of the short- and long-term movements in the premium on the bonus vouchers are worth noting. First, there was an increase over the years in the level of the premium on bonus vouchers. This was due, as explained earlier, to a broadening of the list of imports on the bonus list. Significant changes took place in 1967 with the introduction of the cash-cum-bonus items, which increased the demand for bonus vouchers. Starting in 1966/67 there has been a consistent rise in the level of the premium. Moreover, all items on the licensable and free lists could be imported under the bonus scheme by both commercial and industrial importers. This change in policy allowed entire excess demand for imports of all categories except those that were totally barred from all import lists to keep them from impinging on the bonus market. The safety valve function of the bonus market was thus fully established. The divergence between allocation of imports by the licensing authority and the structure of demand for imports, arising either from misjudgment by the licensing authority about the relative demand for different categories of imports or from changes in relative demand within each shipping period, could now freely be adjusted by resort to the bonus market.

During the five-year period from 1964/65 to 1969/70, which comprised eleven six-month subperiods, the range of fluctuations in the premium on the bonus vouchers was between 10 and 23 percent (as measured by the percentage difference between the highest and lowest quotations within each six-month period) except in one six-month period, when it reached 30 percent. This range of

Table 7.7.   Long-Term Movement and Short-Term Fluctuations in Premium on Bonus Vouchers

	Percentage difference between highest and lowest daily quotations	*Mean*	*Standard deviation as percentage of mean*
1960/61	42.40	125.02	7.48
July–Dec. 1960	28.18	125.35	5.07
Jan.–June 1961	42.40	124.63	9.56
1961/62	120.45	139.65	22.35
July–Dec. 1961	87.50	114.10	17.52
Jan.–June 1962	45.32	165.38	9.56
1962/63	47.21	157.42	8.54
July–Dec. 1962	41.04	148.10	7.61
Jan.–June 1963	23.37	166.67	4.75
1963/64	25.32	152.85	6.29
July–Dec. 1963	13.95	160.33	3.27
Jan.–June 1964	17.19	145.25	4.55
1964/65	26.78	151.75	6.28
July–Dec. 1964	13.30	144.72	2.61
Jan.–June 1965	23.40	159.21	5.03
1965/66	41.10	149.61	5.32
July–Dec. 1965	30.08	144.10	4.81
Jan.–June 1966	14.63	155.12	2.74
1966/67	21.09	158.80	4.54
July–Dec. 1966	9.18	153.34	1.43
Jan.–June 1967	17.69	164.22	3.84
1967/68	20.35	171.92	5.28
July–Dec. 1967	15.36	178.13	3.75
Jan.–June 1968	19.87	166.06	4.15
1968/69	29.30	180.54	5.85
July–Dec. 1968	15.05	171.72	3.42
Jan.–June 1969	15.03	189.56	2.85
1969/70 (up to Dec. 1969)	11.65	184.85	2.32
July–Dec. 1969	11.65	184.85	2.32

Source: State Bank of Pakistan, Karachi, *Daily Quotations on Bonus Vouchers in the Karachi Stock Exchange.*

fluctuations was caused partly by speculation; it was caused mainly by the divergence between the time path of the generation of the bonus vouchers and their placement in the stock exchange, on one hand, and the time pattern of the demand for imports, on the other. Second, against this, the range of fluctuation, as measured by the percentage difference between the highest and lowest quotation, of the premium on the bonus vouchers within each twelve-month period (which included changes in policies) was much higher; in the post-1964 period, it ranged from 20 to 40 percent—almost twice the range of fluctuations evidenced within a six-month period. The conclusion seems inescapable that the most important reason for wide fluctuation in the levels of the premium was the change in policies regarding the bonus rates and the list of bonus imports between six-month shipping periods. Third, there was a decline in the range of fluctuations over the years; this was true for the fluctuations within a year as well as within each six-month shipping period. The most significant decline occurred in the post-1964 period. The range of fluctuations within any twelve-month period during these early years was between 40 and 100 percent.

Two factors contributed to this instability in the bonus market. First, this was the period when the licensing authorities were gaining experience with regard to the responsiveness of the bonus market to the variations in the composition of the import list and second, the market for the bonus vouchers was as yet a narrow one because the number of vouchers dealt with, and the number of items imported, under the bonus list were quite limited. With time, the market widened and diversified, thus increasing the possibility that fluctuations in the demand and supply of one commodity could be offset by contrary fluctuations in another. In the late 1960s the authorities had seemed to have concluded that a premium rate higher than 200 percent on bonus vouchers led to an undesirable or a politically unacceptable rise in the cost of bonus imports. The regulation of bonus rates and import lists was constantly manipulated to ensure that the premium did not go above this ceiling.

The ad hoc and piecemeal fashion in which the cost of imports, as to item and industry, was raised under the bonus scheme created considerable problems of short-term adjustment in the allocation of resources between industry and products because their relative profitability recorded drastic changes. The changes in the costs and prices of imported raw materials when they were placed on the bonus list were quite drastic and occurred in one or two import intensive industries at a time. This threw their cost and price structure temporarily out of line with that of the other import intensive industries, whose imported raw materials had either moved to the cash-cum-bonus rate earlier or had not moved to the cash-cum-bonus rate yet. Consumer resistance to these price increases resulted in short-term demand problems of considerable magnitude in the industries affected. This was particularly true in the engineering industry.[23] The frequent changes in cost and prices were not limited to the industry whose raw material cost went up; the industries purchasing inputs from the industry affected in the first place were also affected in the next round and so on. As the next group of raw materials or industries was put on the bonus list, a second round of changes

23. E. H. Smith, "The Export Bonus Scheme—Declining Effectiveness over Time," unpublished paper (Rawalpindi: USAID, Aug. 1971).

in cost and prices took place and so on. This made it difficult to make a rational decision regarding the composition of output as well as the allocation of investment.

The experimentation with import liberalization in Pakistan provides a number of lessons. Import liberalization, which is conditional upon the availability of an increased flow of commodity assistance from abroad, is an uncertain venture partly because an increase in capital inflow can seldom be guaranteed for a long period. The rate of capital inflow is subject to vicissitudes of international economic and political relations to which an important measure of economic reform in the domestic economy can rarely be securely linked. Second, a more durable move toward the liberation of import controls needed to be linked up with an increase in the effective exchange rate for imports, buttressed by restraint on domestic demand within the limits of foreign exchange availability. It is in the context of such a long-term move toward the adjustment of the relative costs and prices via changes in exchange rate and fiscal and monetary policies that short-term foreign assistance may play a useful role. Foreign assistance provides the necessary cushion against unforeseen changes in the supply and demand for foreign exchange, including short-run speculative increases in demand for foreign exchange. A liberalization of imports is often associated with, as the Pakistan experience shows, an increase in demand for imports for speculative purposes. The fluctuations in exchange earnings also detract from the possibility of a move toward liberalization. The uncertainty in exchange receipts emanates mostly from the uncertainty in the flow of external aid but also from fluctuations in the price and volume of primary exports. The vagaries of nature affecting agriculture make sudden and great demand on foreign exchange resources for imports of food grains. A period of affluent foreign exchange reserves is more likely to be a favorable environment for the adoption of liberalization. Alternatively, any provision of ready and assured access to foreign exchange resources from abroad such as a stand-by foreign credit designed to cushion the effects of an unforeseen shortfall in, or increase in demand for, foreign exchange resources in the wake of import liberalization, may provide the assistance needed to embark upon a policy of dismantling controls.

There is a serious qualification to the usefulness of aid in the process of liberalization. To the extent that imports are financed by (a) tied aid and (b) barter agreements, the scope for liberalization was limited because of the way these financing arrangements are administered. In the late 1960s, of the private sector imports which were regulated by the Chief Controller of Exports and Imports, about 12 percent were financed by barter agreements and 26 percent were financed by foreign economic assistance. Barter agreements, to the extent that they specified the kinds and quantities of commodities that could be imported from bilateral trading partners, left no room for choice in the determination of volume, composition, and source of imports. In Pakistan the barter licenses specifying the source and quantity of imports were distributed among the category holders by the licensing authority. There was the alternative, of course, of auctioning the barter licenses among competing importers, but there were problems. There would have to be several auction markets, each with a few licenses to auction because they would deal with licenses specified not only by country but also by commodity and the quantity of commodity concerned.

The situation was similar to that of imports financed by commodity aid. Some aid donors specified the recipient of their aid within the country. An example was the United States Agency for International Development (USAID) stipulating that the Pakistan Agricultural Development Corporation must receive the licenses for low lift pumps administered under commodity assistance for pumps. In such cases no freedom of action was available at all. Other donors specified the quantities of specific commodities they were willing to supply. Some others specified a list of commodities from which Pakistan could choose the individual commodities in quantities they desired. Whenever the donor country allowed a choice in terms of commodities and quantities, the import licenses, which were country specific but not commodity specific, were for all practical purposes entitlements to specific amounts of currencies of the donor country concerned. Even this could permit some freedom of choice among alternative sources of imports if the lists of commodities permitted by the donor countries were sufficiently wide and overlapping. The broader the range of commodities that a donor country allowed to be imported under commodity assistance, the greater was the possibility that the private importers would bid for licenses for those commodities which were comparatively cheaper in that country. Under tied commodity aid, as it was administered in Pakistan, there was no effective switching of demand for common items from the more expensive to the less expensive source of supply. In view of a narrow list of commodities, if Pakistan was to restrict its purchases of various items to their cheapest sources of supply, demand for many other aided commodities would remain unused. Moreover, the donor countries often could not supply certain items in quantities required by Pakistan; each preferred to supply large quantities of those commodities either of which it was saddled with large stocks or for which it had considerable excess capacity in the industrial sector.

8

Domestic Policy Instruments and Controls

An analysis of the impact of exchange control and foreign trade regimes on the growth and allocation of resources would be incomplete or may even be misleading if they are not placed in the proper context of the associated policy instruments and controls that influenced the use and allocation of resources in Pakistan. The domestic policy instruments, in particular the direct licensing of investment activity as well as price and physical controls on the production, marketing, and distribution of various commodities, did affect the relative profitability of various economic activities and, therefore, the incentives for investment and production in various sectors of the economy. While quantitative restrictions and exchange controls affected the relative levels of profits or scarcity premiums earned by the import competing activities, whether resources were in fact to move into more profitable or move out of less profitable activities was governed by other domestic policy instruments as well. Given the same level of import restrictions on different economic sectors or activities, the sector or activity subject to less restrictive investment licensing or having access to more liberal financing facilities was most likely to expand faster. In the absence of a long-term private credit market and a well-developed stock exchange, private investment was heavily dependent on the provision of credit facilities by government financial agencies. Again, the extent to which the public sector directly undertook investment and production activities did not necessarily follow the incentive structures set up by the exchange control regime. In view of the external economies public sector investment was not guided by purely market considerations or by the criteria of private profitability. It had to meet income distributional objectives as well as the objective of balanced regional development.

Again, whereas the exchange control regime, including exchange rate policy, might determine the relative profitability of investment and production in industry and agriculture, the domestic pricing policy regarding the pricing of outputs and imports through subsidies and price controls affected the profitability of investment in alternative activities within the agricultural sector. For example, the relative profitability of different crops, import competing and export crops, was affected by differential price, distribution, and acreage controls exercised on them. Although exchange rate policy in Pakistan for the major part of the period under discussion reduced the relative profitability of jute cultivation vis-à-vis rice, the domestic controls over price, procurement, and distribution, including food aid policy, adversely affected the incentives for food production.

The foremost domestic policy instrument affecting the allocation of resources was investment licensing policy. Public sector investment, combined with production and price controls, was the next important category of domestic policy instruments that deserve analysis.

INVESTMENT LICENSING AND THE PATTERN OF INVESTMENT

Even though Pakistan had formulated its First Five Year Plan in 1955 there was no systematic attempt until 1960 either to administer, or to present a detailed intersectoral allocation in the field of industry.[1] Permission was often granted on an ad hoc basis. The policymaking apparatus for industrial investment was systematized only in the 1960s, as shown in the diagram.

National Economic Council
Executive Committee of the National Economic Council
Central Investment Promotion and Coordination Committee (CIPCC)
Investment Promotion Bureau

Financing agencies
(Foreign Aid Funds)

Provincial governments
(Pakistan's own foreign
exchange resources)

The National Economic Council, which was the highest policymaking body and was headed by the President of Pakistan, was a subcommittee of the Cabinet. The Executive Committee of the National Economic Council, a smaller body composed of the ministers in charge of the Economic Ministries and headed by the Finance Minister, functioned as a working group that went into detailed examination of public and private sector investment projects prior to their approval. The Central Investment Promotion and Coordination Committee was the principal organ for coordinating the industrial investment program in the private

1. M. T. Durrani, "The Pattern of Private Industrial Investment in Pakistan During the Second Five Year Plan," Pakistan Institute of Development Economics, Research Report no. 54 (May 1966).

sector. It was headed by the Minister of Industries and composed of the provincial Department of Industries, the Development Chief Secretaries, representatives of the Industrial Financing Institutions, Export Promotion Departments, the Defense Ministry, the Planning Commission, the State Bank of Pakistan, and the Ministry of Finance and Commerce. The Investment Promotion Bureau was the secretariat of this committee and prepared the Industrial Investment Schedule in consultation with the agencies concerned. This schedule provided a framework within which the financing agencies and the provincial governments were to accord permission to individual investors.

Over the years, the actual procedure for the sanctioning of industrial investment proposals underwent changes, especially in terms of the relative role of (a) financing institutions and (b) the provinical governments vis-à-vis the central licensing authority.

During the Second Five Year Plan a consistent industrial development program was formulated for the first time. An industrial investment schedule was designed to provide guidelines for investors. The schedule covering 107 groups of industries set forth details of investment targets in each group. The schedule for the Third Five Year Plan was more elaborate and provided additional analysis to serve as a better guide to private investment decisions in terms of (a) the foreign exchange component of investment, (b) the breakdown of total investment between the creation of new capacity and the modernization or balancing of existing equipment, and (c) the geographical distribution of investment between East and West Pakistan. The provision for modernization and balancing, including retooling, was intended to facilitate the maximum use of existing capacity. Although the breakdown of the investment targets was not given for each region within each province of East and West Pakistan, the sanctioning agencies were expected to bear in mind the need for reducing disparity in industrial development, not only between East and West Pakistan but also among the different areas within each region. The schedule not only intended to quantify the existing output and productive capacity but also to estimate the prospective market at home via import substitution and the market abroad through export promotion.[2] The investment schedule, whenever information was available, indicated a detailed breakdown of products or by-products that a particular industry was ordinarily expected to produce during the Third Plan. A certain flexibility was permitted so that actual sanctions could diverge within limits from the allocations provided in the schedule. The investment schedule further distinguished between medium- and large-scale industry on the one hand and small-scale industry on the other

2. The Third Plan schedule indicated detailed investment targets, along with the above mentioned data, for a total of 200 individual industries, which were shown in 23 separate groups.

and specified investment targets separately for each. But no detailed allocations by industry were made for the small-scale sector.

There have been changes over the years in the mechanics of sanction and implementation of the Industrial Investment Schedules. The sanctioning procedure during the first three years of the plan period distinguished primarily between industries that used domestic inputs and those that did not, and among the latter, between those that exhausted these schedules and those that did not.[3]

By 1963 it was apparent that the investment demand and available resources were greatly underestimated. Under the Revised Schedule of 1963, which covered 114 industries in two categories,[4] the responsibility for sanctioning investment was distributed chiefly according to industry and the source of foreign exchange that was to be used. Investors using foreign collaboration or direct foreign loans were sanctioned by the Investment Promotion Bureau, while those using bonus vouchers required only a clearance certificate from the Bureau. Some "specific industries" required prior approval by the CIPCC. On the other hand those industries that were not mentioned in the schedules or whose allocations were exhausted could be sanctioned after scrutiny by the CIPCC.[5]

Sanctioning procedures under the Third Plan Schedule underwent a number of changes. Following a hard core schedule declared in 1965, a comprehensive Industrial Investment Schedule for the Third Five Year Plan was issued in April 1966. It listed targets for 200 industries as well as the relative shares of the two provinces. There were also separate schedules for small-scale units. A significant change in procedure was that the financing institutions were given full freedom to implement the schedule without referring any project to the government. Indi-

3. (1) Units based entirely on domestic machinery and raw materials did not require any prior permission from the licensing authority.

(2) For all other industries, if the scheduled ceilings had not been reached, investors had to approach one of the two Development Banks or the provincial industries department. If permission was given, it meant the right to set up a new unit.

(3) To set up industries that were outside the Industrial Investment Schedule or that had exhausted the allocations, permission from the Investment Promotion Bureau was required. Once this was granted, the applicant automatically received foreign exchange (and a rupee loan, if necessary) from one of the two Development Banks.

4. (i) Industries for which the Investment Promotion Bureau was able to estimate the investment targets for the remaining period of the plan and for which monetary provisions were made in the Revised Schedule, and (ii) thirty-six "specific" industries, for which no specific provision was made because the necessary investment was to be determined only after detailed study and investigation. These industries, for which the schedule could not make specific allocations because their requirements had not been investigated, included many items of mechanical and heavy industry, fertilizers, oil refining, soda ash, boilers, pipes, steel rerolling, pumps, and cement.

5. Such projects normally required approval by the Economic Coordination Committee of the Cabinet.

vidual cases did not have to be referred to the licensing authority, provided the limitations regarding the ceilings and nature of the product manufactured, as laid down in the schedule, were adhered to. Furthermore, they were "advised to ensure" that credit facilities were placed increasingly at the disposal of newcomers and small investors.

Within two years of the publication of the Third Plan Schedule, Pakistan faced severe foreign exchange stringency arising out of the import needs of a greatly enlarged defense budget, large imports of food grains, and a decreased flow of foreign assistance. Thus priorities were reevaluated and a priority list including 90 industries was formulated.[6] Even within the priority list used, better utilization of existing capacity was given preference over the creation of new capacity by providing explicitly for modernization requirements, and in some cases by limiting the provision to such requirements only.

No prior approval of the central government was needed for the priority industries "except where so indicated in the list itself." These exceptions affected 29 out of the 41 industries in this group, including most chemicals, iron and steel, heavy engineering, and electronics.[7] In other respects as well, the priority list indicated a restriction of freedom of private enterprise.[8]

Allocation, Sanction, and Utilization

Experience of the two Plan periods indicates that the allocations made in the investment schedule were revised in the middle of each Plan period, in the light of progress of the sanctions made. This demonstrated that the licensing authority was flexible in its approach and that it responded to the growth of private investment demand. The cost benefit analysis that the licensing authorities applied in sanctioning investments was very vague and general. There were such criteria as the productivity of capital, positive impact on the balance of payment, generation of employment, and so on but without any specific weights attached to any of them. Further, all criteria stipulated by the investment schedule related to domestic inputs vs foreign imports, large scale vs small scale, and fair share to regions as important considerations. They rarely referred to the social rate of return or used the method of shadow pricing. The vagueness of the criterion, lack of stipulated trade-offs between conflicting objectives, and insufficient use of

6. For example cotton spinning had a minimum number of spindles prescribed for it; tanning and curing could not be developed on a small scale; spooling and threadball manufacturing was similarly restricted and so on.

7. Except in the Priority List of 1968, when "foreign exchange saving or earning" was the sole criterion to be used.

8. For example the larger groups received an inordinate share of licenses irrespective of economic criteria.

uniform economic criteria permitted considerable discretion to sanctioning agencies. Thus, opportunities for manipulation were ample and noneconomic biases inevitable. The financing agencies also seemed to screen applications for investments on normal banking criteria.

The original allocations, both total and intersectoral during the Second Plan Period, were only partly reflected in actual investment decisions. Moreover, there was divergence between original allocations and sanctions given by the licensing authority. A comparison between industrial allocations and sanctions indicates that in eight cases sanctions exceeded allocations by as much as 90 percent, whereas in other cases they fell short by as much as 58 percent. However, actual investment was no more than 55 percent of total sanctions. In all sectors, use or actual implementation fell short of sanctions. The sectors with a ratio of utilization to sanctions of about 80 percent or so were beverages, tobacco, jute and cotton textiles, rubber goods, and leather goods. Most of the other sectors had a utilization ratio between 50 and 60 percent. A high proportion of utilization to sanctions tended to be true of those sectors in which the deviation among the sanctions based on the scheduled and unscheduled sanctions were at a minimum (tables 8.1 and 8.2).[9]

Investment licensing was not undertaken in the context of a rigid framework or on the basis of clearcut criteria. Thus, there were significant divergences among the sanctions granted by the government on the one hand and actual investment undertaken by private investors on the other.

Allocations for the investment schedule during the Third Plan Period totaled Rs 10.885 million, less than half of which was sanctioned in three years. Sanctions dropped in 1966/67 and 1967/68 due to the shortage of foreign exchange. This led to the reformulation of the schedule with greater emphasis on the export-oriented industries and less on import substitution.

The export-oriented industries mainly consisted of jute textiles, cotton textiles, canned and preserved food, footwear, and leather tanning, while import substituting industries consisted of a very varied assortment of agrobased industries such as wheat and rice milling, poultry and dairy farming, and the production of sugar, baked goods, edible oils, cigarettes, tea, woollen textiles, paper, and packaging materials (table 8.3). The bias toward export industries were incorporated via easier processing of their applications compared to more rigorous scrutiny of import substitution industries. For the first time, explicit investment criteria were introduced in the new schedule for the purpose of screening investment projects. These guidelines related to increases in income, and im-

9. But there were cases of sanctions of private investment in the Second Plan period for which no provisions were made in either the original schedule or the revised one. These were ad hoc sanctions by the licensing authorities that were subsequently included in the schedule ex post facto.

Table 8.1.   Allocations, Sanctions, and Utilization of Industrial Investment during Second Five Year Plan (1960–65)

Industry	Ratio of planned and unplanned sanctions to total investment allocation	Ratio of actual investment to total planned sanctions	Ratio of actual investment to planned and unplanned sanctions
Food manufacturing	1.95	1.43	0.75
Beverages	1.79	1.18	0.81
Tobacco	1.54	0.84	0.85
Textiles	1.34	0.85	0.64
Jute			
Other			
Footwear	1.57	0.75	0.80
Wood and cork manufactures	0.87	0.92	0.80
Furniture			
Paper and pulp manufactures	6.74	3.95	0.52
Printing, publishing	0.77	0.93	0.66
Leather goods	0.47	0.95	0.84
Rubber goods	1.08	0.62	0.81
Chemicals	1.94	1.05	0.58
Petro-chemicals	1.48	2.21	0.67
Nonmetallic minerals	1.26	0.91	0.52
Basic metals	3.75	0.04	0.04
Metal products	1.88	1.37	0.70
Machinery (nonelectrical)	0.66	0.90	0.71
Electrical machinery	2.01	0.95	0.53
Transport equipment	1.81	1.92	0.50
Miscellaneous	1.63	0.89	0.50
Total	1.72	0.77	0.55

Sources: International Bank for Reconstruction and Development, *The Industrial Development of Pakistan,* June 15, 1966, p. 17; S. R. Lewis, Jr., *Pakistan: Industrialization and Trade Policies* (London: Oxford University Press, for OECD, 1970), p. 102, table 4.19; M. Durrani, "The Pattern of Private Industrial Investment in Pakistan during the Second Five Year Plan Period," Research Report 54 (PIDE, May 1966).

Note: Sanctions included those for which no allocations were made in the investment schedule.

provements in the balance of payments. There were additional criteria as well: to encourage the location of industries in the underdeveloped regions within each wing of the country and to discourage the concentration of industrial ownership. The priority list of industries in 1968 provided explicit investment criteria in that it stipulated that foreign exchange saving or earning would be the sole criterion for selecting industrial projects. Net foreign exchange saved or earned was to be estimated on the basis of both direct and indirect import requirements.[10]

10. Foreign exchange saving in an import substituting industry was based on the CIF cost of equivalent product from the cheapest source, while earnings in an export industry were based on FOB

Table 8.2. Private Industrial Investment: Sanctions and Implementation during Second Plan Period (Percentage distribution)

Industry	Sanctions in the schedule	Scheduled and unscheduled sanctions	Implementation
Food	7.5	8.9	12.2
Beverages	0.5	0.4	0.6
Tobacco	1.6	1.0	1.6
Textiles:	31.2	25.8	30.4
(a) Jute	13.3	—	—
(b) Other	17.9	—	—
Footwear	0.7	0.4	0.6
Wood and cork	0.4	0.3	0.5
Furniture			
Paper and pulp	1.8	8.4	7.9
Printing and publishing	0.8	0.7	0.9
Leather goods	0.4	0.3	0.5
Rubber goods	1.2	0.6	0.9
Chemicals	11.0	12.5	13.2
Petrochemicals	3.3	6.7	8.2
Nonmetallic minerals	6.1	6.7	6.4
Basic metals	21.0	12.6	0.1
Metal products	1.9	2.4	3.0
Machinery (nonelectrical)	2.1	1.7	2.1
Electrical machinery	2.5	2.8	2.7
Transport equipment	1.0	2.3	2.1
Miscellaneous	5.1	5.6	5.1

Source: See table 8.1.

Whenever the allocations made in the schedule for certain sectors fell short of the number of applications received, the licensing authorities were usually inclined to sanction investment in excess of the investment schedule. They were eager to avoid any discouragement to private investment, even at the cost of departing from intersectoral priorities laid down in the schedule. Because the determination of the intersectoral priorities was often based on judgment rather than on any objective criteria or on any detailed analysis of the costs and benefits, the authorities often responded to investment demand as reflected in the applications submitted by the prospective investors. These market signals were the result

---

prices per unit of export. However, the domestic resource cost was conceived only in terms of direct cost of the domestic raw materials, costs of labor, and depreciation on fixed assets financed from local resources. For imported equipment the cost of amortization in terms of foreign exchange was to be deducted from the gross foreign exchange earning.

Table 8.3.   Interindustry Distribution of Allocations, Sanctions, and Utilization during Third Plan
Period (1965–70) (Percentage distribution)

	Allocation in original schedule (1)	Priority list (2)	Total sanctions (3)	Total utilizations (4)	Ratio of utilization to sanctions (5)
Food	6.8	3.8	9.4	7.8	0.54
Beverage	0.1	very small		very small	0.25
Tobacco	0.4	0.9	0.7	0.5	0.53
Textile	30.1	39.8	40.9	38.1	0.61
Footwear and wearing apparel	0.6	0.6	0.4	0.2	0.35
Wood and cork	0.2	0.2	0.1	0.1	0.77
Furniture and fixtures	0.2	0.1	0.1	0.1	0.69
Paper and paper products	1.8	1.6	4.6	3.4	0.48
Printing and publishing	0.6	0.4	0.9	0.7	0.55
Leather and leather products	0.6	0.7	0.3	0.2	0.45
Rubber products	0.5	0.3	0.2	0.1	0.32
Chemicals	12.8	18.8	26.7	37.1	0.76
Oil and coal products	5.9	—	0.3	0.4	0.95
Petrochemicals	1.8	—	1.7	2.6	0.99
Nonmetallic minerals	9.7	5.7	3.7	2.8	0.49
Basic metal	4.3	14.6	0.4	2.8	1.00
Metal products	4.5	1.1	1.2	0.9	0.51
Nonelectrical machinery	3.6	2.8	1.5	2.0	0.86
Electrical machinery	2.8	1.3	1.3	2.5	0.75
Transport equipment	4.2	1.5	1.4	2.2	0.99
Miscellaneous	4.6	4.7	1.0	0.8	0.49
Service industry	2.1	0.3	2.0	1.8	0.57
Unclassified	1.6	0.9	1.3	1.8	0.90
	100.0	100.0	100.0	100.0	

Source: Pakistan Planning Commission, *The Fourth Five Year Plan* (July 1970), p. 358. The
utilization figures were obtained from unpublished data of the Government of Pakistan, Investment
Promotion Bureau.

of various market imperfections, including exchange rate policies and other
interventions by the government in prices and production.

ROLE OF FINANCIAL INTERMEDIARIES AND PRIVATE INVESTMENT

The institutions that financed private investment were basically of two types:
one type, consisting of the Industrial Development Bank and Pakistan Industrial
Credit and Investment Corporation, primarily channeled foreign loans to private
industries. They also lent some domestic funds. The second type, such as the
Investment Corporation of Pakistan, which did both underwriting and investment

in equities, and the National Investment Trust, which invested in industrial shares and debentures, dealt exclusively in domestic funds and served as financial intermediaries to mobilize private (both household and institutional) savings for investment in industrial undertakings. Investment by the first set of financing institutions was closely related to the sanctions granted by the industrial investment licensing authorities. In fact, as described earlier, these financial organizations increasingly became the primary agencies for the implementation of a large part of the investment schedule. The distribution of investment among the different industrial groups by these four financing agencies can be seen in table 8.4.

The distribution of investment by the four leading financial agencies was more skewed than the pattern of total private investment. During the Second Plan, financial institutions invested about half their funds in the textile industry and about 60 percent of the total funds in the food manufacturing and textile industries. The corresponding percentages of the total private investment in these two sectors was 38 percent during the same period. The chemicals and pharmaceuticals had a larger share in total private investment than in the investment that was financed by these specialized agencies. The same pattern holds for the Third Five Year Plan.

Table 8.4.   Percentage Distribution of Investment
by Financing Agencies

Industry

Food products (including edible oils and sugar)	13.5
Tobacco	0.1
Textiles	47.7
Wood products	n.a.*a*
Paper and paper products, printing and publishing	7.5
Leather and rubber products	0.5
Chemicals and pharmaceuticals	9.4
Nonmetallic minerals	3.5
Electrical machinery	0.3
Transport and communication	1.6
Engineering and construction	4.9
Fuel and power	1.7
Minerals and mining	0.5
Miscellaneous	8.3

Sources: Annual Reports of Industrial Finance Institutions, i.e., I.D.B.P., PICIC, ICP and NIT. Also IBRD, *Industrialization of Pakistan, The Record, the Problems and the Prospects,* vol. 3, Special Studies, annex 2 (1970), pp. 7–42.
    a Not applicable.

Table 8.5.   Pattern of Distribution of Scheduled Bank's Advances (Percentage distribution)

Industry	1960	1964	1969
Food manufacturing	7.5	6.0	6.9
Beverage	—	0.8	0.8
Tobacco	0.7	1.2	1.9
Textiles	37.2	45.1	43.2
Footwear and made-up textile goods	4.8	1.7	1.0
Wood and cork	0.2	0.3	0.2
Furniture and fixtures	0.2	0.1	0.2
Paper and paper products	3.2	0.7	1.4
Printing and publishing	0.8	1.8	1.5
Leather products	1.6	1.7	1.5
Rubber products	1.2	1.2	1.1
Chemicals and chemical products	2.6	4.9	7.0
Petroleum and coal products	—	0.4	1.1
Nonmetallic mineral products	0.9	0.7	0.7
Basic metal	0.8	1.1	1.0
Metal products	6.6	7.8	6.7
Machinery (nonelectrical)	2.1	2.9	1.2
Electrical machinery	1.9	3.4	2.9
Transport equipment	4.6	2.0	3.5
Miscellaneous	23.1	16.2	16.2

Source: State Bank of Pakistan, *Banking Statistics of Pakistan 1964–65*, pp. 76–77, and *1969–70*, pp. 80–81.

While the pattern of investment by the industrial financing agencies was highly skewed, the pattern of investment by the commercial banks was more widely dispersed, as table 8.5 shows.

INDUSTRIAL INVESTMENT IN THE PUBLIC SECTOR

It is essential to remember that public investment played a major role in determining the growth as well as the structure of industrial development in Pakistan. During 1960–65, the public sector accounted for 22 percent of total industrial investment whereas during 1965–70 it totaled 30 percent. There are two important points to take into account when assessing the role of government in Pakistan's industrialization. First, except for specific types of infrastructure[11] there was no industrial sector exclusively reserved for the government on either ideological or socioeconomic grounds. Second, the government was to undertake industrial projects where private initiative was lacking because of either a long gestation period or skill constraints. The predominant consideration always was

11. Railways, air transport, telecommunications, and the production of atomic energy.

the dearth of private investment, not the problem of concentration of ownership and control.[12]

The Pakistan Industrial Development Corporation (PIDC) initiated pioneering ventures in many new fields of industry and supplemented private enterprise where the existing number of private units was insufficient in relation to demand. PIDC in its original charter was entrusted with the responsibility of developing twelve industries.[13] It bore the risks and high costs of the early years of experimentation in hitherto untested fields. It participated in the share capital of private firms that were initiated and run by private entrepreneurs but that failed to attract sufficient capital from private sources.

Private industrialists often felt induced to participate in new joint ventures with the PIDC, partly because it ensured easy access to foreign capital and technical expertise and partly because it could secure the necessary government sanctions more speedily and successfully. Many of these joint enterprises or purely public enterprises were later sold to private individuals or industrialists. The transfer of an enterprise to private hands after it had successfully overcome teething troubles helped private enterprise immensely. The process of disinvestment reflected the government's policy of providing scope for private enterprise whenever the latter was willing and able to take over. However, one of the results of disinvestment was the aggravation of concentration of industry control. Only a few private entrepreneurs could afford the PIDC enterprises and they resorted, in some cases, to price manipulations.[14]

Questions were often raised regarding the relative efficiency of the private and public enterprises. What must be recognized, however, is that the criteria governing the operations of public enterprises were not always those of short-run profitability. Public enterprises were expected to take into account external economies and indirect benefits to the economy as a whole. The public sector by the very nature of its task had to undertake projects that did not attract private enterprise and that might not be profitable for some years. Frequently they were located for regional balance. Also, additional costs were involved in attempts to be a model employer by offering additional benefits to workers without commensurate higher productivity. In the early years, more than half the PIDC enterprises were located in less developed areas of the country. The uneconomic location led to higher cost in transport and inventories. In some cases even roads,

12. Attention to this problem is of recent origin (see Pakistan Planning Commission, *Fourth Five Year Plan*, pp. 11–18).

13. Jute paper, heavy engineering including iron and steel, shipbuilding, heavy chemicals other than fertilizers, sugar, cement, textiles, natural gas, chemicals, pharmaceuticals and dyestuff, and development of power from gas.

14. J. T. Hexner, *EPIDC: A Conglomerate in Pakistan: The Spin Off Process* (Cambridge: Harvard University, Development Advisory Service, Aug. 1969).

power, and housing had to be provided. The public enterprises that the government was able to hand over to private investors were always near large urban areas and seldom in isolated areas. Also the operation of public enterprises was not free from bureaucratic control, even though such freedom was the rationale behind the creation of autonomous corporations.

The pattern of investment by the public sector was different from that of the private sector.[15] Public sector industry tended to concentrate on those industries that had high capital requirements, were new to Pakistan, or were technologically complex. This is evident from the composition of their investment. During the Second Five Year Plan about 58 percent of total public investment was in the chemical and basic metal industries. The next most important industrial groups were food manufacturing and textiles, which constituted 12.9 and 8.6 percent, respectively, of total public sector investment. Only about 23 percent of the total private sector investment was in chemicals and basic metals during this period. Similar composition held true during the Third Five Year Plan. There was a shift of public investment toward the machinery and engineering industries during the Third Plan, constituting about 25 percent as against 2 percent during the Second Plan. By that time private investment in chemicals and basic metals had increased to about 29 percent of the total private investment. There was a more widely dispersed distribution of public investment in different kinds of industries.

OTHER DIRECT CONTROLS

In addition to industrial licensing there was a broad range of other direct controls operative in Pakistan, especially in the 1950s. Production, distribution, and prices were all controlled directly. Controls in some form were considered essential due to conditions of acute scarcity and the preference for direct controls stemmed not only from historical experience of wartime prepartitioned India but also from a feeling that supply and demand respond to price variations only slowly and inadequately. Under conditions of scarcity, very large price changes would be necessary if primary reliance was placed on prices to bring demand in line with supply—which was acutely scarce.

It is interesting to analyze the rationale of controls expounded by various policy pronouncements from time to time. The First Five Year Plan states:

> Administrative and social conditions are not favourable for the successful operation of physical controls, and we do not in general favour them. It will, however, clearly be necessary to continue the controls on imports, foreign

15. IBRD, *Industrialization of Pakistan*. See also Pakistan Planning Commission, *Fourth Five Year Plan*.

exchange, new industrial enterprises and capital issues, in order to make sure that the scarce resources of foreign exchange and capital are directed into the uses that would yield the largest contribution to development. Direct physical controls may be needed to meet shortages of import commodities which cannot be countered by the application of the various possible monetary and fiscal measures. In particular, price controls and rationing may become necessary when essential supplies are short and the ordinary price mechanism threatens to cause serious hardships to the more vulnerable elements of the community.[16]

This Plan pointed out three different kinds of situations that necessitated resort to direct controls. First was the danger of inflation. In a period of rapid development a lag between supply and demand could create inflationary pressure, especially in articles of common use such as food and clothing. Second, apart from overall inflation, there might develop local scarcities and consequent distress, arising from "the unsatisfactory and ineffective working of the distribution mechanism. . . . Slowness and irregularity of transport, combined with depleted working stocks in the hands of the distributing agencies, can cause temporary shortages of a local character."[17] Third, direct controls may be needed in the presence of unforeseen imbalances such as fluctuations in available resources induced by unfavorable harvests, rising or falling world prices, and variations in the rates of foreign aid.

Control on production was primarily employed with regard to jute and cotton. For jute the attempt was to stabilize and maintain remunerative prices for the growers via output restrictions. The acreage of jute under cultivation was controlled until the 1960s by means of licensing of the jute growers. However, subsequent analysis revealed that the licensing regulations were not very effective, certainly not during all the years, and that the relative prices of jute and rice were the principal determinants of the land area devoted to these two competing crops.[18] The licensing of jute acreage was thus abolished in 1959, partly because control was not effective and partly due to considerable administrative cost.

The regulation of the production of cotton had a narrower scope. It was concerned with regulating the relative output of the various types of cotton produced rather than total output. The growing areas were divided into zones, in each of which a particular variety was allowed to be grown and in which the government agencies distributed seeds for that variety. In the case of tea, the Pakistan Tea Board was entrusted not only with the responsibility of regulating and

16. *The First Five Year Plan*, p. 88.
17. Ibid., p. 89.
18. A. K. M. G. Rabbani, "Economic Determinants of Jute Production in India and Pakistan," *Pakistan Development Review* 5, no. 2 (Summer 1965).

establishing new tea gardens but also of issuing directives to private tea gardens to plant or replant tea in such minimum areas as may be specified by it from year to year.

Government intervention in the distribution of cash crops was also common in the 1950s. The Cotton Board was established in the early 1950s to fix minimum prices for cotton and to help stabilize them via open market operations. The board also regulated trading practices, including all matters concerning storage, transport, insurance, and so forth, as well as regulated baling, ginning, and pressing charges. The price support schemes were abandoned in the early 1960s. The Jute Board had similar functions, but by 1957 its marketing functions in the internal market were largely taken over by yet another agency, the Jute Marketing Corporation. The Jute Board had the responsibility of fixing the minimum export prices for raw jute. The Jute Marketing Corporation was to carry on internal trading in jute with a view to stabilizing the internal price of raw jute. State intervention in the marketing of sugar cane was intended to encourage the cultivation of sugar cane in new areas and to ensure an adequate and well-timed supply of cane to the sugar factories. The supply was fixed at a higher level in the areas where farmers were unused to the cultivation of sugar cane and were to be induced to cultivate it in preference to other crops. The controlled prices were regionally differentiated with a view to securing a wider geographical distribution of the sugar factories, including those areas where the cost–price considerations did not favor the production of sugar cane.

FOOD GRAINS CONTROL

There were extensive controls on the distribution and prices of food grains. During the 1950s the government undertook extensive rationing and price control to combat the shortage of food grains. The government organized the distribution of grains through their authorized agents and obtained the necessary supplies by compulsory procurement from domestic producers as well as by imports from abroad. Two different methods of procurement were employed by the government: (1) a voluntary method in which the government bought at a fixed price from producers and market intermediaries without any coercion, and (2) a compulsory method that required delivery of a predetermined quantity to the government by producers and occasionally by market intermediaries at a fixed price. The latter method involved coercion; the degree of coercion depended on the divergence between the procurement price and the market price on one hand and the quantity of obligatory delivery on the other. A component of the compulsory procurement was known as border delivery, which was extensively used in the five-mile border zones of East Pakistan to curb smuggling of food grains to eastern India. In these areas the government procurement was a much higher proportion of farmers' output than in the other areas and procurement was strictly enforced. Throughout the 1950s procurement prices were lower than the prices prevailing in the open market. This situation served as a disincentive to production, especially in the surplus areas, where the procurement was often compulsory. The surplus areas were cordoned off so that prices fell to the low levels at which the procurement took place. Thus the pricing policy for food grains kept prices low and ignored the relative prices of alternative crops and of manufactured foods. This policy worked in a way that discouraged an increase in agricultural production during the 1950s.

Public intervention in the food grain distribution system through rationing started in 1943 with the object of alleviating the wartime shortages of food grains in the cities; this policy continued throughout the 1950s and 1960s. Throughout the whole period no major deviation was observed in the urban biased objective of the public distribution of food grains, although emphasis shifted toward supporting the consumption of the poor in general and stabilizing market prices. An implicit political objective was to satisfy the most vocal groups in the society, the urbanites. The public distribution of food grains comprised mainly the statutory and modified rationing, although supplies to government employees, such as police, and for relief operations were also important. Under the statutory rationing system the people of the major urban centers were given ration cards that entitled them to a weekly quota of rice, wheat, sugar, and edible oils. Under modified rationing the people of other areas, i.e., the rural areas and smaller towns, were entitled to a ration quota that varied according to the level of household income. The average supplies under modified rationing were much lower than those under statutory rationing. Sales to the groups covered under rationing were made at prices below the procurement or import prices. In areas under modified rationing, open market sales or purchases were allowed to authorized agents at prices different from the ration or procurement price.

With the imposition of martial law in Pakistan in October 1958 the most comprehensive price controls were introduced. Under this regulation the retail prices of 14 essential commodities including rice, wheat, and sugar were fixed. It was a belief in the efficiency of martial law in enforcing economic controls without loopholes that led the authorities to undertake the wide extension of controls in 1958 in order to achieve a more equitable distribution of critically scarce commodities. Indeed, immediately after the promulgation of these controls there was a decline in prices consequent on dishoarding of commodities by traders.

During the 1960s food grain distribution continued to play a significant role but the supplies were obtained mainly through imports. The controls over prices were slackened and the internal procurement of food grains was considerably reduced. In West Pakistan toward the end of the 1960s there was little

Table 8.6.   Procurement, Prices, and Distribution of Food Grains

	Prices (Rs/maund)			Goverment control over supply (in thousand tons)		Goverment control as percentage of net domestic production
	Harvest price	Procurement price	Ration shop price	Domestic procurement	Imports	
West Pakistan (wheat)						
1964/65	16.3	13.5	15.0	0.5	1,492	33.0
1965/66	15.2	13.5	15.0	21.0	744	21.3
1967	24.1	13.5	17.3	9.0	1,146	27.0
1968	16.3	17.0	17.3	781.0	1,148	30.5
1969	16.4	17.0	18.6	992.0	16	16.0
1970	17.8	17.0	17.0	1,001.0	227	17.1
East Pakistan						
	Rice			Rice and wheat		
1964/65	26.25	20.93	25.4	12	1,002	10.5
1965/66	29.14	21.71	26.1	93	923	10.6
1966/67	38.75	26.63	28.2	8	1,100	11.2
1967/68	34.30	28.21	30.2	22	1,019	8.9
1968/69	38.14	29.79	30.8	9	1,190	9.3
1969/70	37.87	29.79	30.4	9	1,547	10.9

Sources: C. H. Gotsch and G. Brown, Prices and Subsidies in Pakistan Agriculture 1960–76 (Washington, D.C.: World Bank, 1978); R. Ahmed, Foodgrain Supply, Distribution and Consumption Policies within a Dual Pricing Mechanism: A Case Study of Bangladesh (Washington, D.C.: International Food Policy Research Institute, 1978).

difference among the harvest price, the procurement price, and the ration shop price. In fact, starting in the mid-1960s the price policy was used to provide incentives to producers who were suspecting a drastic fall in prices resulting from the great impact of the new technology on increased cereal production. So the government started purchasing the surplus grains at a fixed support price so that prices did not fall below that level. As a result internal procurement of wheat rose quite sharply and reduced imports in West Pakistan toward the end of the 1960s. In East Pakistan internal procurement continued to be low because of a low procurement price compared to harvest price and slackened government emphasis on compulsary procurement. The government distribution of food grains was, however, kept at around 10 percent of domestic production chiefly through imports of wheat and rice, the absolute levels of which were increasing toward the end of the 1960s (table 8.6).

Along with the exchange control liberalization which started in 1959, the government also started relaxing controls on the domestic front.[19] Beginning in

19. For details of the food grain policy during the Second Plan period, see W. P. Falcon and C. H.

February 1959 controls on profit margins were drastically reduced. In January 1960 rice rationing was virtually abolished in East Pakistan and rice procurement was placed on a voluntary basis, except in a five-mile border belt. Even larger decontrol took place in April 1960, when direct controls on wheat movements, wheat prices, and wheat rationing were abolished in West Pakistan. Distribution was left instead to the private traders without any of the previous licensing restrictions. A buffer-stock system was initiated under which the government guaranteed farmers a minimum price of Rs 13.50 per mound of wheat. Sales to the government were voluntary, and the government entered usual market channels only when prices dipped below the statutory minimum. The government also placed a ceiling on wheat price movements by establishing Rs 16 per mound as the price at which it released wheat into the market. In the early 1960s the bulk of the wheat came from the PL 480, but in the later years domestic procurement under the price support scheme became a vital component of the government supply.

Gotsch, *Agricultural Development in Pakistan: Lessons from the Second Plan Period* (Cambridge: Harvard University, Center of International Affairs, 1966).

PART 3
EFFECTS OF TRADE AND ECONOMIC CONTROLS
ON GROWTH, EFFICIENCY, AND EQUITY

9

Introduction

The system of trade controls and associated domestic policy measures and instruments of control, as examined in the foregoing chapters, had wide-ranging effects on the performance of the foreign trade sector as well as that of the domestic economy. The direct impact of the system of controls in terms of delays, administrative costs, inflexibility, and uncertainty in economic decision making have already been analyzed and are worth summarizing in order to put the subsequent chapters in this part into their proper perspective.

Even though one could argue that the administration of the licensing system and of direct controls should, in principle, involve no more time than implementation of decisions relating to tax and subsidy schemes in a price system, in practice the former was more time consuming. The task of definition of priorities under conditions of general scarcity of foreign exchange was very difficult once price signals were abandoned as a guide to priorities in allocation. Bureaucracy tended to procrastinate and, faced with a broad scope for the exercise of judgment, delayed difficult decisions in the absence of simple guidelines for the determination of priorities. No less important was the multiplication of bureaucratic apparatus. Because administrative decisions had significant consequences for gains obtained or losses sustained by the affected parties, there were opportunities for graft. Negotiations of illegal transactions took time. Honest administrators, fearful of the possible stigma of corruption, tended to multiply the number of persons they wanted to associate with decision making so that blame and responsibility could be widely shared.

Apart from the direct costs of operating an elaborate bureaucratic machinery, there were also costs imposed upon the potential entrepreneurs to maintain elaborate and frequent contacts with the licensing authorities.

The ways in which the quantitative controls and licensing system were administered involved a considerable degree of inflexibility in the composition of inputs as well as their utilization. Even though attempts were made to introduce flexibility from time to time, the commodity composition of import licenses could seldom respond to changing patterns of supply and demand. There were instances of unutilized licenses, on the one hand, and on the other, excess demand for import licenses in the case of specific commodities. The resale of import licenses by the users or importers was banned. This created problems for industrial licensing because the specification of individual items of intermediate inputs in the import licensing system for each industry or for each unit deprived the latter of its freedom to undertake substitution among imports to minimize costs or to innovate changes in input mix.

The inflexible pattern of eligible imports and the nontransferability of licenses created a certain rigidity, leading to economic inefficiency. The commodity allocations of import licenses to individual units based on outdated surveys of requirements and notions of equity left no room for freedom of choice in the determination of the optimum input mix in the production process. Surveys could seldom be done often enough; there was a built-in bias in favor of the use of imported inputs rather than their domestic substitutes.

There was uncertainty about the availability of imports, both its quantum and composition, owing to changes in the balance of payments. There were, in addition, changes in the effective rates of exchange for imports and exports. This contributed to inefficiency in the planning of production and investment, especially for the import intensive industries. Many industries required specific raw materials to turn out a product of constant quality for which the particular processes or machinery was designed, and a variation in the basic specification of raw materials adversely affected the quality of production and productivity of the enterprise. Quality was also adversely affected by restrictions on procurement that tied import licences to a particular source.

Of course, the uncertainty of the balance of payments would not have disappeared upon the absence of controls. The adjustment to changes by the users of imports would have been probably more of a continuous process, and would not have been based upon second-guessing the reaction of licensing authorities to the fluctuating state of balance of payments. Under a pricing system the changes in the rate of exchange and variations in the price of imports would bear the brunt of uncertainty of fluctuations in balance of payments; uncertainty regarding decisions by authorities on their amount and composition created an additional element of unpredictability. To the extent that changes in the licensing procedure added another element of uncertainty to the uncertainties of trade balances and changes in prices, there was a tendency for overaccumulation of inventories, especially on the part of the industrial units having direct license to imports rather than through the importing intermediaries.

There were further inefficiencies in the trade control system arising from relative discrimination in favor of import substitution vis-à-vis export promotion and from restraint in the working of competitive forces. Import substitution was preferred over export promotion. The limited size of the domestic market hindered the full realization of economies of scale wherever they were important. The possibility for innovation and experimentation that the challenges of an export market provided to domestic enterprises was passed by. The inflexible import licensing system hampered the efficiency of export activities in yet another way. Because of rigidities or difficulties in securing the right composition of input mix imposed by the licensing system, export industries often had to work with inferior substitutes and hence failed to produce the quality products required by foreign buyers. The Export Bonus Scheme initiated during the 1960s introduced greater flexibility in the import licensing system, partially offsetting this particular disability of the export industries.

The import licensing system did favor the use of imported inputs in lieu of domestic substitutes that were protected, high cost products. The direct licensing of imported inputs, which did not pay a premium, allowed the imported inputs to have a competitive advantage vis-à-vis domestic inputs. The quantity of import licensing was inversely related to the domestic availability of inputs; thus an industry using domestic inputs was at a disadvantage.

The import allocation system either eliminated or restricted the possibility of competition, either foreign or domestic. Foreign competition was ruled out because often imports were banned or were restricted. The possibility of domestic competition was also minimized by the method of industrial licensing on the basis of a fair share or of historical requirements, which eliminated free entry into an industry by new firms. The effects, therefore, were to eliminate incentives to reduce per unit cost of output as well as to prevent production from being concentrated in the most efficient units (and industries).

The following chapters are designed to examine in greater detail the impact of trade and economic controls in Pakistan on allocational efficiency, on savings and investment and growth, and on equity, among individuals or groups as well as among regions, which in the case of Pakistan constituted a unique characteristic of its economy and posed a distinct set of problems in development and in regional equity. The attempt is made, as far as possible, to trace the relationships of the broader aspects of economic development in Pakistan to the system of trade and associated controls. In many instances it was not possible within the limitations of data, and without straying further from the main theme of the book, to deal more effectively with a few of the issues of Pakistan's development experience and policies delineated in this book. It needs to be borne in mind, however, that although the trade controls were the most important types of controls with a persuasive effect on the economy (because imports and foreign exchange were a major bottleneck to Pakistan's growth and because both aid and foreign exchange earnings were administered through a system of controls), they were not the only controls. The trade controls—their nature, magnitude, and characteristics—must be viewed in the context of overall domestic economic controls and other policy instruments. They substituted as well as reinforced one another; there were occasions when they might have contradicted one another. As controls proliferated it was not easy to ensure that they were consistent as well as mutually reinforcing in relation to overall policy objectives.

There were diverse agencies to implement them and each set had its limited objectives, which could not be and were not always set and weighed against the objectives and effects of other controls. There was no central mechanism to sift and to coordinate the licensing mechanism and the system of controls. Planners were scarcely in a position to do so; they did not have a programming framework for checking and monitoring consistency and efficiency of controls.

10

Exchange Control Regime and Allocational Efficiency

INTRODUCTION

The impact of the exchange control regime on economic growth and the efficiency of resource allocation has attracted a great deal of attention. The efficiency of the exchange control regime in Pakistan could be analyzed in several ways. First, one could compare the costs of production of different activities, i.e., ex-factory prices, with the CIF prices of competing imports.[1] Second, one could estimate the effective rates of protection enjoyed by various activities within Pakistan. Third, one could estimate the domestic resource cost of earning or saving foreign exchange. However, in most of these exercises, the limitations of data prevent the analysis from being carried out for the entire period of industrialization in Pakistan. The effective rates of protection and the domestic resource costs have been estimated only for one year, 1963/64. This was in a sense the high point in Pakistan's industrialization efforts. Therefore, the period of the mid-1960s provides a very useful and appropriate vantage point from which to analyze the efficiency of Pakistan's efforts at import substitution.

---

1. The ratio of ex-factory price to the CIF price of the competing imports was not identical to the ratio of the domestic wholesale price of the imported products to their CIF prices for a number of reasons. For one thing there was imperfect substitutability between the imported and domestic products. The price differentials derived from the two methods therefore did not necessarily relate to the same product. Second, even when the foreign and domestic products were very close substitutes, the quotations for the domestic prices of the imported products related to the wholesale prices, which were in any case different from the domestic ex-factory prices. Wholesale prices included the profit margins of wholesale traders. The ex-factory prices used in this study were averages of the prices of a number of firms in an industry, including high and low cost firms. The domestic wholesale prices are likely to be higher (excluding the wholesaler's profit margins) than those based on an average of ex-factory prices of different firms by an amount equal to the excess of marginal producer's cost over the average cost in the industry. See Nurul Islam, "Comments on Planning Experience in Pakistan," *Pakistan Development Review* 8, no. 3 (Autumn 1968): 379–80.

COMPARATIVE COST RATIOS

A study based on the reports of the Tariff Commission of Pakistan between 1951 and 1966 investigated the ex-factory prices and the prices of competing imports in the case of 115 industries, which produced about 359 individual products. Thirty percent of the total number of industries had ex-factory prices that were 50–100 percent higher than the corresponding CIF prices whereas about 15 percent had 100–200 percent higher prices.

If the industries are divided into three broad groups, consumer goods, intermediate goods, and capital goods, the cost ratios are as given in table 10.1. Because various industries were investigated during different time periods, it is possible to analyze the pattern of cost ratios over time, even though the composition of the industrial groups within different periods varied (table 10.2). The cost ratios do not indicate any trend over time. The simple average cost ratios of all the industries as well as that of each industry were higher in the last period than in the first period. However, about 10 out of 115 industries had cost ratios less than one; 3 out of 60 industries during 1961–66, 2 out of 29 during 1951–55, and 5 out of 24 during 1956–60 were highly competitive and did have ex-factory prices no higher than the CIF prices of the competing imports.

A crucial question relating to the competition in Pakistani industries is the behavior of cost ratios over time, i.e., whether the industry improved in efficiency over time and to what extent.[2] In a young industrializing economy, it is expected that infant industries that begin with high costs would experience a decline in costs with the acquisition of skill and experience in terms of management and technical knowledge. Accordingly, the cost ratios may be found to be related to the age of individual industries. The cost ratios of different industries (on the basis of the number of years of their operation) could be combined for a limited number of broad groups (table 10.3).

There does not appear to be any clear relationship between length of operation and comparative cost ratios. Conceivably, different industries have different periods of infancy and some develop competitive efficiency earlier than others. The time pattern of the cost behavior of the individual industries is not very different if one compares age groups of 1–5 and 11–20 years. The cost ratios of only such industries as bakery products, paints, varnishes and polishes, pharmaceuticals, rubber and rubber products, nonmetallic mineral products, electrical machinery, transport equipment, textiles, and miscellaneous industries register a decline. But this is not true for the rest of the industries, some of which suffer a rise in cost ratios with an increase in the number of years in operation.

2. The following discussion on interfirm cost differences is based upon Nurul Islam, "Comments on Planning Experience in Pakistan," *Pakistan Development Review* 8, no. 3 (Autumn 1968): 375–89.

Table 10.1.   Comparative Cost Ratios (Excluding domestic indirect taxes)

	Consumer goods	Intermediate goods	Capital goods
Simple average	1.58	1.78	1.70
Median value	1.40	1.58	1.62
Weighted average	1.00	1.87	1.77

Source: Nurul Islam, "Tariff Protection, Comparative Costs and Industrialization in Pakistan," Pakistan Institute of Development Economics, Research Report no. 57 (Karachi, Jan. 1967).

The above analysis therefore does not appear to provide any satisfactory or conclusive answer to the problems of the behavior of cost ratios over time. These comparisons are constrained since each industry group combines a large variety of products and activities, whose cost behavior may differ widely over time. An earlier analysis of 15 specific industries for which the cost ratios were reviewed by the Tariff Commission indicated an improvement in comparative efficiency in the course of 10 to 15 years. They covered about 40 individual products. For 7 industries and 16 products, the cost ratios declined by 25–60 percent. The rest of the cost ratios declined by 5–24 percent.[3]

By itself, an analysis of the cost ratios over time may not provide an adequate test of the infant industry hypothesis. Cost ratios may turn unfavorable even when there is an improvement in efficiency and productivity within the domestic industry, merely because the costs of competing imports might fall faster as a result of more rapid technological progress in the advanced countries. The problem is then one of the speed of technological advance in developed countries and a lag in the developing countries in the catching up process. This suggests that a more detailed analysis of the changes in the productive efficiency of domestic industries over time is necessary; this necessitates an identification of the changes in costs that are not due to changes in (1) wage rates, (2) profits, and (3) input prices over time. This is the case because it is an improvement in efficiency in the use of inputs through a learning process, as distinguished from a technological advance, that is involved in the infant industry argument.

As is well known, the high ratios of domestic ex-factory prices to the CIF prices of competing imports, as an index of efficiency of the domestic industries, suffer from a number of limitations. This index fails to isolate the effect of taxes on inputs, both imported and domestic. Neither does it isolate the effect of the high cost of the domestically produced intermediate inputs. A more reliable measure of interindustry differences in efficiency would be to consider the efficiency of the production process or economic activity involved in the particular industry. A comparison of the value added in domestic prices with the value

3. Islam, "Tariff Protection, Comparative Costs and Industrialization," p. 11.

Table 10.2.   Time Pattern of Comparative Cost Ratios

	1951–55	*1956–60*	*1961–66*
Consumer goods	1.44	1.27	1.79
Intermediate goods	2.19	1.76	2.04
Capital goods	1.48	1.46	1.71
Simple average	1.56	1.40	1.83

Source: N. Islam, "Studies on Comparative Costs, Factor Proportions and Industrial Efficiency in Pakistan," in Nurul Islam, *Studies on Commercial Policy and Economic Growth,* Pakistan Institute of Development Economics, Readings in Development Economics no. 2 (Karachi, 1970), p. 213.

added in world prices in different industries,[4] as measured by the effective rates of protection, however, confirms the high levels of inefficiency in many Pakistani industries. The comparisons between world and domestic prices, used either in a comparison of the ex-factory prices with the CIF prices or in the estimation of effective rates of protection, are made at the existing exchange rate. The levels of price differentials, as well as the rates of effective protection, should be adjusted downward if a correction is to be made for overvaluations of the existing exchange rate.

The effective rates of protection for different industries for 1963/64 are given in table 10.4. They are compared with the rates of nominal explicit protection measured by tariffs and with nominal implicit protection measured by price differentials between import and domestic prices that were reported in chapter 5. The ranking of industries by nominal explicit protection is widely different from ranking by effective protection. The nominal implicit protection (price differentials) or nominal explicit protection (tariffs) greatly underestimates the degree of effective protection received by the industries (table 10.4).

Nine industries had negative value added in terms of world prices, i.e., the world market value of the material inputs exceeded that of output. The number of industries with negative value added was reduced to three when the traded inputs were included in the value added. The median value of effective protection was 139 percent under the former method and 365 percent under the latter. However, the rates of effective protection were reduced if an adjustment was made for the overvaluation of the exchange rate (see table 10.4). The average value of the effective rates of protection for the entire manufacturing sector was reduced from the high level of 155 percent to 70 percent if an adjustment was made on an

4. For details on the measurement of effective protection, see R. Soligo and J. J. Stern, "Tariff Protection, Import Substitution and Investment Efficiency," *Pakistan Development Review* 5, no. 2 (Summer 1965): 257–66.

Table 10.3.   Comparative Cost Ratios of Industries

			Comparative cost ratios	
No. of firms	*No. of products*	*No. of years in operation*	*Unweighted*	*Weighted*
41	131	1–5	1.54	1.61
25	112	6–10	1.61	1.65
23	49	11–20	1.46	1.61
2	4	21–30	1.34	1.34
2	12	31 and above	1.61	1.83

Source: Nurul Islam, ''Comparative Costs, Factor Proportions and Industrial Efficiency,'' *Pakistan Development Review* 8, no. 3 (Autumn 1968): 375–89.

assumption based on a 50 percent overvaluation of the exchange rate; the median value fell from 133 to 55 percent (table 10.5).

The rates of effective protection do not distinguish between inefficiency and high profitability, both of which might contribute to high rates of effective protection. Three industries (sugar, edible oils, and motor vehicles) that were found to have negative value added in world prices were known to be high cost and inefficient ones; a few among them earned very high profits, a fact discovered by an independent investigation of their cost structure and profits. It was not only that the cost of the production of sugar was the highest among the industrial products but also that the price of sugarcane was higher than world prices. Both the price of the finished product as well as the price of the raw material was fixed by the government. The price for manufactured sugar, fixed by the government at a level sufficient to cover the high costs of the East Pakistani mills, provided a very high rate of return or profit to the industry in West Pakistan, which had lower costs.

Therefore, the high rates of effective protection in the sugar industry included a high rate of profit—as high as 24 percent internal rate of return—in West Pakistan, which produced two and half times the output in East Pakistan during the 1960s.[5] The opportunity cost of sugarcane production was very high especially if an alternative to sugarcane growing, i.e., cotton growing, was considered. In 1966 the net income from the growing of sugarcane in West Pakistan was kept substantially higher than that from cotton growing because the government fixed a very high price for sugarcane; the net income from sugarcane was three times that from cotton.[6] The world price of refined sugar, imported mostly

5. Government of Pakistan, Planning Division, ''The Economics of Sugar Industry in Pakistan,'' unpublished memorandum, 1969.

6. IBRD, *The Industrial Development of Pakistan* (1966), chap. 8, p. 120.

Table 10.4.   Levels of Nominal and Effective Protection from All Sources Compared with Levels of Tariff Protection in Pakistan, 1963/64

| | | | *Effective implicit protection* | |
Industry	*Nominal explicit protection*	*Nominal implicit protection*	*(Undeflated, nontraded inputs)*	*(Nontraded inputs in value added)*
Consumer and related goods				
Sugar	55	208	−198	−329
Edible oils	45	104	−125	−189
Tea	−2	23	−10	−6
Cotton textiles	127	30	733	213
Silk and silk textiles	174	304	−626	9,900
Footwear	76	60	85	59
Wearing apparel	223	218	−470	1,900
Printing and publishing	0	28	22	16
Soaps	35	60	178	223
Matches	33	0	11	9
Plastic goods	94	223	669	335
Sports goods	72	60	92	75
Pens and pencils	46	140	245	186
Electrical appliances	82	286	−3,433	72
Motor vehicles	78	234	−164	−2,100
Average	78	103	−350	883
Intermediate goods				
Jute textiles	51	27	406	183
Thread and threadball	84	60	163	82
Sawmilling	61	73	1,150	92
Tanning	61	56	567	96
Rubber products	25	137	−555	525

from the East European countries that might be selling below their domestic costs of production, was particularly low. While the CIF cost of imported sugar was $60 per ton in 1968 from the East European countries, the principal source of imports, the import price from the rest of the world was $80 (Rs 380) per ton and the domestic price fixed by the government was Rs 1,701 per ton.[7]

The assembling of motor vehicles (especially commercial vehicles) was associated with very low value added and high profits, which worked out at 20 percent of the sales price. The rate of profit on trucks averaged about 17 percent of the sale price. A comparison between the components of the ex-factory price of an assembled commercial wagon and the CIF price as well as the local price of

7. IBRD, *The Industrialization of Pakistan, The Record, The Problems and The Prospects* (1970), vol. 2, p. 54.

Table 10.4 (*Continued*)

			Effective implicit protection	
Industry	*Nominal explicit protection*	*Nominal implicit protection*	*(Undeflated, nontraded inputs)*	*(Nontraded inputs in value added)*
Fertilizer	0	15	−688	186
Paints and varnishes	23	60	257	133
Chemicals	24	65	300	113
Petroleum products	−23	27	−7	−5
Paper products	62	79	376	144
Average	29	47	187	88
Investment and related goods				
Nonmetallic mineral products	49	134	355	72
Cement	38	44	64	49
Basic metals	9	58	525	194
Metal products	59	88	−869	270
Nonelectrical machinery	13	89	355	170
Sewing machinery	85	60	138	82
Electrical machinery and equipment	22	60	89	72
Average	31	71	423	155
Average for all industries	59	85	· · ·	271
Median	51	60	365	139

Sources: B. Balassa et al., *The Structure of Protection in Developing Countries* (Baltimore: Johns Hopkins Press, 1971), pp. 223-60. See also P. S. Thomas, "Import Licensing and Import Liberalization in Pakistan," *Pakistan Development Review* 6, no. 4 (Winter 1966): 500-44; Goverment of Pakistan, Ministry of Commerce, *Pakistan Customs Tariff, 1968-69* (Islamabad, 1969); S. R. Lewis, *Economic Policy and Industrial Growth* (Cambridge: M.I.T. Press, 1969), p. 104, and *Pakistan: Industrialization and Trade Policies* (Oxford: Oxford University Press, 1970), p. 72.

the same commercial wagon, when imported directly, confirms the low value added and high profits made in the local assembly of the commercial vehicles (table 10.6). The value added in the local assembling of this particular type of commercial wagon was not negative when estimated in world prices. In fact, the difference between the world price of the vehicle and that of the completely unassembled parts, which were imported into Pakistan for assembling, indicates the magnititude of value added in world prices, which was about Rs 2,384, whereas in domestic prices the value added was about Rs 10,322, of which profits constituted 53 percent.

There also was a group of industries that were the principal export industries of Pakistan and at the same time were the recipients of high rates of effective protection, such as jute, cotton, and leather manufactures. The rates of effective protection for the jute and cotton textiles were higher than the effective rates of

Table 10.5.   Rates of Effective Protection (Ranges in number of industries)

	Official exchange rate	Foreign exchange 50% more expensive
1. Negative value added in world prices	3	3
2. Above 1,000%	2	2
3. Above 200%	5	1
4. Between 100 and 200%	8	3
5. Between 60 and 100%	8	10
6. Below 60%	4	8
7. Negative protection or net taxation	2	5
	32	32

Sources: See table 10.4.

export subsidy, calculated in terms of value added. Protection awarded to these industries partly originated from export taxes on their principal raw materials, cotton and jute, thus helping the manufacturing industry to obtain raw materials at subsidized prices. Again, evidence indicates the existence of high profits in these industries in addition to some inefficiency.[8] Moreover, these industries, faced with an imperfectly competitive market at home, indulged in price discrimination between home and domestic markets.[9]

While on the subject of relative inefficiency of different industries, it is important to note that there were considerable differences in costs among the individual firms within an industry. For one thing, if the effective rates were used as an index of inefficiency, one would find higher rates of effective protection for those firms within an industry that received their imports under direct industrial licensing and therefore did not pay the high scarcity premiums as the bonus premium. There were smaller firms within each industry that did not have such direct access to imported inputs and had to buy from the commercial traders at local prices, which included high premiums. The effective rates of protection for such nonprivileged firms were, therefore, often substantially lower.

The free list contributed further to the diversity in the effective rates of protection. The overwhelming proportion of the free list imports consisted of raw materials and intermediate goods. Prior to the introduction of the free list the rates of import duty on raw materials was lower than that on the rest of the imports. A lowering of the effective rate of protection for the import-competing sectors, while leaving the rates for the other sectors unchanged or enhanced,

8. Ibid., pp. 10, 26.
9. Islam, "Comparative Costs, Factor Proportions and Industrial Efficiency," pp. 226–32.

Table 10.6.   Comparison between Imported Vehicle and Locally Assembled Vehicle (Rs)

	Imported vehicle	*Locally assembled vehicle*	
CIF price	10,064	Imported inputs (CIF)	7,680
Import duties and other surcharges	4,120	Import duties	2,721
Bonus premium	17,759	Bonus premium	6,777
Handling charges	297	Handling charges	287
	32,240	Total cost of imported inputs	17,465
		Domestic inputs	963
		Wages and administration costs	4,882
		Profits	5,440
			28,750

Source: IBRD, *The Industrialization of Pakistan, The Record, the Problems and the Prospects* (1970), appendix IV, pp. 2–3.

increased the degree of dispersion of the effective rates of protection and to that extent contributed to the misallocative effects of the prevailing exchange rate system. The liberalization via the free list, by reducing the effective rates of protection of some sectors and increasing them for others, had the effect of creating a greater diversity in the structure of effective protection. Consequently, it reduced the relative attractiveness of domestic production and of investment in the industries competing with the free list items.

Was the pattern of investment related to the structure of effective protection? One would expect that, given the differential incentives represented in the pattern of effective protection, the private investors would invest more in the industries with higher rates of effective protection than in those with lower rates of effective protection. Did the Industrial Investment Licensing System reinforce or offset the differential stimulus provided by the structure of effective protection? An attempt was made to see if interindustry distribution of sanctions of investment licenses or the ratio of use of these licenses, during both the Second and Third Plan periods, was correlated with the interindustry differences in the effective rates of protection. The ranking of industry by effective rates of protection was not correlated with their ranking by the percentage share of total sanctions, or by the ratio of utilization to industrial sanction or licenses in either of the Plan periods. The rank correlation coefficient was small and insignificant. However, while there was no correspondence in terms of detailed industrial classification between the pattern of industrial sanctions or their utilization and that of effective protection, industries with more than an average level of effective protection received a major part of the sanctions and undertook a major part of the investment during both the Second and Third Five Year Plans. But the average ratio of implementation to sanctions was higher for industries with less than the average effective rate of protection. Again, industries that had received higher than the median value of effective protection had approximately the same ratio of utilization to sanctions during the Third Plan as those with lower than the median value of effective protection. During the Second Plan, however, industries with less than the median value of effective protection had a higher rate of utilization or implementation of the investment sanctions.

DOMESTIC RESOURCE COST

It is only natural that an economic system so crucially dependent on direct control of imports and of investment would show different social return on different activities. Social profitability and private profitability diverge, with the latter being the net result of a number of detailed regulations.

The index that would be most appropriate to indicate the interindustrial disparities is the domestic resource cost (DRC) per unit of foreign exchange. Apart from its known qualifications three points should be mentioned.

1. A reallocation of resources that is intended to reduce differences in DRCs may not necessarily improve allocational efficiency. This is because activities to which reallocation is directed may run into sharply increasing costs and diminishing returns. Therefore, even large spreads of DRCs among alternative sectors do not necessarily yield a corresponding measure of social losses.
2. The DRC estimates are not adjusted by the use of shadow prices for domestic inputs. Moreover, international prices used for the domestic resource cost of foreign exchange are average international prices rather than marginal prices. The DRC estimates should ideally be based on shadow prices of domestic inputs as well as on marginal rather than average world prices; to the extent that they do not, they are directly related to conventional estimates of effective rates of protection.
3. The scarcity premiums that are estimated from interviews are not without limitations. They are used frequently to derive world prices indirectly from domestic prices. Their reliability is not unquestionable.
4. The input coefficients used are expressed in value terms, but then the prices of inputs and outputs vary between years.

This estimation of DRC must be used with caution. Despite the approximations the DRCs were adequate to indicate whether there were high coefficients of variation in the returns on different activities. Because the data base for these estimates was not very firm and the economy was in a state of disequilibrium and flux, the variance of DRCs, by themselves, would be an inadequate basis for providing a conclusive answer as to the extent to which the system was suboptimally organized. But the conclusion that the exchange control system ignored opportunity costs in making allocational decisions is strengthened not only by the evidence of domestic resource costs but also of detailed analysis made earlier of comparative cost ratios and effective rates of production of various industries.

The domestic resource cost of import substitution or of export promotion is estimated in the following different ways:

(a) The resource cost was defined as V/W, where V was the value added in domestic prices and W was the value added in world prices. Two sets of the domestic resource cost ratios corresponding to the two versions of effective protection (corresponding to two different treatments of nontraded inputs) were estimated. None of these methods of estimating the DRC included the costs of intermediate inputs, supplied by other industries to the given economic activity, but included only the costs of primary inputs directly used in the particular activity.

(b) The domestic resource cost was estimated by taking into account the direct and indirect inputs of the primary factors in the given economic activity. In this version the direct and indirect wage and nonwage costs of a unit of gross value of output were estimated for 1963/64 by means of an input–output analysis. The net foreign exchange earnings or savings were estimated from the price differential between the domestic and world price of the final products. This method assumed that an expansion of output in any one sector involved a corresponding expansion, via the input and output relationship, in all the other activities. The import requirements were expressed in world prices (i.e., CIF prices). The domestic inputs were expressed in domestic prices. An alternative formulation of the domestic resource cost was estimated in an attempt to adjust for the fact that market wage rates were most probably higher than their social opportunity costs. In this version of the domestic resource cost, it was assumed that the opportunity cost of labor was 50 percent of the market wages, and hence the direct and indirect wage costs per unit of output were scaled down by half.[10]

The distribution of industries by domestic resource cost (in terms of its various formulations) is shown in table 10.7. All the different versions of domestic resource cost confirm a very wide degree of dispersion among different industries. The average (mean) value and the corresponding coefficient of variation of domestic resource cost for all the manufactured exports in their various formulations are given in table 10.7.

These estimates of domestic resource costs of earning or saving foreign exchange are based on aggregative data. A more disaggregated analysis of the domestic costs (direct resource costs only) of earning foreign exchange in the

10. The rationale for this particular decision was based on evidence relating to the average income of rural labor or the lowest income groups in the rural areas compared with the average urban wage.

Table 10.7.   Alternative Estimates of Domestic Resource Cost
(Rs per dollar)

	Mean	*Coefficient of variation*
Direct resource cost (nontraded inputs not in value added)	21.59	0.84
Direct resource cost (nontraded inputs in value added)	34.06	2.54
Direct and indirect resource cost	17.91	1.23
Direct and indirect resource cost (wages adjusted)	17.68	0.66

Sources: A. Bergan, "Personal Income Distribution and Personal Savings in Pakistan: 1963/64," *Pakistan Development Review* 7, no. 2 (Summer 1967): 196–200, and A. R. Khan, "What Has Been Happening to Real
Wages in Pakistan," *Pakistan Development Review* 7, no. 3 (Autumn
1967): 317–47.

case of nineteen narrowly defined manufactured products confirms the findings
based on the more aggregative data.[11] The structure of the social costs is shown
by table 10.8.

DOMESTIC RESOURCE COST IN AGRICULTURE

During the 1960s, under the impact of new policies as well as new technological advances, important shifts took place in the comparative costs of different
crops. So the social costs of earning or saving foreign exchange through import
substitution and export promotion in agriculture deserve careful examination.

Table 10.9 suggests a few interesting conclusions. The new variety of rice in
East Pakistan was the lowest cost earner of foreign exchange. The new variety of
rice in both East and West Pakistan had lower costs than new varieties of wheat
and cotton. The new variety of wheat had the highest rank or costs among the
alternative food crops. Its domestic cost was lower only than the traditional rice
varieties, maize, and sugar; the last named crop was the least efficient user of
scarce resources. In spite of new varieties of seeds, rice (Boro) in East Pakistan
was the most efficient user of scarce resources among all the agricultural crops in
East Pakistan. It ranked higher in costs than the new variety of jute. However, it
did not provide competition to jute because jute and this particular rice crop
(Boro) were not grown in the same season. It was the second rice crop (Aus) that

11. K. Ikram, "Export Policy in a Developing Country: A Case Study of Pakistan" (Ph.D. diss.,
Harvard University, 1971).

Table 10.8.   Distribution of Industries by Range of Social Costs

Range of costs (Rs per dollar)	Unadjusted social cost (no. of industries)	Adjusted social cost (no. of industries)
4.76–6.00	5	6
6.01–900	6	9
9.01–12.06	2	1
12.01–18.00	2	1
18.01 and above	3	2

Source: K. Ikram, "Export Policy in a Developing Country: A Case Study of Pakistan" (Ph.D. diss., Harvard University, 1971).

competed with jute but that did not have the benefits of technological progress. Not only the new variety of jute but also the traditional variety was a more efficient user of scarce resources than the traditional rice crop, from which each faced effective competition. The net result of import substitution in food grain production based on the insulation of the domestic market from the world market was that domestic prices were widely different from the world prices, as table 10.10 indicates.[12]

The price of cotton was also lower in the world market in the late 1960s than in the domestic market.[13] The low price abroad was largely a function of low quality. Among all the cotton exporters Pakistan received the lowest price per pound for its cotton. This was not only because the cotton was short staple but also because of (a) intermixing of varieties, (b) high alien matter content (due to lack of a grading system), and (c) lack of a classification system to stipulate the quality of each bale.

The combination of the domestic prices of crops that were at variance with the world market prices, and the subsidized input prices, resulted in a pattern of production within agriculture that was very different from what would otherwise have taken place if production of the different crops were governed by the world market prices of inputs and outputs.[14]

12. C. H. Gotsch and W. P. Falcon, *Agricultural Price Policy and the Development of West Pakistan* (Cambridge, Mass.: Organization for Social and Technical Innovation, Feb. 1970), vol. 2. See also IBRD/World Bank, *Prices and Subsidies in Pakistan Agriculture: 1960–1976,* 2 vols., AGREP Division Working Paper no. 5 (June 1, 1978).

13. IBRD/World Bank, *Prices and Subsidies,* vol. 2, *Prospects for Pakistan's Exports.* Eighty-two percent of Pakistan's cotton was medium staple length—a category that accounts for 22% of world production. Pakistan accounts for 21% of the world's supply. As far as world trade was concerned, there was a strong presumption that relatively more of longer staples entered the export market from the rest of the world, leaving Pakistan's shorter staple cotton at a disadvantage. Pakistani cotton ranked at the middle to the lower end of the spectrum with a price roughly equal to nonirrigated Texas cotton, which until recently constituted much of U.S. cotton stocks.

14. Programming exercises relating to West Pakistan agriculture were undertaken to compare the optimal cropping pattern that resulted from the use of domestic prices with the cropping pattern that

Table 10.9.   Social Cost of Earning or Saving Foreign Exchange in Agriculture

Commodity	Social cost (Rs per dollar)
Rice (IRRI, Boro, East Pakistan)	1.88
Rice (traditional Amman, East Pakistan)	2.34
Rapeseed (West Pakistan)	2.47
Fine rice (West Pakistan)	2.82
Jute (new variety, East Pakistan)	3.08
Rice (IRRI, West Pakistan)	3.34
Cotton (West Pakistan)	3.84
Mustard (East Pakistan)	4.17
Jute (present variety)	5.21
Wheat (Mexi-Pak)	5.25
Rice (traditional, Boro, East Pakistan)	5.39
Rice (traditional, Aus., East Pakistan)	7.02
Maize	7.47
Sugar	8.69

Sources: R. Lawrence, "The Comparative Costs of Pakistan's Major Crops" (Islamabad: USAID, 1969) (mimeographed), and Government of Pakistan, Ministry of Agriculture, "The Costs of Production of Major Agriculture Commodities in West Pakistan" (Islamabad, 1969) (mimeographed).

Note: The calculation of social costs was based upon the following assumptions: (a) the social cost of labor was half the market wage rate, i.e., Rs 1.50 per day in West and Rs 1.25 in East Pakistan, (b) market rental charges for bullocks were used as the cost of power, (c) irrigated land was priced at Rs 2,000 per acre in West Pakistan, and unirrigated land was priced at Rs 1,000 per acre; in the East land was priced at Rs 1,500 per acre, reflecting the lack of alternative uses of land during dry seasons for lack of water. A social discount rate of 10% was used. Traded inputs such as fertilizers and pesticides were priced at the world price, and the nontraded inputs, the most important of which was water, were priced at their real cost of production. The latter was obtained by shadow pricing the inputs used in producing tube-well water in West Pakistan and water from the low lift pumps for the Boro crops in East Pakistan.

CONCLUSION

The foregoing analysis of the allocative efficiency of the exchange control regime, buttressed by domestic policies and instruments of control, suggests a number of conclusions.

---

would have been optimum under a regime of world prices. The objective function was to maximize the net return (net of costs) from a 12.5-acre farm, given the constraints on resources availability in terms of land, labor, water, and bullock. See ibid., pp. 414–21.

Table 10.10. Comparison between Domestic and World Prices (Rs per maund)

	Domestic price		
Commodity	Primary market	Ex Karachi (FOB)	World price
1. Wheat	17.00	20.00	12.00
2. IRRI rice	19.00	22.00	13.50
3. Maize	14.50	16.50	7.00

Sources: See table 10.9.

The exchange control regime favored import substitution over export promotion. The bias in favor of import substitution was evident from effective rates of protection that were higher than effective rates of export subsidy as well as evident from higher effective import rates of exchange than export rates of exchange. This was true throughout the two decades of development under study; there was a narrowing of the gap during the early 1960s, which again widened toward the end of the decade.

Import substitution under the shelter of a protected domestic market meant less competition; an equal if not greater range of incentives for export promotion would have enabled nascent Pakistani industries to face the forces of competition and technological innovation required for selling in the export market; it would have hastened the process of learning by doing. In fact, in view of the risks and uncertainties of the export market, which are subject to events, developments, and policies outside the control of a national government, a positive discrimination in incentive systems and effective exchange rates in favor of export markets was worth serious consideration.

Secondly, there was a great degree of differentiation in terms of effective exchange rates for both import substitution and export promotion. No sooner had an attempt been made to reduce the dispersion of exchange rates and to promote a greater uniformity of incentive structures for individual commodities than there were set in motion tendencies for proliferation and differentiation of rates. This was partly due to the pressures of vested interest groups that wanted to secure relatively greater advantage or gains vis-à-vis others; moreover, the possibility of differentiation by commodities and markets widened the discretionary power of the bureaucracy administering the system of controls and licensing. Both the vested interest groups and the bureaucracy promoted and supported the system of differentiation, which often resulted in less efficient industries receiving greater protection or subsidy. In the absence of concrete evidence on the quantification of differential external economies or different degrees of "infancy," differentiation for the purposes of protection and subsidy depended upon the bargaining or negotiating strength of the affected industries, or upon the predilection of the administrative authorities. Under these circumstances, differentiation by broad categories of commodities was more logical, to the extent that their distinguishing characteristics could be identified.

An analysis over time of comparative costs (ratio of domestic prices to CIF prices of competing inputs for a large number of industries) indicates no systematic downward trend, implying that there was in general no systematic evidence of the increasing efficiency or decreasing inefficiency, as measured by cost ratios, of Pakistani industries. There were, however, exceptions when cost ratios declined; these cases were not necessarily those which received the highest rates of protection or effective export rates of exchange.

Effective rates of protection were in general very high in Pakistan. A few industries had negative value added calculated in world prices. The pattern of interindustry variation in effective rates of protection was not correlated with the relative importance of different industries, measured either by their share in total industrial output or by the relative growth rates of individual industries. Industrial investment licensing was a very important instrument in determining the pattern of industrialization. In many instances the imposition of high rates of protection provided the initial impetus for the establishment of a domestic industry by creating the possibility of profits high enough to cover domestic costs in excess of import prices. Industrial investment licensing, which controlled or determined entry into a particular field of activity, limited the number of enterprises in a particular field and hence the degree of competition and the extent of excess profits in the industry. Thus while protection determined the desire to invest in domestic activity, investment licensing determined the extent of investment that took place and thus influenced the level and magnitude of profits. In other cases investment licensing led to the establishment of an industry; subsequently the industry concerned sought and received protection against foreign imports or received subsidies or incentives for exports. In any specific instance it was, therefore, not clear how far high profits earned by an industry were due to imports being kept out by high protection and how far they were due to the limitation on the extent of investment and hence on the supply of domestic output imposed via restriction on entry by means of licensing.

Effective protection concealed both inefficiency and high costs as well as high profits. Two elements were not clearly distinguished in the minds of the policymakers. In some cases the degree of protection granted was more than necessary to cover the cost differential, the excess of domestic costs over the international price of competing products. The range and level of effective protection that resulted from the interaction of tariffs and quantitative restrictions on inputs and outputs were not predetermined; an ex post examination of the resultant pattern of effective protection did not serve as a guide in the determination of quantitative restrictions and tariffs. The analysis of these effects on the efficiency of the allocation of resources seldom provided the basis on which these policies were evaluated or formulated. Although in a number of cases the deliberations of the Tariff Commission took note of the tariffs on inputs as well as on outputs in a general way in order to compare the costs of domestic outputs with the prices of competing imports, imposition of quantitative restrictions was seldom based upon the recognition of their effects in terms of the degree of effective production. The quantitative restrictions were predominantly imposed in response to balance of payments considerations; only in a few cases were they imposed for reasons of protection based on cost factors investigated by the Tariff Commission. Moreover, the interindustry distribution of the intensity of import restrictions was based upon considerations of essentiality and need; it was also related to policy objectives about the broad patterns of industrialization, in terms of the relative emphasis on consumer goods and capital goods, without any particular reference to comparative cost factors.

There was substantial dispersion in domestic resource costs among individual industries; they confirmed the dispersion that was reflected in the structure of the effective rate of production. The estimates of domestic resource costs were closely related to those of the effective rates of protection except that an attempt was made to use the shadow price of labor and to include nontraded inputs in value added. Not all interindustry divergence in domestic resource costs was accounted for by inefficient or suboptimal allocation of resources between industries and economic activities. It was, however, possible that if reallocation did take place, marginal costs would rise in some cases and prices would fall in others, so that divergencies in domestic resource costs would disappear or shrink significantly. The marginal costs could not be estimated for lack of data, and the assumption regarding the shadow price of inputs was not entirely without reservations.

In spite of these shortcomings and reservations the overall picture is one of major misallocation of resources not only within the manufacturing industry but also within the agricultural sector. In the case of agriculture, domestic pricing policies buttressed by controls over marketing and distribution were the principal policy instruments, whereas import restrictions on agricultural imports, including government monopoly of such basic import items of cereals, oil, and sugar, combined with export taxes in a few major agricultural exports and export control or prohibition of many others, created a pattern of relative prices for alternative agricultural crops or other agricultural activities that were very different from the pattern of relative international prices for the same or similar products.

11

Factor Intensity, Scale, and Productivity

TRADE POLICIES AND FACTOR INTENSITY

Factor Intensity of Manufactures

Two features of the exchange rate system are worth recalling. First, the imported capital goods were relatively cheaper, especially to those who directly imported capital equipment under the system of investment licensing. The relative proportion of capital good imports, which were directly imported under the system of investment licensing, was considerably greater than that for other categories of imports, such as raw materials, which were directly licensed to the actual users. The entire public sector investment and a large proportion of private investment were based upon imported capital goods that were licensed directly to the investors. The direct importation of capital goods by the actual users meant that the latter did not have to pay the scarcity margin on the imported goods. Moreover, it was large-scale industry that had the exclusive privilege of direct access to imports of capital goods without the intermediation of the traders. Large-scale firms imported at the official exchange rate plus import duties that were lower on equipment and machinery than on raw materials and consumer goods. The price at which imported capital goods were available to large-scale industry was lower than the price at which they were available to small-scale industry because the latter purchased imported capital goods from the commercial importers.

The availability and price of imported capital goods were critical in their impact on the choice of technology. This was because the domestic machinery and equipment industry was small. In fact, the low effective rate of exchange for imported capital equipment discouraged the establishment of a domestic capital goods industry. Furthermore, the low rates of interest discussed earlier, compared with the high rates of return on capital, tended to encourage a more liberal use of capital equipment.

The capital/labor ratios in the manufacturing industries in Pakistan compared with that in two other countries are shown in table 11.1. Although in view of the

Table 11.1. Capital/Labor Ratios in Manufacturing Industries (Value of fixed assets in US dollars per worker)

Sector	East Pakistan	West Pakistan	Japan	USA
Cotton textiles	1,713	2,418	475	2,760
Jute textiles	2,130	—	—	—
Paper	11,424	—	508	7,310
Leather goods	960	1,164	422	1,010
Rubber goods	1,122	2,764	269	3,730
Fertilizer	35,503	37,503	—	—
Other chemicals	826	4,082	—	—
All chemicals	4,440	8,831	1,100	8,320
Basic metals	843	1,546	2,558	8,600
Machinery	3,306	1,023	478	4,800
Wood products	1,236	652	367	—

Source: A. R. Khan, ''Capital-Intensity and the Efficiency of Factor Use,'' *Pakistan Development Review* 10, no. 2 (Summer 1970): 261.

relative factor endowment of Pakistan compared to that of the United States and Japan, capital intensities of the Pakistani industries should have been lower than in Japan or the United States, the reverse seemed to hold true (table 11.2). The capital intensities were invariably higher for the two regions of Pakistan than for Japan. The only exception was basic metals. Even more surprising was the fact that in many sectors, the capital intensities in Pakistan were close to those of the United States while in some (paper, chemicals, and leather goods) they were higher.[1]

Attempts to estimate the elasticity of substitution between observed capital/ labor ratios and relative factor prices in Japan and the United States have found the numerical value of elasticities to be just above or below one. If they are reasonable indicators of the true elasticities of substitution, Pakistan with her relative factor endowments should have far lower capital intensity than that displayed in a corresponding activity in an economy such as Japan's. Apart from factor prices, capital and labor prices in Pakistan being out of line with her relative factor endowments, two other factors might have accounted for the high capital intensity of Pakistani industry. One was the existence of excess capacity or unutilized capital equipment, which is discussed in greater detail later in this chapter. Second was the limitation of Pakistan's freedom of choice of techniques

1. A. R. Khan, ''Capital Intensity and the Efficiency of Factor Use,'' *Pakistan Development Review* 10, no. 2 (Summer 1970): 240–44. The above comparison of the capital intensities suffers from two limitations: (1) use of the official exchange rate and (2) lack of comparability of products among different countries. However, because a very large proportion of capital equipment is imported at the official rate in Pakistan, it is hoped that these limitations will not create very serious distortions.

Table 11.2.   Ranking of Sectoral Capital Intensities

	USA	Japan	East Pakistan	West Pakistan
Coal and petroleum	1	1	1	1
Chemicals	3	3	3	2
Basic metals	2	2	12	7
Paper	4	8	2	10
Textiles	11	7	6	6
Machinery	7	6	55	11
Transport equipment	6	5	7	5
Leather products	12	11	11	9
Rubber products	8	9	10	4
Wood, etc.	9	10	9	12
Industry, n.e.s.	10	12	8	8
Food, drink, manufactures	5	4	4	3

Source: E. R. Khan, "Capital-Intensity and the Efficiency of Factor Use," *Pakistan Development Review* 10, no. 2 (Summer 1970): 262.

imposed by tied aid under which purchases of capital equipment, most of which were financed by foreign assistance or, more accurately, foreign project aid, were tied to the sources of aid. As is evident from table 11.2, capital intensity was lower in Japan than in the United States. Pakistan could not procure equipment from Japan using less capital intensive techniques with aid funds supplied by the United States or any other country. Again, Pakistan could conceivably buy capital equipment of older vintage or secondhand machinery from the aid-giving country. Apart from the fact that Pakistan banned the import of secondhand machinery it is not clear whether a particular aid-giving nation could supply secondhand machinery of satisfactory quality.

Factor Intensity of Exports

The trade policies of Pakistan, as discussed earlier, aimed at promoting not only industrialization but also exports of manufactured goods. Did Pakistan succeed in promoting exports of labor intensive manufactures? What was the factor intensity of the commodity composition of her exports. Studies on capital/labor ratios of manufacturing exports are not available. But an alternative analysis of factor intensity was undertaken on the basis of value added criteria.[2] An increase in the value added per employee is assumed to reflect an increase in

2. N. Islam, "Factor Intensities in Manufacturing Industries in Pakistan," *Pakistan Development Review* 10, no. 2 (Summer 1970): 147–73; idem., "The Manufactured Exports of Pakistan: Factor Intensity and Related Characteristics" (Karachi: Pakistan Institute of Development Economics, 1969).

Table 11.3.   Factor Intensity of Manufactured Exports (Percentage of manufactured exports)

Index of factor intensity	*1961/-1963/64*	*1964/65-1966/67*
Less than average value added per employee	87.48	87.89
Less than average wage value added per employee	87.22	89.60
Less than average nonwage value added per employee	89.00	88.43

Source: N. Islam, "The Manufactured Exports of Pakistan: Factor Intensity and Related Characteristics" (Karachi: Pakistan Institute of Development Economics, 1969).

the use of physical capital relative to labor. All industries or commodities that yielded less value added per employee than the average for the manufacturing sector as a whole were treated as labor intensive and those with more value added per employee than the average were treated as capital intensive in a broad sense. The relative importance of labor intensive commodities in the manufactured exports of Pakistan is shown in table 11.3.[3]

Because both cotton and jute textiles dominated the manufactured exports of Pakistan, constituting about 72-74 percent of the total manufactured exports during the 1960s, the average factor intensity of the manufactured exports, excluding these two items, has also been estimated (table 11.4).[4]

Thus, with the exclusion of cotton and jute textiles, the relative significance of the labor intensive manufactured exports declined over time and those using relatively more capital and skill increased in importance.

The results obtained in table 11.4 on the basis of value added per employee conform to the results obtained on the basis of alternative estimates of factor intensity. The alternative indices are the ratio of production workers to total employment and the ratio of wages and salaries to the total cost of output, i.e., the gross value of output.[5]

Those manufactured exports that had a ratio of the employment costs to the value of total output greater than the average for all the manufacturing exports

3. Islam, "Manufactured Exports."

4. Ibid.

5. The production workers are defined in the Pakistan Census of Manufactures as those engaged in manual work directly associated with actual production, i.e., fabricating, processing, and assembling, whereas the nonproduction workers consist of administrative, professional, clerical, and service staff. See Central Statistical Office, *Census of Manufacturing Industries, 1959-60* (Karachi, 1962), pts. 1 and 5, and D. B. Keesing, "The Impact of Research and Development on the U.S. Trade," *Journal of Political Economy* 75, no. 1, (Feb. 1967): 42. The distinction between different categories of employees on the basis of skill has also been made by D. B. Keesing in his earlier studies.

Table 11.4.   Factor Intensity of Manufactured Exports (Excluding jute and cotton textiles)

Factor intensity	Percentage of exports excluding jute and cotton textiles	
	1961/62–1963/64	*1964/65–1966/67*
Less than average value added per employee	53.29	59.69
Less than average wage value added per employee	54.18	65.36
Less than average nonwage value added per employee	59.10	61.49

Source: N. Islam, "Factor Intensities in Manufacturing Industries in Pakistan," *Pakistan Development Review* 10, no. 2 (Summer 1970): 149–74.

taken together, i.e., the labor intensive ones, constituted about 83.37 and 79.63 percent of the total manufactured exports during the two three-year periods in the 1960s. If jute and cotton textiles are excluded, the labor intensive exports, according to this criterion, constituted about 38 and 32 percent of the rest of the manufactured exports in the two periods. The proportion of the total export industries employing more than the average proportion of the production workers to total employment was about 78–82 percent during both periods.

The labor intensive exports, including jute and cotton textiles, (which have less than average value added per employee) increased at an average compound rate of 16 percent during the 1960s. Excluding jute and cotton textiles, the labor intensive commodities grew at the same rate as the rest of the manufactured exports, i.e., about 31 percent per annum. Among these, however, exports that use relatively less skilled labor, i.e., had wage value added less than the average, grew faster (36%) than those that use more skilled labor (26%).

How does the factor intensity of manufactured exports compare with the factor intensity of total industrial or manufactured output in Pakistan? The labor intensive commodities played a much greater role in the export market than the rest of the industries did. Their relative importance in the export market was not a mere reflection of their relative importance in the total manufactured output of the economy; they were less significant as a constituent of total output than they are as a source of manufactured exports.

What proportion of Pakistani manufactured exports is constituted by those commodities that are labor intensive in the U.S. economy, i.e., which yielded less than the average value added per employee of the U.S. manufacturing industries as a whole? About 88 percent of the Pakistanis' manufactured exports are labor intensive judged by this criterion. If jute and cotton textiles are excluded from the total manufactured exports, the percentage of labor intensive exports is, respectively, 55 and 64 percent in the two periods in the 1960s.

Even though the majority of Pakistani manufactured exports were labor intensive, it is worth examining whether the differential export performance of the individual exports was in any way related to their factor intensity or other economic characteristics. The relative performance of the individual exports was measured alternatively by (a) the proportion of each individual export to the total exports, and (b) the ratio of export to output in each sector.[6]

The ratio of export to output, as a measure of the export performance or competitiveness in the export market, appears to be inversely related to the value added per employee, i.e., the lower the value added per employee, the higher the percentage of output that is exported, as seen below:

$$\log \left(\frac{X}{O} \right) = 1.27 - 1.79 \ \log X_1 \quad R^2 = 0.20,$$

where X is export, O is output, and X_1 is value added per employee. This significant relationship also holds true if the wage and the nonwage components of the value added per employee are used separately as the independent variables:

$$\log \left(\frac{X}{O} \right) = -2.86 - \underset{(1.52)}{2.93} \ \log (X_0) \quad R^2 = 0.11$$

$$\log \left(\frac{X}{O} \right) = -2.41 - \underset{(0.50)}{1.43} \ \log (X_7) \quad R^2 = 0.21.$$

X_6 and X_7 are the wage and the nonwage components of the value added, respectively. This is equally true if the value added per employee, based on the U.S. data, rather than the value added per employee, based on Pakistan data, is used as an index of factor intensity.[7]

6. The proportion of each individual export to the total exports relates to the average of the last three years (1964–67), by which time the manufactured exports had become more diversified, as evidenced by an increase in the value of the miscellaneous exports. The ratio of the export to output applies to 1963/64, the latest year for which the comparable output data for any significant number of exportable items were available.

7. The number of employees per establishment or the value added per establishment as an index of economies of scale is subject to the limitation that this is influenced by such factors as market imperfections and the existence of differential monopoly rents and profits. One can argue that the

Export performance, measured by the ratio of individual exports to total exports, is not related to factor intensity if a simple relation between export performance and factor intensity is used, but when it is used in conjunction with domestic output as an additional explanatory variable, there is a negative relationship, implying that the higher the labor intensity of an export, the greater is its relative importance as shown by the following:[8]

$$\log \frac{X}{T} = 6.69 + \underset{(0.24)}{0.65} \log O - \underset{(0.67)}{1.48} \log X_1 \quad R^2 = 0.24.$$

Choice of Technology in Agriculture

Exchange rate policy, combined with the interest rate policy and the pricing policy in agriculture, had an important effect on the choice of production techniques in agriculture. This was especially evident in the spread of mechanization in agriculture. Under the prevailing system of exchange control and commercial policy the agricultural machinery imported from abroad was sold below the scarcity price, partly because there was an overvaluation of the exchange rate in Pakistan and partly because there were no offsetting taxes or duties on the imports of agricultural machinery. The average cost of agricultural machinery, let us say a tractor, was about $65 per horsepower in West Pakistan as against $74 in Malaysia and $81–110 in the United States.[9] The prices of other imported inputs such as fuels were underpriced, even though this was partly offset by import duties and indirect taxes. To the extent that the machinery, spare parts,

---

relation between export performance and factor intensity may be due to the effect of the variables excluded from the estimating equation but in turn related to the index of factor intensity. One such important factor is the scale or size of the industrial establishments, which indicates the presence or absence of economies of scale. However, the size of establishments per industry used either singly or in combination with the value added per employee as an explanatory variable does not seem to add anything to the explanation of the interindustry variations in export performance.

8. The ratio of individual exports to total exports is based on the average values of three years (1964–67).

9. S. R. Bose and B. H. Clark, "Some Basic Considerations in Agricultural Mechanisation in West Pakistan," *Pakistan Development Review* 9, no. 3 (Autumn 1969): 273–84, and W. P. Falcon and C. H. Gotsch, "Agricultural Development in Pakistan: Lessons from the Second Plan Period," in G. F. Papanek, ed., *Development Policy Theory and Practice* (Cambridge: Harvard University Press, 1968). See also W. P. Falcon and C. H. Gotsch, "Relative Price Response, Economic Sufficiency and Technological Change: A Study of Punjab Agriculture," in W. P. Falcon and G. F. Papanek, ed., *Development Policy II—The Pakistan Experience* (Cambridge: Harvard University Press, 1971).

and fuels were not imported directly by the actual user but were imported through commercial importers, who in view of quantitative restrictions on such imports earned the difference between the domestic and landed cost, the actual user paid more than the landed cost and to that degree the undervaluation of the imported machinery and its parts was offset. However, the big landholders often directly imported machinery because there was substantial integration, both vertical and horizontal, among the agricultural, industrial, and commercial enterprises in Pakistan.

Agricultural commodities, such as wheat and rice, were also overpriced in the domestic market in comparison with their world prices, even if the latter were converted at any reasonable estimate of the scarcity price or shadow price of foreign exchange. At the prevailing official rate the domestic prices of wheat and cotton were, of course, considerably above the world market price (see table 10.10). The world prices for agricultural commodities such as wheat and cotton were lower than their domestic prices by more than the differential between the domestic and foreign prices of agricultural machinery. The result was that the ratio of the prices of agricultural machinery to output prices in the domestic market was different from that in the world market. In the domestic market, in terms of wheat or cotton, agricultural machinery was cheaper than in the world market. The relative price differential in favor of agricultural machinery quickened the pace of mechanization in West Pakistan and had an adverse effect on rural employment.

In various studies in Pakistan the shadow wage rate was assumed to vary between one-half and one-third of the market wage rate.[10] Whereas labor was overpriced, capital available to the owners of large farms in agriculture was underpriced not only because they had access to the imported agricultural machinery at relatively low price but also because such farmers had access to borrowed capital from credit institutions at a rate of interest of about 6.5 percent per annum. This low rate of interest capital compared with the shadow price of capital, which was estimated to be between 10 and 15 percent.[11] The opportunity cost of agricultural machinery such as a thresher, after correction for the overvaluation of foreign exchange and for the underpricing of capital, was estimated to be 40–60 percent higher than the market price at which it was available to the agriculturists in West Pakistan. Similarly, a tractor was available at 40–100 percent below its opportunity cost.[12] The combined result of the above factors was that from the private point of view mechanization in agriculture was profit-

10. R. Lawrence, "Some Economic Aspects of Farm Mechanization in Pakistan," unpublished memorandum (Islamabad: USAID, Aug. 1970). See also Bose and Clark, "Agricultural Mechanisation."

11. Lawrence, "Farm Mechanization."

12. Ibid. See also Bose and Clark, "Agricultural Mechanisation."

able; however, its profitability was in serious doubt from the social point of view. According to one estimate, the social cost of tractor mechanization (evaluating all inputs including prices of tractors in world prices and labor at zero social cost) exceeded social benefit by 43–60 percent, depending upon the intensity of tractor use, which varied between 2 and 3 acres per horsepower. The social benefit consisted of output evaluated in world prices and of the opportunity cost of fodder that would be saved consequent on the replacement of the bullock by the tractor.[13]

However, private costs were not much higher than social costs evaluated in world prices because tractors were available until recently at the official rate of exchange with little or no duty. While the social rate of discount used was 10 percent, the big farmers who were using tractors could borrow at 6.5 percent. The only significant element of private cost not included in social cost was the cost of labor. Total private costs in domestic prices were about 14 percent higher than social costs, excluding labor, in terms of world prices.

But private returns were considerably higher than social returns. The evaluation of agricultural output in domestic prices was 30 percent higher than world prices, and hence private returns from output were 30 percent higher than social returns, excluding the additional value of output released from the production of fodder. Furthermore, there was the saving of labor costs, especially in the displacement of sharecroppers or tenant farmers, who received a larger share of output than wage laborers. The precise calculations of the private versus the social costs and benefits of mechanization would require further studies but the broad orders of magnitude are clear from the discussion above. The fact remained that the price structure for scarce inputs, i.e., capital foreign exchange, had the effect of increasing the private returns of mechanization above the social returns.

If the above estimate of social cost was increased by evaluating labor cost not at zero but at half the market wage rate, the excess of social cost would have turned out to be more than twice the social benefit unless mechanization could be shown to increase substantially the farmer's income in world prices. To say that mechanization through the use of tractors was promoted in West Pakistan because of an overestimation of private profitability at the cost of social benefit is not to suggest that there were not specific agricultural operations where the use of machines could be profitable from both private and social points of view. An important social consequence of mechanization through the use of tractors in West Pakistan was the increasing polarization between big and small farmers. It was the big farmers who took to tractor mechanization in a substantial way because the use of tractors was economical for large-sized farms and also because they had access to large amounts of capital, from their own sources as well as from

13. The following discussion of private and social costs and returns is based upon Bose and Clark, "Agricultural Mechanization," p. 281, table 1-4; p. 787, table 11.4; pp. 294–95.

credit institutions. Already, the green revolution, using improved seeds, water, and fertilizer, had spread, mainly among the big and medium-sized farmers, thus accentuating the inequalities of income distribution in the rural areas of West Pakistan. The use of machines, concentrated as it was among the large farmers, contributed to the aggravation of income inequality. However, because there were no significant economies of scale in the use of seeds, fertilizer, and water, the possibility of the seed–fertilizer revolution spreading to the small farmers was very great, provided that the supply of credit and extension services for the small farmers could be organized. The small-scale peasant farmer could adopt these innovations with relatively minor adjustments in his institutional framework, whereas technological innovations involving tractors, threshers, and combines involved major adjustments. The latter necessitated large management units, standardization of output, and sophisticated organization and cooperation. Mechanization of selected agricultural operations, coupled with a more intensive use of better seeds and fertilizers, held much greater prospects for the maximum spread of new technology in agriculture to all economic groups. The benefits from the use of capital in spreading the fruits of biological-chemical innovation among a very large number of the small farmers were greater than that from mechanization by large farmers. As new technology spread widely among the agriculturists, there would be considerable demand for capital investment in storage, transportation, and processing of agricultural products that would yield high social returns.

The greatest social problem created by mechanization was the possibility of increasing unemployment in agriculture as a result. Various surveys conducted in the areas where tractor mechanization took place at a rapid rate suggest that the labor force on land was reduced by about 50 percent.[14] This was a socially disturbing phenomenon, particularly when what was needed was to increase labor use and to make a net dent in the unemployed agricultural labor force. However, with the spread of biological-chemical innovations and a consequent increase in output, it was suggested that some areas in West Pakistan were experiencing labor shortages at harvest time. Evidence for this was not conclusive. Even if there was a rise in wages in the peak season above the level prevailing prior to the seed–fertilizer revolution, large-scale mechanization would not be socially justifiable if scarce inputs were not so heavily underpriced. Moreover, the rise in wages in the peak season was often a local phenomenon with pockets of scarcity of labor during the peak season in West Pakistan rather than a universal, uniform scarcity of labor. This was due to the different cropping patterns in the different regions and argued the need for measures designed to increase the mobility of labor in the rural areas during the peak season.

Moreover, the use of selected agricultural implements for a specific agricul-

14. Ibid, p. 289.

tural operation to overcome the seasonal labor shortage, which did not involve imports of larger scale machines from abroad but which could be produced at home with simple labor intensive techniques and with the already available indigenous skill, was expected to be socially less costly. Furthermore, such use would stimulate development of indigenous labor intensive industries and would increase total employment in the economy. This was the pattern of the agroindustrial relationship during the early stages of the green revolution, consequent on the widespread use of tube-well irrigation in the villages of West Pakistan.[15] In the rural areas of the Punjab arose shops and factories that produced the spare parts and components of tube wells. The external economic effects of the use of large tractors within the domestic economy of West Pakistan were likely to be extremely limited; it was unlikely that the number of machines and tractors in use in West Pakistan's agriculture would justify and lead to the development of an efficient machine-building industry in Pakistan. Moreover, the requirements of skill, capital, and foreign exchange for the development of such a large capital goods sector were substantially more than in the case of widely dispersed small-scale industries producing simpler agricultural implements.

Capacity Utilization

Because of its effect on imported capital equipment and raw materials, exchange rate policy had an appreciable impact on the degree of utilization of installed capacity. There was considerable excess capacity in virtually all categories of industries. A few arguments relating import controls to capacity utilization are as follows. First, the link between industrial licenses and installed capacity used by the Exchange Control System created an incentive to establish more capacity. If lack of imported inputs restrained output expansion, creation of capacity was a way to overcome it. Larger capacity implied larger total value of industrial licenses for raw materials at lower prices. The question was often raised as to why expansion of existing capacity was sanctioned by the investment licensing authorities while existing capacity was underutilized because of the shortage of imported raw materials. The answer was sought in terms of the existence of market imperfections and the criteria that governed the allocation of foreign exchange resources among the competing uses. To a certain extent the licensing authorities helped generate the consequences of an imperfect market when new firms were licensed while existing firms operated with excess capacity. This was done on the doubtful assumption that increasing the number of firms necessarily increased the degree of competition as well as made the system

---

15. H. Kaneda, *Mechanization, Industrialization and Technical Change in Rural West Pakistan,* University of California, Davis, Economics Department, Working Paper Series no. 8 (Jan. 1971).

fair in some sense. From the point of view of an efficient allocation of resources, a growth in the number of firms (each with excess capacity) involved a waste of resources. Also, underpricing of capital imports owing to overvalued exchange rates led to suboptimally increased intensity of capital vis-à-vis labor. Second, in an economic system where allocation was determined by efficiency, efficient firms could bid away intermediate goods from the inefficient. The former would have greater utilization of capacity while the latter would cease operation. This process, which leads to higher overall utilization rates, failed to function in a trade regime where allocation ignored the efficiency criterion. Another way in which the quantitative restrictions affected capacity use was the creation of bottlenecks. This was due to lack of speedy availability of imported inputs—which is an inevitability in a direct control system.

Most studies on Pakistan indicate that capacity utilization was significantly affected by import controls. Two studies on capacity utilization have come to the same conclusion.[16] The concept of capacity was not a simple one. It was based upon the entrepreneurs' judgment as to what was full capacity.[17] There was a wide variety in the number of shifts a firm considered normal. Therefore, the level of operation a firm reported to any data collecting agency as "full utilization" differed from one firm to another. In terms of single-shift output, the utilization rates in the period (1951–68), on the basis of independent and scattered surveys over the period, appeared to be as shown in table 11.5. One observes from the table that for most of the period about 60 percent of industries operated at less than 40 percent of single-shift capacity until 1967/68, when it fell to only 23 percent of industries. Of course, there are problems of comparison because data for the period 1951–66 were from a limited sample of industries, all seeking protection, whereas the data for the 1967/68 period cover a more comprehensive range and number of establishments. However, the conclusion that a significant change in utilization rates occurred in the 1960s appears reasonable. This is confirmed by comparison with more comprehensive data for 1964/65 (table 11.6). For two-and-half-shift output as capacity, the percentage of industries that had utilization rates of less than 40 percent fell from more than 70 percent of industries in 1964/65 to just more than 30 percent in 1967/68. Corresponding percentages for those operating over 60 percent of capacity were 11 and 23 percent. More industries were working at higher capacity than in the earlier period, although substantial excess capacity still remained.

16. G. Winston, "Capital Utilization in Economic Development," *Economic Journal* 81 (Mar. 1971): 36–60, and A. R. Kemal and T. Alauddin, "Capacity Utilization in Manufacturing Industries of Pakistan," *Pakistan Development Review* 13, no. 3 (Autumn 1974); 231–44.

17. Winston, "Capital Utilization." The unadjusted utilization rate is based on single-shift maximum output whereas the adjusted utilization rate is based on two-and-a-half shift maximum output.

Table 11.5.   Percentage Distribution of Industries according to Capacity Utilization

Utilization rates	1951–55	1956–60	1961–66 [a]	1967/68 [b]
Below 20	17	20	35	10
20–40	50	40	29	13
41–60	12	20	16	26
61–80	17	7	10	32
81–100	4	13	10	19

Note: The industries investigated above constituted a small sample. Moreover, because most of the data for 1951–66 were collected from Reports of the Tariff Commission, they related to industries that sought protection. Data for 1967/68 were comprehensive because they were from the Department of Promotion and Supplies and concerned all industries.

[a] Nurul Islam (for data between 1951–66), "Factor Intensities in Manufacturing Industries in Pakistan," *Pakistan Development Review* 10, no. 2 (Summer 1970): 149–54.

[b] A. R. Kemal and T. Alauddin, "Capacity Utilization in Manufacturing Industries of Pakistan," *Pakistan Development Review* 13, no. 3 (Autumn 1974): 231–44. (calculated from data on 2-½ shift capacity output concept).

It is interesting to note that there does not seem to be any significant difference among groups of industries, i.e., consumer goods, intermediate goods, and capital goods, in terms of capacity utilization (table 11.7).

In a detailed study of capacity utilization Winston finds imports as a percentage of total supply a significant variable affecting capacity utilization.[18] The association between the two variables was found to be negative. A higher ratio of imports to the total supply worked from the sides of both supply and demand to lower the degree of utilization of capacity. It not only reduced demand for the output of the import competing, domestic industry but also encouraged investment in the process of import substitution, thus adding to capacity at a faster rate than elsewhere. Past import ratios were more significant statistically as explanatory variables, suggesting the dominance of the supply relationship. A negative correlation was also found between the availability of imported raw materials and the capacity utilization rate.

SCALE AND PRODUCTIVITY

The main focus of Pakistan's exchange rate policy, insofar as industrialization was concerned, was on large-scale enterprises in trade and industry. The import licensing policy was mainly concerned with the allocation of imports among large-scale commercial importers or large-scale industrial establishments. Even though in the late 1960s attempts were made to introduce into the import trade newcomers from the underdeveloped regions and from the interior centers, the

18. Winston, "Capital Utilization," p. 42.

Table 11.6.   Utilization Rates in Manufacturing Industry

Range of utilization rates	1964/65 No. of industries	(%)	1967/68 No. of industries	(%)
Below 20	9	34.6	9	15.0
20–30	8	30.8	12	20.0
30–40	2	7.7	11	18.3
40–50	2	7.7	9	15.0
50–)0	2	7.7	5	8.3
60–70	2	7.7	7	11.7
70–80	1	3.8	5	8.3
80 and above	—	—	2	3.4
Total no. industries	26	100	60	100

Sources: 1964/65: G. Winston, "Capital Utilisation in Economic Development, *Economic Journal* 81 (Mar. 1971): 36–60; 1967/68: A. R. Kemal and T. Alauddin, "Capacity Utilization in Manufacturing Industries of Pakistan, *Pakistan Development Review* 13, no. 3 (Autumn 1974): 231–44.

emphasis was always on large size. This was because it was easier for the licensing authorities to deal with a few large establishments than to deal with numerous small-scale enterprises in either trading or industrial activity. In the industrial field, both in investment licensing and in the licensing of imported raw materials and capital goods, the focus was on the large-scale manufacturing sectors. This was true not only of the exchange rate policy but also of fiscal, credit, and financial policies. This situation was particularly remarkable because in terms of both employment and income the small-scale industrial sector was important. Was this concentration on the large-scale sector justified on the grounds of either efficiency or equity?

A systematic and comprehensive study of the relative efficiency of the industrial enterprises by size in Pakistan is hard to locate. Some scattered evidence and a few selected studies confirmed that from the point of view of equity or effi-

Table 11.7.   Capacity Utilization in Different Industry Groups (1951–66)

Percentage of capacity utilization	Percentage distribution of industry in each group Consumer goods	Intermediate goods	Capital goods
0–20	28	35	11
20–40	34	44	39
40–60	10	17	22
60–80	10	—	22
80–100	18	4	6

Source: N. Islam, "Comparative Costs, Factor Proportions and Industrial Efficiency," *Pakistan Development Review* (Summer 1967), reprinted in N. Islam, *Studies on Commercial Policy and Economic Growth* (Karachi: Pakistan Institute of Development Economics, 1970), p. 226.

ciency, the relative neglect of small-scale industry in the policy framework of Pakistan was unjustified. A survey of four industries in Karachi in 1960 showed that although the large-scale enterprises employed more capital per unit of labor, the productivity of labor did not increase uniformly with an increase in size (see table 11.8). In most cases the small-scale enterprises had higher profitability in terms of rate of return per unit of capital. Capital intensity increased with size. Insofar as capital productivity was concerned, the smallest size had the highest output per unit of capital but between the remaining size groups there was no necessary correlation between size and capital productivity.

The above findings regarding the absence of any monotonic and consistent relationship between productivity or capital intensity and size are also confirmed by an analysis of the census of large-scale manufacturing industry by size reported in table 11.9.[19] One can observe that the highest labor productivity was reached in the size group of 250 and fewer than 500 employees. From then on labor productivity declined. This pattern was repeated in the case of most of the individual industries.

As table 11.8 shows, the capital intensity was lower for small-scale industry than for large-scale industry in almost all the cases in East and West Pakistan.[20] In all cases the productivity of capital was higher for the small-scale industry than for the large-scale industry. The productivity of labor, however, was not necessarily lower for every small-scale industry. In some categories of textiles and rubber products, labor productivity was higher in the small-scale than in the large-scale industry. The above findings should be treated with caution because of differences in the product mix between the large- and the small-scale industry. Whereas the large-scale paper industry was engaged in papermaking its small-scale counterpart was engaged in bookbinding and the making of paper articles. Sugar produced in the large-scale industry was more refined than that produced in the small-scale industry. Even in the sectors in which products were close substitutes (textiles, leather products, wood, cork, and furniture) capital intensity was lower and capital productivity higher for the small-scale industry.

An alternative way of analyzing the influence of size on factor intensity and factor productivity was attempted on the basis of data in the Census of Manufacturing Industries relating to the size distribution of large-scale manufacturing industries. The value added per establishment was used as an index of size, whereas wage value added per employee and nonwage value added per employee were used as indices of labor and physical capital intensity, respectively. The

19. Central Statistical Office, *The Census of Manufacturing Industries: 1959–60* (Karachi, 1962), pp. 48–52.

20. Small-scale industry in this context is defined as establishments that use motive power and do not employ more than 50 workmen and whose fixed assets, including land, do not exceed Rs 250,000.

Table 11.8.   Characteristics of Firms by Size

Industry by scale	Capital per manhour (Rs)	Average productivity of capital (Rs)	Output per manhour
Textiles			
0- 9 workers	0.32	1.58	0.50
10–19 workers	3.92	0.34	1.33
20–49 workers	3.78	0.27	1.03
50–99 workers	4.14	0.36	1.49
100 and over	3.85	0.29	1.11
Total	3.82	0.29	1.11
Light engineering			
0- 9 workers	0.97	1.03	1.00
10–19 workers	2.56	0.27	0.70
20–49 workers	3.51	0.39	1.35
50–99 workers	3.14	0.42	1.31
100 and over	6.72	0.20	1.34
Total	4.76	0.27	1.28
Plastics			
0- 9 workers	3.41	0.74	2.52
10–19 workers	1.94	0.24	0.46
20–49 workers	4.46	0.26	1.18
50–99 workers	8.28	0.20	1.65
100 and over	2.09	0.44	0.93
Total	3.67	0.49	1.07
Leather and leather goods			
0- 9 workers	0.30	2.98	0.91
10–19 workers	0.67	1.35	0.90
20–49 workers	1.65	0.67	1.10
50–99 workers	1.18	1.25	1.47
100 and over	—	—	—
Total	1.31	0.89	1.17

Source: G. Ranis, *Industrial Efficiency and Economic Growth: A Case Study of Karachi*, Pakistan Institute of Development Economics, Apr. 1961, pp. 6–23, tables 1, 3, 11, 13.

rank correlation coefficient between size and either of these two indices was insignificant. The former was -0.1414 (t = 0.9054) and the latter was 0.1823 (t = 1.1955). The productivity of capital, however, had no discernible relationship with size and ratio of value added to fixed assets. Labor productivity, defined as value added per man, was positively and significantly related to size.

The lower capital intensity of small-scale industries was understandable. The small-scale industry was faced with a different set of factor price ratios than the

Table 11.9.   Labor Productivity in the Manufacturing Sector

Size distribution of industry	Value added per employee (Rs)
Fewer than 20 persons	2,814
20 and fewer than 50	3,216
50 and fewer than 100	3,946
100 and fewer than 250	3,755
250 and fewer than 500	4,905
500 and fewer than 1,000	3,929
1,000 and more	3,107

Source: Central Statistical Office, *The Census of Manufacturing Industries: 1959-60* (Karachi, 1962), pp. 45-52.

large-scale industry.[21] As indicated earlier, the small-scale industry had more restricted access to credit than the large-scale industry. The direct licensing of imported capital equipment was restricted to large-scale industry. The small-scale industry either bought from the trading intermediaries, paying the scarcity margins on the imported goods or substituted domestic capital goods for imported equipment and paid a higher price. A comparative analysis of the component of capital stock or fixed assets of large- and small-scale industry shows that the proportion of machinery in total assets is far less for the small-scale industry than for the large.[22] Moreover, the small-scale enterprises paid lower rates of wages than the large-scale ones. This was partly due to locational and environmental factors. Large-scale enterprises tended to concentrate in a few large centers, where supply/demand balance for labor was less favorable. The need for workers' housing and/or transport was imperative. Where small-scale enterprise was a family enterprise, a greater proportion of labor was supplied by family and the wage rate was not related to marginal productivity. In the case of raw materials also, the large-scale industry enjoyed certain advantages over the small-scale industry. The former had organized marketing facilities available to it and did enjoy economies of scale in the purchase of its inputs, which were not available to the small-scale industry. The small-scale industry suffered from similar disadvantages in the purchase of imported raw materials. The ratio of imported to total raw materials was found to be higher for the larger firms than for the smaller firms in the survey mentioned earlier.[23] Furthermore, data from the Census of Manufacturing Industries indicated that the ratio of raw material

21. Khan, "Capital Intensity," pp. 232-63.
22. Ibid.
23. G. Ranis, *Industrial Efficiency and Economic Growth: A Case Study of Karachi,* Pakistan Institute of Development Economics (Apr. 1961), p. 5.

costs to total output was higher for the smaller firms than for the larger firms. This was consistent with the hypothesis that the small firms paid a higher price for raw materials than the larger firms.

The small-scale sector suffered from unfavorable or discriminatory treatment in terms of fiscal, financial, and exchange rate policy, examples of which are given below:

(a) Small industries, which were set up as partnerships, or proprietorships were not eligible for any tax holiday.

(b) Even if set up as private limited companies, small industries enjoyed a rebate of 5 percent of income tax whereas bigger units set up as public limited companies enjoyed a higher rebate of 10 percent.

(c) The small industries' source of financing their expansion was mainly through the ploughback of reserves rather than public issue of shares. Consequently, the requirement of compulsory distribution of profits for small industries under the tax holiday provision was tantamount to denying them the means for expansion.

(d) Small industries, being too small, were not well organized for export and could not qualify for the rebate of up to 30 percent on export incomes although their exports were substantial.

(e) Difficulties in getting refunds of taxes from the government were faced by all, but small industries were especially inconvenienced because of their poor resources in staff and money. Consequently, many of their claims were not pursued.[24]

The limited financial resources of small industries and their limited access to bank financing (due to insufficient collateral) restricted the size and raised the cost of inventories, especially because they had to pay high prices for imported raw materials. The lack of working capital also contributed to insufficient capacity utilization. Small industries could not afford the bulk purchase of raw materials and could not take advantage of wholesale pricing and bulk shipments.[25] A recent survey of the small-scale engineering industry producing components of tube wells, such as pumps, strainers, and diesel engines, as well as fodder choppers, cane crushers, harvesters, and other agricultural implements, named the shortage of imported raw materials as the greatest single obstacle to the growth of this sector (see table 11.10).

The importance of import policy and of the availability of raw materials for small-scale industry can be seen from the following quotation from the above survey.

24. IBRD, *The Industrialization of Pakistan, the Record, the Problems and the Prospects* (1970), vol. 3, pp. 71–72.
25. Ibid, vol. 2, pt. 2, pp. 30–31.

Table 11.10.   Complaints of Shortages (Survey of agriculture-related small-scale industry)

	Times mentioned (%)
Imported raw materials	60
Credit	21
Skilled labor	13
Machinery	6

Source: H. Kaneda and F. C. Child, *Small-Scale, Agriculturally Related Industry in Punjab,* Working Paper Series no. 11, University of California, Davis, Economics Department (Sept. 1971), p. 23.

Many of the firms in the industry do not apply for an import license on the probably correct assumption that, even if technically qualified, their application would be entrapped by the bureaucratic morass and invitations to *bakshish* (bribery). Some of the larger and older firms in the small-scale engineering industry import raw materials; as licensed industrial users they are entitled to a semiannual quota of imports. All other firms depend upon a market supplied by commercial importers who are allocated similar quotas. In addition a substantial share of the imports of licensed industrial users, in this industry or elsewhere, are resold, sometimes as castings, often without any processing. It is interesting to note that the open ("black") market price of pig iron, for example is about 10–12 percent less in Lyallpur than in other areas. It will be recalled that Lyallpur has a disproportionate share of the older, larger firms with import quotas and none of the new expanding diesel engine firms.[26]

This survey found little or no evidence of economies of scale in this industry.

Small firms coexist with large ones, providing a competitive product by similar methods. There were only two observable differences between the production methods of the very small and the larger firms. (1) The workers in the medium and larger firms are more specialised, with the Smithian benefits; 78 of the 100 diesel engine producers said that their workers specialise in particular tasks. (2) The larger firms with the larger outputs were able to utilise some specialised, and of course, indivisible machine tools for particular operations. The net advantage of size appears to have been modest. The major consequence appears to be a somewhat more generous profit margin (economic rent?) for the larger firms and perhaps slightly higher wages or more regular employment for the production workers.[27]

26. Ibid., p. 24.
27. Ibid., p. 19.

It is remarkable that, in spite of various handicaps in regard to the supply of credit and other inputs, the small-scale enterprises in many industries did well in competition with the large-scale enterprises. The one outstanding example was the case of the engineering industry, in which the small-scale enterprises, widely dispersed geographically, registered considerable growth in the 1960s. According to one estimate there were 800 small-scale production units employing 2,680 machine tools as against 1,700 large-scale production units employing 21,000 machine tools.[28] The small-scale industry in this sector was found to be fairly competitive with foreign imports.[29]

To summarize, the trade policies put the small-scale industries in a disadvantaged position, although their factor intensity was in line with the factor proportions of the country and they were *not* less efficient than their large-scale counterparts. In the face of adverse policies the small-scale industries were able to survive because of their lower labor cost. The family enterprises, which many small-scale industries were, had to be satisfied with very low family income to withstand the competition of the favored children of the Pakistani industrial and trade authorities.

28. IBRD, *Industrialization of Pakistan,* pp. 30–31, 71–72.

29. IBRD, *Proposed Credit to Pakistan for the East Pakistan Small Industries Project* (May 1970), annex 1, p. 23.

12

Exchange Control, Savings, Investment, and Income Distribution

Exchange rate policy in Pakistan contributed to the redistribution of income among sectors and income groups and thereby affected the magnitude of domestic savings. The effect of exchange rate policy on the allocation of resources, and consequently on real income, was also an important factor. This was particularly true of output originating in the manufacturing sector.

INTERSECTORAL RESOURCE TRANSFER

Exchange rate policy had discriminated in favor of and shifted resources to the manufacturing sector. It provided lower returns to exporters of agricultural goods and thus to the growers, and increased the returns of those engaged either in import trade or in industries producing import substitutes. The importers earned the excess profits arising from import restrictions, which amounted to 40–50 percent of the landed cost of imports during the 1960s.[1] Imports on private accounts were about Rs 2 billion annually and profits would therefore amount to about Rs 1 billion. This was about 6 percent of the annual nonagricultural GNP in current prices.[2] Similarly, high profits were earned throughout the period by the industrialists producing import substitutes for the domestic market. Profit rates, which were about 50–100 percent in the 1950s, declined to about 20–50 percent by the 1960s.[3]

The effective exchange rates for the agricultural sector were between Rs 3.00

1. In the early 1950s, when the exchange restrictions were at their peak, the scarcity margins on the landed cost of imports were probably in the neighborhood of 60%. Total private imports in the 1950s were about Rs 800 million annually, yielding a total annual profit of about Rs 480–500 million to the private traders engaged in import trade, which constituted about 5% of the annual income of the nonagricultural sector then.

2. For nonagricultural income, see Ministry of Finance, *Pakistan Economic Survey 1969-70*, p. 4.

3. G. F. Papanek, *Development Policy: Theory and Practice* (Cambridge: Harvard University Press, 1968), pp. 39, 195.

and 4.25 per dollar during the 1950s, whereas for imported and domestically manufactured goods, part of which the agricultural sector purchased, they were between Rs 9 and 10 per dollar. In the 1960s the agricultural sector received between Rs 4.50 and 5.00 per dollar for its sales and paid between Rs 10.00 and 12.00 per dollar for its purchases. In other words, for every dollar's worth of sales the agricultural sector did not receive more than 47 cents worth of manufactured output in the first decade and no more than 50 cents' worth of goods in the next.[4]

In other words, if agriculture had operated freely in the international market, it could have obtained more for its sales in terms of industrial goods than that which it obtained in the domestic market.[5]

The trends in intersectoral resource flow in the domestic economy over time can be further gauged from the movement of domestic terms of trade between agriculture and manufacturing. The terms of trade had no consistent movement during the period. The movement during the entire period is shown in table 12.1.

The deterioration in the terms of trade during the early 1950s was the combined result of a fall in agricultural prices and a rise in the prices of manufactured goods. The former was partly the result of the post-Korean War slump in international prices, which greatly affected the price of cotton and jute. The continuation of export taxes on principal export crops under those conditions had a further depressing effect on their domestic prices. The drop in jute prices led to a diversion of land to the production of rice, resulting in an increase in its supply and consequent downward pressure on its price. The rise in the price of manufactured goods was the result of severe import restrictions, especially on cotton textiles, which had a very heavy weight in the price index. Rapid import substitution in the protected consumer goods sector during this period caused an increase in the price of these domestically produced goods. The rise in prices of manufactures was not entirely due to the protective effect of import restrictions; partly it was the result of increased domestic demand and indirect taxes.

There was an improvement in the terms of trade of agriculture during the latter half of the 1950s. The favorable movement cannot be attributed to a fall in industrial prices due to increased efficiency but rather to the slower rate of rise in industrial prices compared to agricultural prices. Rapid urbanization and increasing population raised the demand for marketable surpluses against the background of a stagnating agriculture with the inevitable upward pressure on grain prices. The returns to agricultural exports were increased particularly by the devaluation of 1955 and to a lesser extent by the reduction of export taxes. Thus

---

4. See chaps. 4 and 5.

5. S. R. Lewis, "Effects of Trade Policy on Domestic Relative Prices: Pakistan, 1951-64," *American Economic Review* 58, no. 1 (Mar. 1968): 60-78.

Table 12.1. Index for Manufucturing and Agricultural Prices and Terms of Trade

| | West Pakistan | | | East Pakistan | | |
| | | | Terms of trade (agriculture / manufacturing) | | | Terms of trade (agriculture / manufacturing) |
	Manufacturing	Agriculture		Manufacturing	Agriculture	
1951/52	85.29	96.05	112.62	95.31	87.67	91.98
1952/53	91.26	89.63	98.21	94.83	69.87	73.68
1953/54	98.15	85.58	87.19	107.11	69.67	64.95
1954/55	86.31	77.16	89.40	95.57	58.52	61.23
1955/56	88.22	82.72	93.77	96.55	75.07	77.75
1956/57	93.03	92.39	99.31	99.00	112.17	113.30
1957/58	97.81	100.35	102.60	105.51	98.59	93.44
1958/59	95.26	95.29	100.03	98.32	91.68	93.24
1959/60	100.00	100.00	100.00	100.00	100.00	100.00
1960/61	98.34	108.45	110.28	99.12	130.03	131.18
1961/62	100.08	108.91	108.82	100.92	103.99	103.04
1962/63	102.44	108.22	105.64	101.93	103.07	101.12
1963/64	103.18	110.44	107.04	98.85	98.74	99.89
1964/65	103.67	118.99	114.78	99.56	114.58	115.09
1965/66	108.09	116.96	108.21	105.73	125.40	118.60
1966/67	113.35	128.45	113.32	108.71	147.33	135.53
1967/68	114.42	118.82	103.85	111.42	129.35	116.09
1968/69	117.13	120.05	102.49	114.92	145.70	126.78

Sources: 1951–64 from Stephen R. Lewis, Jr. and S. Mushtaq Hussain, *Relative Price Changes and Industrialization in Pakistan, 1951–64,* Monographs in the Economics of Development, no. 16, Pakistan Institute of Development Economics (June 1967), pp. 62–65; 1964–69 from Stephen R. Lewis, Jr., ''Recent Movements in Agriculture's Terms of Trade in Pakistan,'' *Pakistan Development Review* 10, no. 3 (Autumn 1970): 392.

domestic prices of export crops registered some improvement. Substantial deficit financing generated inflationary pressures, which had a more pronounced impact on agriculture owing to lags in supply response. Although industrial prices also increased, the rate was lower due to greater availability of consumer goods as a result of higher output and imports.

When analyzing the movement in the terms of trade during the 1950s it is important to remember that the government during this period directly participated and/or intervened in the production and marketing of a number of agricultural commodities. Prices of agricultural goods were thus adjusted to a level lower or higher then warranted by the supply and demand situation. Food grain prices were kept low in the first half of the 1950s while cash crop prices were stabilized in the later half. The 1950s witnessed extensive controls on food grains. The government undertook extensive rationing and price controls in view of the prevailing shortage. The supplies required for the public distribution system were obtained by direct compulsory procurement from the producers. In some years sales to urban dwellers and low income rural groups covered under rationing were made at prices below procurement prices, which were also lower than those prevailing in the open market. This served as a distincentive to production, especially in the surplus area, where procurement was often compulsory. The surplus areas were "cordoned off" so that prices fell to low levels, at which time procurement took place.[6] On balance, the policy worked in a way such that whereas, on the one hand, prices were low in the surplus areas, they were high and wildly fluctuating in the deficit areas. This resulted in the worst of both worlds. Thus overall prices were low despite poor output. The regulation of jute acreage by means of licensing used to stabilize prices via output restrictions was not very effective in the early 1950s. However, in the latter part, when domestic prices improved as a result of devaluation, this regulation of supply maintained higher prices. Similar controls existed on cotton varieties but did not have much effect on prices.

The terms of trade in the agriculture of West Pakistan rose sharply in 1960/61, continued upward slowly and reached a peak in 1966/67,[7] and then declined at the end of the 1960s. Rapid growth in imports and in the domestic output of manufactured goods moderated the rise in their prices. The price support policy for wheat, coupled with heightened urban demand for food and for the reduction of export taxes on agricultural items, permitted a larger increase in agricultural prices despite continued growth in its output. The latter part of the decade witnessed a reduction in industrial growth.[8] Together with steady agricultural prices, except for 1966/67, this led to a decline in the agricultural terms of trade. The terms of trade in East Pakistan also rose sharply and continued at a higher level than in West Pakistan. The reason is primarily a relatively stagnating agriculture, which resulted in rising agricultural prices and relatively stable price of industrial goods. Thus, although the terms of trade for agriculture were favorable in both wings, the level in East Pakistan was slightly better.

So, during the early 1950s, when restrictive trade policies were followed, the internal terms of trade were an important mechanism for intersectoral resource transfer in favor of industry. However, growing industrialization and urbanization enlarged the demand for food and also checked the rapid advance in the prices of manufactures, thus changing the terms of trade in favor of agriculture. However, it should be noted that in the absence of exchange control and other direct controls, agriculture's terms of trade could have been more favorable than they were. Thus, resource transfer from agriculture continued despite some improvement in the terms of trade.

6. N. Islam, "The Economic System of Pakistan," in C. B. Hoover, ed., *Economic System of the Commonwealth* (Durham: Duke University Press, 1962), pp. 442–56.

7. Largely owing to bad harvests.

8. Owing to the Indo-Pakistan War and the subsequent fall in foreign assistance and imports.

Aside from the terms of trade loss, resources from the agricultural sector also flowed into the industrial sector in the form of an export surplus enjoyed by the former. The total resource transfer from agriculture in terms of world prices may be expressed by the following relation:

$$\frac{E}{P_e} - \frac{M}{P_m} = \frac{E-M}{P_e} + \frac{M}{P_m}\left(\frac{P_m}{P_e} - 1\right)$$

where E and M are the exports and imports of the agricultural sector, respectively, valued at current domestic prices. P_e and P_m are the ratios of the domestic prices of the exports and the imports to the corresponding world prices. An estimate of E-M puts it as high as 15 percent of rural income in 1964/65.[9] The estimates of P_m and P_e during 1961–64 were 1.71 and 1.00 for East and 1.75 and 1.10 for West Pakistan.[10] In averaging for all Pakistan, one can approximate the estimates of P_e and P_m at 1.05 and 1.75, respectively. Therefore, the total transfer was estimated at about Rs 7.546 billion in 1964/65, of which

$$\frac{E-M}{P_e} = \text{Rs 3.488 billion and } \frac{M}{P_m}\left(\frac{P_m}{P_e} - 1\right) = \text{Rs 4.058 billion.}$$

From the above, it appears that more than half the transfer was due to terms of trade loss. The total loss was more than twice the nominal loss in terms of the balance of trade surplus of agriculture in domestic prices.[11] It is worth noting that the transfer of surplus from the agricultural to the manufacturing sector was mainly concentrated in East Pakistan. An estimate for West Pakistan turns out to be around Rs 300–400 million.[12] The estimates of the quantum of resource transfer from agriculture, given above, are subject to qualifications. The estimate of the balance of trade surplus of agriculture is subject to serious statistical inadequacies relating to the flow of goods between agriculture and the rest of the economy; for example, it omits the payments for services, both in the public and private sectors, which the agricultural sector purchases from the rest of the economy. The benefits of government expenditures must be split between the agricultural and nonagricultural sectors, and payment by agriculture for the ser-

9. K. B. Griffin, "Financing Development Plans in Pakistan," *Pakistan Development Review* 5, no. 4 (Winter 1965): 609–14. E = Rs 14.425 billion and M = Rs 10.763 billion.

10. Lewis, "*Effects of Trade Policy*," p. 65.

11. A. H. M. Nuruddin Chowdhury, "Some Relfections on Income Redistributive Intermediation in Pakistan," *Pakistan Development Review* 9, no. 2 (Summer 1969): 99–101.

12. P. Eklund, "An Analysis of Capital Flows between the Agricultural and Non-Agricultural Sectors of West Pakistan," IBRD, unpublished monograph (Apr. 1969).

vices it receives must be accounted for. The saving–investment gap method used to estimate the intersectoral resource transfer in West Pakistan, quoted above, was based on the indirect estimates of investment and private savings in agriculture and excluded capital transfers from the nonagricultural sectors to agriculture; it also included investment by the farming families in nonfarming activities. Therefore, both above estimates of resources transfers indicated a range or a rough order of magnitude and need to be used with caution.

Domestic Savings and Exchange Control System

It has been shown that the exchange control system had resulted in the transfer of income and resources from the agricultural to the manufacturing sector and, within the industrial sector, to large-scale manufacturing as opposed to small scale. To determine its net effect on domestic savings, we have to examine the savings efforts of these sectors. The rural to urban income transfer may have affected overall savings negatively because the propensity to save in rural areas seems to be higher, in a few years, than in urban areas in both wings of Pakistan. The savings efforts in the corporate sector may have been quite favorable since more than half their profits were reinvested. However, it is difficult to be categorical about the effect of the exchange control system on total domestic savings because a large part of it was a substitute for public revenue forgone due to large tax concessions. Similarly, noncorporate household savings, especially financial savings, were subject to considerable fiscal incentives. Yet their growth was small, perhaps even inadequate to offset the loss in revenue. The composition of government expenditure would determine the extent to which this loss in revenue was significant for public saving. The import control regime, by reducing imports of consumption goods, especially luxury consumption goods, consumed by the higher income groups, was expected to contribute to private savings. However, this was not the outcome, at least certainly not to the extent desired. Insofar as controls leading to reduced imports of consumer goods encouraged substitution at home through an increase in the domestic production of consumer goods, the restriction on consumption could not be effective. Moreover, there was no special step taken to channel domestic production of consumer goods to export markets. On the contrary the exchange rate for exports was unfavorable compared to the import rates of exchange until the 1960s. No serious fiscal attempt was made to restrain or reduce domestic consumption. In fact consumption goods industries in order to increase output required imported inputs to increase output on the one hand and reduced raw material exports on the other; thus the net balance of payments effect was reduced. Equal exchange rates would have encouraged efficiency and would not have discriminated against exports. The only positive effect on savings could have been the generation of excess profits in import substituting industries, which might have contributed to savings.[13]

The trend of the domestic savings rate from 1949/50 to 1967/68 as shown in table 12.2 suggests that during the 1950s it rarely exceeded 5 percent of GNP and on average was considerably below that level. During the 1960s the domestic savings rate touched a peak of 11 percent, with a pronounced upward trend over the second decade (i.e., the 1960s). The increase in savings at the end of the first half of the 1950s was largely the result of institutional improvement in the mobilization of domestic saving. The number of banks and financial inter-mediates increased rapidly and the government's tax machinery improved signif-icantly. In the first five year plan period the rate of savings recorded a decline. This was due to a reduced rate of growth[14] accompanied by an actual decline in per capita income for East Pakistan. The subsequent increase in the rate of savings in the 1960s was accompanied by an acceleration in the growth rate of GNP. Domestic saving fell during the later part of the 1960s, especially 1965/67, despite the growth of income.

Public saving in Pakistan was small; revenue expenditures, excluding nonin-vestment development outlay, ranged between 8 and 10 percent of GNP over the past two decades.

Private Savings

The distinctions important in an analysis of private savings are between the rural and urban elements and between the corporate and noncorporate sectors. Of course their performances have to be seen in the context of large financial incentives offered by the government, as the nature of fiscal policy was geared to that end.

Rural–Urban Saving Rates

Evidence seems to indicate that the rate of rural saving was higher—and certainly no lower—than the rate of urban saving, as table 12.3 reveals.[15] The fact that the data in table 12.3 are limited to a single year prevents one from attaching

13. Azizur Rahman Khan, "Import Substitution, Export Expansion and Consumption Liberaliza-tion: A Preliminary Report," *Pakistan Development Review* 3, no. 2 (Summer 1963): 208–31, and "Some Notes on Planning Experience in Pakistan," *Pakistan Development Review* 8, no. 3 (Autumn 1968): 419–30.

14. Rate of growth of GNP was 2.4% and growth of per capita GNP was not significantly different from zero.

15. A. Bergan, "Personal Income Distribution and Personal Savings in Pakistan, 1963/64," *Pakistan Development Review* 7, no. 2 (Summer 1967): 184–88.

Table 12.2.   Gross Domestic Saving

	GDS (Rs million)	GDS/GNP
1949/50	438	2.1
50/51	1,352	6.2
51/52	511	2.2
52/53	552	2.3
53/54	938	4.2
54/55	974	4.4
55/56	1,316	5.6
56/57	626	2.3
57/58	734	2.5
58/59	1,444	5.0
59/60	1,987	6.1
60/61	2,800	7.7
61/62	3,436	9.1
62/63	4,135	10.7
63/64	4,266	10.3
64/65	5,364	11.1
65/66	3,690	7.9
66/67	5,559	9.8
67/68	6,852	11.3

Sources: M. Baqai, *Pakistan's Economic Progress: Possibilities of Take off,* Occasional Paper Series no. 4 (Montreal: McGill University, 1968), pp. 12–17.

great significance to the absolute magnitude of differences between urban and rural saving. But there was other accompanying evidence to support the view that rural savings were high. Although the higher rate of rural savings was consistent with the transfer of resources from the rural to the urban sector, it was also possible for the rural areas to have lower rates of saving and still transfer resources if the investment rate in the rural areas was less than the saving rate. Independent sets of data for the same year, even though less reliable, indicate the difference in the rates of saving between rural and urban areas. More recent data show a larger differential between urban and rural saving rates than the earlier studies do, with all income groups in the rural areas having higher saving rates than the corresponding income groups in the urban areas.[16] An independent study put the marginal saving rate of the rural families at 20–25 percent, which compared very favorably with the urban marginal saving rate.[17] Also, the rural areas generated a higher rate of saving with a less unequal distribution of income. In

16. T. M. Khan, "Some Reflections on Planning Experience in Pakistan," *Pakistan Development Review* 8, no. 3 (Autumn 1968): 394–97.

17. Ibid., p. 397.

Table 12.3.   Personal Saving in 1963/64

	Gross saving as percentage of gross personal income
East Pakistan	
Rural	12.0
Urban	9.9
Combined	11.8
West Pakistan	
Rural	9.2
Urban	6.7
Combined	8.8

Source: A. Bergan, "Personal Income Distribution and Personal Savings in Pakistan, 1963/64," *Pakistan Development Review* 7, no. 2 (Summer 1967): 184–88.

the urban areas a rise in income beyond a certain income level did not cause a rise in the rate of saving. In the rural areas, saving rates increased monotonically as income increased.[18]

In addition recent experience with the green revolution has shown that savings responded very strongly to profitable investment opportunities in the rural areas. Investments in new techniques were financed to a large extent by farmers' personal savings, especially among medium-sized farmers.[19]

The Corporate Sector

The manufacturing sector as a whole accounted for 12 percent of Pakistan's GNP in 1969/70. Of this the large-scale establishments contributed a little less than 9 percent to GNP and at most a little more than 10 percent to domestic savings. However, because the exchange control regime had its major impact on this sector, it is interesting to inquire whether they were relatively high savers. Because private limited companies account for a small proportion of the total assets of this group, only the public limited companies are discussed.

Corporate profits were a major source of industrial financing. Initial investment in industry in the 1950s was financed to a substantial degree by profits earned in trade. Subsequent expansion was financed partly by reinvestment of

18. Ibid., p. 396. For example, the urban households with monthly income between Rs 500 and 700 saved the same proportion of income as those with income between Rs 700 and 899 as well as those with incomes Rs 900 and above.

19. Ghulum Mohammad, "Private Tubewell Development and Cropping Patterns in West Pakistan," *Pakistan Development Review* 5, no. 1 (Spring 1965): 1–53.

Table 12.4. Reinvestment of Industrial Profits (Gross savings as proportion of gross profits)

	Average 1 *1959-63*	*Average 2* *1964-70*
1. Textiles and allied	49.6	49.6
2. Jute textiles	58.2	50.8
3. Sugar and allied	35.0	49.4
4. Cement	50.4	63.6
5. Chemicals	44.0	31.5
6. Engineering	43.4	44.9
7. Transport and communications	84.6	86.7
8. Fuel and power	47.2	54.3

Sources: (1) K. Haq and M. Baqai, "Savings and Financial Flows in the Corporate Sector 1959-1963," *Pakistan Development Review* 7, no. 3 (Autumn 1967): 298-304. (2) R. Amjad, "Growth, Profitability and Savings of Quoted Companies 1964-1970," *Pakistan Economic and Social Review* 11, no. 4 (Autumn 1573).

profits.[20] On average, gross savings of the corporate sector as a whole were about 50 percent of gross profits,[21] but about 70 percent of post-tax profits, through the period 1959-70 (table 12.4).[22]

Import substitution was the prime result of Pakistan's exchange control system, especially in the earlier period, although the bias against export industries was partially corrected later on. However, a study of both types of industries does not reveal any significant differences in their savings effort.

Except for transport and communications, where the percentage of profits saved was in the eighties, the percentages for textiles, jute, fuel, and power were not significantly different. Cement had a savings rate of about 50 percent in 1959-63 and higher still in the later period; sugar had its lowest savings (35 percent) in the earlier period but was close to 50 later. Only chemicals and engineering had lower rates of savings throughout, less than 45 percent in the latter period and as low as 31 percent in the former.

The differences among the individual industries in terms of rates of reinvestment of profits were not related to whether they were predominantly import-

20. For example, in the period 1962-68 retained earnings (excluding depreciation) formed 11-15% of industrial financing. In 1965-70 total internal savings (retained earnings plus depreciation) financed between 23 and 28% of total industrial investment.

21. Retained earnings plus depreciation = gross savings.

22. Gross savings as a percentage of gross profits were higher in the late 1960s, reaching 58% in 1965. Gross savings as a percentage of post-tax profits were lower in the late 1960s, reaching 65.5% in 1967.

substitute or export-oriented industries. Nor were the differences related to the intensity of import restrictions or rates of implicit or effective protection.

However, the bias of the trade regime was against the small-scale industries as listed in chapter 11. Although no solid evidence was available, a priori theorizing suggested that the propensity to save out of profits in small-scale industries might be low. On the other hand the rate of surplus per unit of invested capital was higher in the small-scale than in the large-scale industry. If the ex post reinvestment of profits was lower in the former sector, this could have been due to its lack of easy access to (a) imported inputs and spares and (b) domestic, supplementary financial facility. Therefore, to the extent that the foreign trade regime induced a flow of resources away from the small- to the large-scale industrial sector, the net effect of policies on domestic saving could have been either way; available evidence in Pakistan was inconclusive.

Corporate savings had rarely exceeded 10 percent of gross domestic savings.[23] Corporate savings mostly hovered around 6–7 percent of total savings and grew at an annual rate of about 20 percent except for 1963/64 to 1967/68; the latter fact is accounted for by the reduction in the growth rate of manufacturing and the lower markup ratios owing to rising raw material costs.[24] The point to note, however, is that the rate of corporate saving was the result not only of the sector's innate propensity to save but also of generous financial and fiscal incentives. Tax incentives were liberally provided to stimulate corporate savings throughout the past two decades, especially since the beginning of the 1960s. Tax holidays for industrial enterprises in the early years of their operation and different tax rebates were common phenomena.[25] A series of additional rebates was provided for corporate income taxation. These rebates were granted from the super tax so that a company paid an income tax of 30 percent (which was the rate of corporation tax) even when allowable rates were more than 30 percent.

It is abundantly clear that tax concessions were exceptionally high and rebates unnecessarily large for an already profitable sector.[26] Thus a substantial part of the savings of the corporate sector occurred at the cost of public revenue. The question that is begged is whether this sector would have saved as much in the

23. Except in 1965/66.

24. Markup equivalent to ratio of gross profit to gross rates. It was 18.5 in 1959–63, 16.0 in 1964–70.

25. Tax holiday implied complete exemption of profits from income tax for a certain initial period, for entirely new enterprises and/or for new identifiable industrial units in old establishments. The rationale was to induce investments in sectors that were not too profitable and to disperse industries to less developed regions of the country.

26. In fact higher than was necessary for the purpose. In one study it has been shown that 40% of the firms enjoying a tax holiday would have invested even without it, on the basis of its already high profitability. See B. A. Azhar and S. M. Sharif, "Effects of Tax Holiday on Investment Decisions: An Empirical Analysis," *Pakistan Development Review* 13, no. 4 (Winter 1974): 415.

absence of such financial incentives. If not, the resource flow directed toward large-scale manufacturing by the trade regime might have contributed much less to savings than the evidence on retained profits for reinvestment suggested.

Household Saving

The performance of household saving was poor. Over the years its increase was slow. For want of data, the examination is confined to its financial saving, which was just over one-third of total household saving. The rate of financial saving, which increased very substantially in the early 1950s owing to improvements in financial institutions, failed to maintain the rising trend despite considerable financial incentives (table 12.5). It fell to 2.9 percent in 1959/60, advanced to 3.7 percent by the end of the Second Plan, and then declined again during the Third Plan period. As a component of total domestic saving it was only 16 percent in 1966/67. The reason was to be found in policies that had contrary effects. On the one hand, income tax deductions were permitted lavishly as incentives to invest in financial assets. On the other hand, interest rate and dividend policy kept returns to those assets low and often negative. Thus households used this situation to avail themselves of investment deductions from taxable income and yet used most of those funds for consumption or for buying ornaments, jewelry, consumer durables, real estate, and luxury housing.

The large tax concessions markedly reduced the progressiveness of the tax rate. Dividend income of RS 1,000 was exempt from taxation in 1960/61, and this limit was gradually raised to 3,000 by 1965/66. Dividend income received by shareholders were exempt from taxes if this income was not subject to taxation at the corporation level, and dividends from two special types of investment were exempt to the extent of Rs 2,000.[27]

It has been shown that urban sectors, especially households, were provided with liberal fiscal incentives to save and invest, particularly in financial assets. The tax system was designed to impose a very light burden on this group, although a large part of the increases in income occurred in this group. The effects of financial and interest rate policies on domestic saving and investment can be seen from the returns to financial assets. The nominal rate of interest paid to depositors was extremely low.

In the mid-1960s there was some improvement in the nominal rates of interest paid on bank deposits. But the real rates of return, adjusted for high rates of inflation, showed in fact a deterioration.[28]

27. N. Islam, "The Tax System of Pakistan," unpublished manuscript, Pakistan Institute of Development Economics (1970).
28. Planning Commission, *The Third Five-Year Plan* (Karachi, 1965), p. 123.

Table 12.5.   Rate of Financial Saving for the Household Sector (Percentage of GNP)

	1949/50	*1954/55*	*1959/60*	*1964/65*	*1967/68*
Household financial saving	1.2	3.2	2.9	3.7	2.7

Sources: B. A. Azhar and S. M. Sharif, "Effect of Tax Holiday on Investment Decisions: An Empirical Analysis," *Pakistan Development Review* 13, no. 4 (Winter 1974): 415; M. Baqai, *Pakistan's Economic Progress: Possibilities of Take Off,* Occasional Paper Series no. 4 (Montreal, Canada: McGill University, 1968), pp. 10–20.

Another instance of low rates of return on financial assets was the rate of dividends received by the shareholders in the corporate sector. Dividends as a proportion of net worth seldom exceeded 6 percent. In view of the rate of price increases this provided a very poor return despite an extremely profitable manufacturing sector. The low rates of interest and the low rate of return on these investments discouraged saving in the form of financial assets. Financial intermediaries could not earn a positive margin after providing a fair return to the depositors and they could not offer diverse forms of assets to suit the needs of various classes of savers. Hence it was highly plausible that the saving propensities of these units in the economy were very depressed.[29]

Thus the noncorporate sector (such as the urban rentiers, professionals, and employers), which benefited from the income redistribution mechanism and which had surplus investable funds, received very scanty reward from investment in financial assets. This situation diverted the potential surplus of these spending units to consumption of items such as ornaments, jewelry, and consumer durables and to real estate and farmlands. Often such surplus was devoted to luxury house construction.[30]

Public Saving

Public saving in Pakistan was small; revenue expenditure excluding noninvestment development outlay ranged between 8 and 10 percent of GNP over the past two decades (table 12.6). Defense, an important component of revenue expenditure, ranged between 3 and 4 percent of GNP over the two decades. Public saving (defined as revenue surplus) has been estimated in two ways (see table 12.6). The A estimate includes and B excludes noninvestment development outlay in revenue expenditure. One can see that public saving is positive only if

29. Ibid.

30. A sample survey in Dacca revealed that as much as 42.5% of personal savings in the urban sector was in the form of gold, ornaments, consumer durables, and housing. Savings released for investment purposes were only a little over half of total savings produced by these recipients of income.

Table 12.6. Public Savings in Pakistan

		Public saving as percentage of GNP	
	Total revenue as percentage of GNP		
Period		*A*	*B*
1950/51/1954/55	8.1	−0.5	−0.2
1955/56/1959/60	9.2	−0.3	0.3
1960/61/1964/65	10.6	−0.9	2.0
1965/66/1969/70	12.3	−0.8	2.3

Source: N. Islam, "The Tax System of Pakistan," unpublished manuscript, Pakistan Institute of Development Economics (1970), pp. 59–63.

one excludes the noninvestment development outlay in revenue expenditure, but even then it is very low. The low tax base and high revenue expenditure, including defense, were responsible for the low rate of public saving. The tax base was small largely due to the inelasticity of the tax system, especially with respect to corporation and personal income taxes. The relative significance of indirect taxes increased over time. While the ratio of direct taxes to GNP was about 2 percent for the two decades, the ratio of indirect taxes to GNP increased from about 4.4 percent in the late 1950s to 5.4 percent in the early 1960s and 6.6 percent during the late 1960s.[31] Duties on trade were the most important component of this trend, even in the late 1960s, when incomes of the large and medium farmers increased substantially, consequent to a technological breakthrough. Pakistan did not succeed in formulating an adequate, efficient, and equitable system of either the land tax or the agricultural income tax to mobilize a part of the large increase in income. In fact the ratio of direct taxes on agriculture compared with the nonagricultural sector declined over the years, as shown in table 12.7.

As explained earlier, Pakistan maintained a wide variety of effective exchange rates for imports and exports which were greatly different from the official exchange rate of Rs 4.76 per dollar. This was done by means of a set of taxes on imports and exports, as well as a particular combination of import licensing and export promotion schemes. With a change in the official exchange rate, a set of effective exchange rates similar to or different from the previous set would be generated by changed rates of taxes, export subsidies, and import premiums. The change of tax rates, which might accompany a change in the official exchange rate, would necessarily affect public saving through its effects on total tax proceeds. Therefore, public saving was very closely related to the exchange rate policy. A sufficient degree of devaluation could eliminate all taxes on imports

31. Islam, "The Tax System," pp. 58–66.

Table 12.7.   Ratio of Direct Taxes to Agricultural and Nonagricultural
Incomes

	Agriculture	*Nonagricultural sector (income and corporation taxes only)*
1959/60	1.7	2.0
1964/65	1.3	2.8
1968/69	1.2	2.3

Source: N. Islam, ''The Tax System of Pakistan,'' unpublished manuscript, Pakistan Institute of Development Economics (1970), pp. 59–63.

unless effective exchange rates on imports were to be raised above the preexisting levels and, indeed, may necessitate subsidies to certain categories of imports.
So long as taxes on foreign trade were vital components of total tax proceeds, the
specific combination of the exchange rate variation and the tax rates used to
establish the desired set of effective exchange rates was crucial for the determination of the magnitude of public saving. Customs duties were in fact very important in the structure of total tax revenue (table 12.8). During the 1960s customs
duties comprised nearly one-quarter of the total tax revenue.

Importers paid import duties and, in addition, paid bonus premiums on that
portion of imports which were covered under the Export Bonus Scheme. Exporters paid taxes on cotton and jute and received bonus payments on all manufactured exports and some primary exports. If the official exchange rate was adjusted downward, nonbonus exports would have to be taxed in order to maintain
the same effective exchange rate as before. Depending upon the degree of devaluation, vis-à-vis the preexisting structure of the effective exchange rates,
some imports would receive subsidies and others would pay lower rates of taxes.
Because imports greatly exceed exports, there would be a loss of revenue and
significant impact on public saving. The government could offset this loss of
revenue either by borrowing from the State Bank or by resorting to taxation on
domestic output and expenditure. In the absence of borrowing and additional tax
measures, the surplus on the revenue account (defined as public saving) would
have changed from a positive to a negative amount, depending on the nominal
exchange rate chosen, as is illustrated in table 12.9 by the example of the tax
position in one year.

INVESTMENT AND EXCHANGE CONTROL SYSTEM

Among the significant issues in the study of trade regimes is whether they have
any discernible effect on the inducement to invest. This is crucial because the
emergence of entrepreneurs is essential for industrialization in a mixed economy
and because the pace of investment itself determines the growth of the country.

Table 12.8.   Composition of Total Tax Revenue

	Direct	*Sales*	*Customs*	*Excise*
1960/61	36.0	21.9	25.3	17.4
1964/65	35.0	18.7	25.8	23.2
1969/70	30.0	10.0	23.6	36.1

Source: N. Islam, "The Tax System of Pakistan," unpublished manuscript, Pakistan Institute of Development Economics (1970), pp. 59–63.

In Pakistan such inducement was important in the early years in view of her lack of industrial entrepreneurs. However, because of the public sector's role in industrial investment, the argument for continued and indiscriminate protection of indigenous entrepreneurs was weak. Thus, with the exception of the early years there was little evidence to indicate that Pakistan could not have sustained the desired levels of investments, without quantitative restrictions augmenting the profits of the private entrepreneurs.

Pakistan, like most other developing countries, lacked industrial entrepreneurs. Muslims in prepartitioned India played a very small role in commerce and banking and a negligible one in industry. Yet industry grew rapidly in Pakistan and was largely developed by private entrepreneurs in the early period. High profits, resulting from quantitative restrictions, were strongly conducive to industrial investment. This situation was buttressed to some extent by the strong disincentives to alternative activities in agriculture or even trade owing to the adverse implicit exchange rates for agriculture and declining profitability in trade.

The exchange control system provided both the means and the rationale for a shift into industry. The means stemmed from scarcity premiums on imports that supplied the initial capital; the rationale sprang from high profits spurred by large effective rates of protection. Two-thirds of the private industrial investment owned by Muslims in 1959 was controlled by families who had been traders previously.[32] Most of these groups were located in or migrated to West Pakistan.[33] These traders were the people who had resources to respond to market incentives. Nearly one-third of the initial private investment in industry in the 1950s was financed by profits resulting from scarcity premiums in foreign trade and one-fifth was funded by profits from internal trade. An additional advantage of trading was access to a distribution system, which allowed evasion of price controls and taxes. Furthermore, profits in protected industrial investments were

32. G. Papanek, "Pakistan's Development: Social Goals and Private Incentives" (Cambridge: Harvard University Press, 1967), chaps. 2 and 7.

33. Private entrepreneurs in East Pakistan were consequently lacking while most private sector developments occurred in West Pakistan.

Table 12.9.   Financial Flows of the Government Sector under Alternative Nominal Exchange Rates, 1964/65 (Rs million)

1. Nominal exchange rate	4.76	6.90	8.90
2. Taxes on foreign trade	1,429.2	1,000.9	1,697.0
3. Subsidies on foreign trade		−548.2	−1,746.1
4. Net taxes on foreign trade	1,492.2	452.7	−49.1
5. Other tax receipts	2,542.4	2,542.4	2,542.4
6. Total tax receipts	3,971.6	2,995.1	2,493.3
7. Ratio of net taxes on foreign trade to total tax receipts	36.0	15.1	−19.7
8. Surplus on revenue account	1,124.0	147.5	−354.3

Source: R. Soligo, "Real and Illusory Aspects of an Over-valued Exchange Rate: The Pakistan Case," *Oxford Economic Papers,* May 1971, p. 102.

phenomenal. In the 1950s most entrepreneurs recouped their entire capital in one and a half years. Profits remained high in the 1960s despite a decline.

However, as some studies have indicated, investment behavior cannot be fully explained by movement in profits. A recent study of investment behavior for the period 1962–70 by Amjad tried to gauge the significance of profits as an explanation of investment behavior in the industrial sector.[34] Profits were expected to be important on both the demand and supply side in the decision to invest. Entrepreneurs wanted to maximize the present value of returns on investment, of which profits were an indicator. In a country with poor capital markets, finance for investment was primarily supplied by profits. A cross section study of relations among profits, sales, and gross investment of industrial firms for each of the nine years between 1962 and 1970 found profits to be a central determinant of investment only in the Third Five Year Plan period (1965–70). Profits were less important in the Second Plan than in the Third Plan. This was attributed to the part played by investment licensing, buttressed by lendings from the government institutions, in financing industrial investment. It was found that on the average for the period 1961–65, 41 percent of gross fixed corporate investment was financed by borrowings in foreign exchange from these agencies compared to 25 percent in 1965–70.[35]

The availability of external finance was considered an important determinant of investment behavior in Pakistan in two ways. The first was that, given the prevailing system of multiple exchange rates and the fact that loans from the two financial institutions PICIC and IDBP were available at the official overvalued exchange rate, in all cases firms would have preferred to finance their investment from these funds rather than from their own internal funds or from any other

34. R. Amjad, "A Study of Investment Behaviour in Pakistan, 1962–70," *Pakistan Development Review* 15, no. 2 (Summer 1976): 134–53.

35. Ibid., pp. 144–45.

source of borrowing.[36] The second was the extent of availability of these loans from these financial institutions. Because availability of these funds varied in the two plan periods, it was found that during the Second Plan period (1960-65), in the case of firms whose investments were financed mostly by funds from these financing institutions, external funds were the more significant variable explaining the investment behavior. For the rest finances for investment were mainly generated by profits. This is seen if domestically owned companies (30 firms) that were dependent for over 40 percent of their total investment on loans sanctioned in foreign exchange from PICIC and IDBP were separated from the rest. Even though the number of firms in the rest of the sample was not large, the profit hypothesis was now far more closely related to investment than if all firms were considered together.

During the Third Plan external finance was more widely available among intending investors; the role of external finance in the explanation of investment behavior was more general and not restricted to the case of those predominantly dependent on financial institutions.

Profits were a major influence on investment by firms during the period covered, although the manner and extent of the influence were different over the two plan periods. During the Second Plan it seemed to be a strong inducement to investment from the demand side whereas during the Third Plan the influences seemed to have worked through the supply side as well, as a source of finance for investment owing to abundant availability of loans at the official "overvalued" exchange rate from financial institutions.

It may be argued that supernormal profits were not always needed to attract resources into a sector. Although no detailed work is available on the utility of incentives that were created for the manufacturing sector to induce additional investment, a study of the tax holiday is revealing and suggestive.[37] The study estimated the present value of an investment with and without tax exemption from the firms' own accounts and classified them into three categories. They consisted of (1) firms whose present value was negative in the absence of exemption but positive with it, (2) firms whose present value was positive even in the absence of the tax holiday, and (3) firms who would not invest with or without the tax holiday. It was concluded from representative samples of 70 firms that only 20 percent invested because of the tax holiday. The remaining firms either would not have invested even with the tax holiday or would have

36. The Industrial Development Bank of Pakistan (IDBP) and the Pakistan Industrial Credit and Investment Corporation (PICIC) were the channels through which foreign aid funds for industrial investment in the medium- and large-scale industries were provided. They provided loans or agents for financing foreign exchange components of private industrial investment. In a few cases they also provided local financing in addition to foreign exchange financing.

37. Azhar and Sharif, "Effects of Tax Holiday," pp. 409-32.

invested anyhow. Similar percentages were obtained for the 20 firms in the cotton textile industry. What seems odd is that nearly two-fifths of the firms are classified as firms "who would not have invested with or without a tax holiday." And yet these were firms that were actually in operation and had invested. Some arbitrary cutoff profit rates seem to have been used by the authors. Even if post-tax profit rates were low with or without exemption, they would become higher with exemption than without. Therefore, except for those creating losses, the rest may be considered as having invested because of the tax holiday. However, despite that caveat the percentage of firms that would have invested anyhow because profits were already high is very large.[38] Assuming that profits' accounts were understated (for tax purposes), this percentage figure, if anything, is biased downward.

In the light of this evidence it is difficult to conclude that the degree of high profits created by the exchange control system and other fiscal and financial incentives was necessary to induce additional investment.

DOMESTIC SAVINGS, EXTERNAL RESOURCES, AND EXCHANGE LIBERALIZATION

Among the developing countries Pakistan was a significant recipient of foreign economic assistance. Annual average per capita external economic aid to Pakistan was only marginally lower than the per capita aid to the developing countries that had special political and military links with the developed, aid-giving countries. Moreover, starting with a low level of assistance in the early 1950s, the rate of flow of gross assistance increased considerably in the 1960s.[39] The country's dependence on aid, measured as the percentage of aid to total imports of goods and services, was greater than the specially privileged, dependent territories. There has been a consistent increase in the ratio of external assistance to GNP throughout the period up to 1964/65. Between 1964/65 and 1969/70 there was a fall in the ratio of assistance to GNP (quite a significant decline) but a small decline in the ratio of foreign assistance to investment and a small increase in the ratio of assistance to foreign payments (see table 12.10). Roughly 57 percent of the total foreign economic assistance was in the form of loans and credits, about 21 percent in grants, and 22 percent was in the form of PL 480 aid, which was a mixture of loans and grants. Project assistance constituted 44 percent and the nonproject, i.e., commodity, assistance constituted 34 percent of total assistance in 1969.[40]

38. Percentage of firms that would have invested without a tax holiday was 40%.

39. N. Islam, "Foreign Assistance and Economic Development—The Case of Pakistan," *Economic Journal* 82 (Mar. 1972): 502–30.

40. Planning Commission, *Report of the Advisory Panel on the Fourth Five-Year Plan* (1970), vol. I, p. 279.

Table 12.10. External Economic Assistance

	Percentage of GNP	*Percentage of foreign payments*	*Percentage of gross investment*
1949/50	1.3		37.6
1954/55	2.5		28.0
1959/60	2.8	(1960/61) 28.5	39.7
1964/65	6.6	(1964/65) 38.3	37.9
1969/70	3.8	(1969/70) 42.8	32.1

Source: See n. 39.

Note: The statistical estimates of aid, foreign payments (which include both visible and invisible payments), and gross investment for the period prior to 1954/55 leave much to be desired and, therefore, should be treated with caution.

An increased capital inflow from several important donors was linked to a policy change in support of liberalization of the exchange control system. This in turn would have had implications for additional domestic saving. Import liberalization, in the sense of bringing official and effective rates of exchange close together, through devaluation, for example, would transfer excess profits from import substituting industries to the export sector. It was not obvious how this transfer would have affected the aggregate rate of savings; it depended upon the relative propensity to save on the part of farmers producing export crops as well as on marketing intermediaries who had a large share in export income. Alternatively, excess profits could be taxed by the government and contributed to public saving. It is not clear whether the rate of private savings out of profits was lower than the rate of public savings out of taxes. The behavior of public savings was very different in different periods. It is interesting to study how far domestic savings were stimulated by the increased inflow of foreign assistance and the trade liberalization measures that accompanied the larger inflow of foreign capital.

The increase in the rate of capital inflow was expected to increase the rate of domestic saving in two ways. First, it raised the rate of investment and hence the rate of increase in income, which in turn raised the marginal and average rates of saving. This was true even when part of foreign assistance went toward encouraging consumption, since at least another part increased investment and income and hence the rate of saving. The net result in terms of a change in the rate of saving depended upon the relative pull of the saving-depressing effect of increased consumption and of the saving-raising effect of the increase in income. No less significant were the policy measures designed to mobilize savings out of greater income. Secondly, an increase in capital inflow was expected to increase the rate of saving by providing the scarce foreign exchange component of investment. In a country such as Pakistan, investment was critically dependent on imported inputs so that domestic savings could be frustrated for lack of foreign exchange resources. It is difficult to assess quantitatively how much savings would have been frustrated if foreign exchange through foreign capital inflow had not been available.

The correlation between the changes over time of savings, and inflow of foreign resources did not follow a consistent pattern. Between 1951/52 and 1954/55, i.e., the years that preceded the inauguration of economic planning in Pakistan, there were substantial annual fluctuations in the rates of both capital inflows and domestic savings, and the relationship was mainly inverse. The improvement in saving rates from 1952/53 onward was associated with a decline in the flow of foreign resources. This advance in saving rates was basically the result of institutional improvement in the mobilization of domestic savings rather than the result of income growth. The deficiencies in the financial infrastructure such as the banking and financial intermediaries and in the administrative apparatus such as the tax collecting machinery were slowly being remedied by the mid-1950s.

In the following period, i.e., the period of the First Five Year Plan (1955/56–1959/60), whereas the rate of capital inflow registered an increase, the rates of both saving and investment recorded a decline. The rate of private saving could not be maintained at the level reached in 1954/55, in view of the slowing down of the growth rate accompanied by an actual fall in per capita income in East Pakistan. The lack of any financial discipline in the public sector, by a government that was highly unstable and changed frequently, was reflected in the inability to raise taxes and to contain increases in nondevelopment expenditure. This resulted in nominal public saving during 1955–60. A large part of foreign assistance was used to import food to meet the domestic shortage. There was a strong presumption that foreign aid in this period contributed primarily to the financing of consumption expenditure. An additional external factor was a decline in the external terms of trade, mainly owing to a rise in import prices. It is thus difficult to establish any close one-way relationship during this period between the rates of domestic saving and of capital inflow.

During the five-year period starting in 1960 Pakistan witnessed marked acceleration in the rate of capital inflow as well as in the rate of domestic savings. She received the biggest push in her history in terms of an increase in external economic assistance. The rate of capital inflow increased to 6.6 percent of GNP in 1964/65 compared with 2.8 percent in 1959/60. It was not only that the rate of capital inflow during this period increased by about 50 percent but also that the rate of savings increased by about 90 percent. This was accompanied by an acceleration of 5.2 percent in the growth rate of income, more than twice the rate in the First Plan period (1955–60). The increase in the rate of saving in this period was attributable to an improvement in all the different forms of saving—

more so in terms of an increase in corporate and public saving as well as in noncorporate nonfinancial saving than in household financial saving. Public saving increased substantially during the Second Plan period. This substantial increase in the rate of domestic saving has often been ascribed to the acceleration in the rate of capital inflow.

There were, however, two factors worth mentioning in this context. First, although the foreign exchange component of current production in a natural resource-scarce economy such as Pakistan was important in increasing the rate of growth, the major reason for the accelerated growth during the 1960s was the breakthrough in agriculture, which was not import intensive. At the same time there was considerable excess capacity in the industrial sector due mainly to the shortage of imported raw materials. The imbalance in the composition of foreign assistance in favor of project assistance in relation to commodity assistance contributed to the scarcity of raw materials in relation to the availability of capital equipment. Secondly, the increase in foreign exchange availability during this period was also partly due to a large increase in Pakistan's own foreign exchange earnings.[41] While an acceleration in the growth rate of income during the Second Plan provided the resources for increasing the saving rate there were important favorable changes in economic environment, institutions, and policies not directly related to the flow of aid that increased the saving rate in the early 1960s. Compared to the widespread political instability in the 1950s, the 1960s witnessed a stable, authoritarian government with a heavy bias toward economic development. The discipline of public investment planning was practiced to a much greater extent than in the earlier years. Financial discipline was reflected in an ample increase in public saving. Agriculture received considerable attention. The earlier bias against export promotion inherent in the import substitution policy was partially corrected through the introduction of the Export Bonus Scheme. One could even suggest that better export performance and improvement in the domestic saving rate encouraged a greater aid flow rather than the other way around. Along with an improvement in economic performance there was an enhanced ability to initiate and formulate aid-worthy projects as well as to negotiate aid due to the strengthening of the planning machinery.[42] One could hypothesize a two-way relationship between domestic saving and foreign capital inflow during this period. The accelerations in the rate of capital inflow provided the impetus to the growth of income, savings, and investment and stimulated associated institutional and policy changes. The growth of income and savings in their turn had a beneficial cumulative effect on the rate of capital inflow. The

41. Compared with the virtual stagnation in export earnings during the First Plan, Pakistan's exports grew at the rate of 7% per annum during the Second Plan period.

42. J. White, *Pledged to Development* (London: Overseas Development Institute, 1967).

question might legitimately be asked whether during the 1960s Pakistan could not have increased its rate of saving more than it in fact achieved if it was determined to reach her plan targets with a lower capital inflow. Other countries at Pakistan's level of per capita income generated higher levels of saving. Moreover, an examination of its imports revealed that there was scope for providing greater foreign exchange resources for current domestic production and investment by reducing nonessential imports.

During the latter part of the 1960s both the rate of domestic saving and the rate of foreign capital inflow slowed. Whether the positive relationship was a causative one is difficult to say because other independent circumstances and factors depressed the rates of both inflow of capital and domestic savings. The outbreak of Indo–Pakistan hostilities resulted in the suspension of economic assistance. The international climate for foreign aid worsened during the same period. In respect to domestic saving, the most immediate factor was the impact of the war on domestic public saving. There was a considerable rise in defense expenditure, which increased from 29.1 percent of nondevelopment expenditure and 2.4 percent of GNP in 1964/65 to 48.4 percent of nondevelopment expenditure and 5.4 percent of GNP in 1965/66.[43] The second factor tending to reduce the rate of saving was the incidence of two consecutive years of bad harvest in 1965/66 and 1966/67. The fall in agricultural output adversely affected income and saving rates in the first two years of the Third Plan in the rural areas, whereas the rise in food prices increased the cost of living and depressed the saving rate in the urban areas. Third, the political agitation against the Ayub government, associated with massive riots, demonstrations, and industrial strikes all over the country during 1968 and 1969, created great uncertainty among the investors about the future of the economic policy as well as that of the political system. This dampened the rate of investment and hence the rate of reinvestment of profit.

The liberalization of controls was expected to affect domestic savings in a number of ways. First, in the corporate sectors greater imports would have increased domestic investment by making a substantial supply of raw materials available to the domestic industrialists. This would have stimulated savings, especially through a larger reinvestment of profits. Second, import controls replaced either by tariffs or by an auctioning of imports would have augmented government revenue and reduced the scarcity premium of imports. So there would have been a redistribution of income from the importers to the government, and the impact on savings would have depended on the savings behavior of the two sectors. Third, if liberalization is achieved through devaluation, there

43. Government of Pakistan, Ministry of Finance, *Budget in Brief, 1969–70* (1970). Even though the relative importance of defense expenditures declined in subsequent years, it was substantially higher than it was in 1964/65; it averaged about 40% of nondevelopment expenditure and 3.5% of GNP during the rest of this period.

would be redistribution of income from the importers to the exporters, and also to the government if devaluation increased the total import bill. Thus, depending on the savings behavior of the three groups, domestic savings are expected to change. So although the first factor is expected to increase domestic savings the net effect is not clear.

To study the relationship between domestic savings and liberalization efforts the following regression equation was estimated on the time series for 1949-68:

$$S = a_0 + a_1Y + a_2D,$$

where S is the domestic savings (in billion rupees), Y is the gross national product, and D is a dummy variable that has a value of 1 for trade liberalizing years and 0 otherwise. The following result was obtained:

$$S = -2.889 + 0.150\,Y + 0.812\,D \quad R^2 = 0.94.$$
$$(0.009) \qquad (0.235)$$

The figures in parentheses are standard errors of estimate. The coefficient of D is positive, indicating that liberalization was associated with higher domestic saving, and the value of the coefficient was statistically significant. Thus, in Pakistan's case liberalization of controls seems to have stimulated domestic change.

Trade liberalization years were also the years when associated measures were taken to stimulate public savings through reduced expenditures. This was also the period when agricultural development was accelerated and special measures were taken to stimulate rural savings and investment.

INCOME DISTRIBUTION AND CONCENTRATION OF CONTROL

The foreign trade regimes of Pakistan with their accompanying policies have also had their effect on the size distribution of income. As has been demonstrated in earlier chapters the exchange control regime led to misallocation of resources within sectors and, in conjunction with direct controls, effected intersectoral resource transfers. This aggravated inequalities among sectors and accentuated the unequal income distribution within rural and urban areas. It will be shown that the burden of redistribution of income from agriculture to industry was borne by the poorer sectors of rural areas. At the same time, the benefits of such transfers did not go to the industrial workers of the urban sector. Within agriculture and industry, the trade regime militated against employment and small-scale activity in favor of capital, rather than labor, therefore enhancing existing inequalities in the distribution of income.

The static picture of the nature of income distribution in 1963/64 in rural and urban areas is shown in table 12.11. One can note that there was a considerable disparity of income between rural and urban sectors. Urban income was about 38

Table 12.11.   Pattern of Income Distribution in Rural and Urban Areas of Pakistan, 1963/64

Monthly income group (Rs)	Rural households		Urban households	
	Percentage of households	Percentage of income	Percentage of households	Percentage of income
Less than 50	5.6	1.3	2.0	0.3
50–99	26.2	12.1	14.7	5.0
100–149	26.3	19.5	24.1	12.9
150–199	17.0	17.8	18.8	14.0
200–249	9.5	12.7	12.1	11.6
250–299	6.1	10.0	7.3	8.6
300–399	4.5	9.3	8.7	12.8
400–499	2.2	6.0	4.5	8.6
500 and above	2.6	11.3	7.8	26.2
All groups		167		230

Source: Computed from T. M. Khan, "Some Reflections on Planning Experience in Pakistan," *Pakistan Development Review* 8, no. 3 (1968), tables I, II, pp. 395–96.

percent higher than rural income. The inequality in the distribution of income, although not very acute compared with the level for many other developing countries, was very high, especially in the urban sector. The bottom 40 percent of urban households had a share of only 18 percent of the total income, whereas the top 12 percent enjoyed about 35 percent of the total income. In the rural sector about the same proportion of income (36%) at the upper end was shared by a larger proportion of households (15%), indicating a lower degree of inequality in the distribution of rural income.

Direct information on changes in income distribution is hard to get. For want of data the analysis on changes of income distribution must rely on indirect information such as trends in employment, output, and wages. An attempt is made below.

Trend in Rural Income Distribution

Available indirect evidence shows that there had been a deterioration in the inequality in income distribution in both East and West Pakistan. In East Pakistan the inequality in the distribution of land, which is a major determinant of the pattern of income distribution in rural areas, worsened during this period. Landless laborers as a percentage of total cultivators rose from 14.3 percent in 1951 to 17.6 percent in 1961 and further to 19.8 percent in 1967/68.[44] Average income and employment for the lower income brackets might have fallen because of the

44. A. R. Khan, *Poverty and Inequality in Rural Bangladesh*, International Labor Organization, Working Paper (Geneva, 1976).

adverse effect of trade policy on jute cultivation. In East Pakistan the jute grow-ers, who constituted the poorer rural households, suffered a drop in income from low prices owing to price discrimination at home and a slump in markets abroad. Further lower production of jute because of poor returns and the consequent substitution of rice made for decreased employment, as labor input per acre in jute was about 92 percent higher than in the growing of traditional variety of rice.[45] Although jute acreage as a proportion of total cropped acreage in the region was small, it was nearly one-quarter of the total in the mid-monsoon season. Consequently the effect on employment and wages in that season could be substantial.

There was no consistent improvement in East Pakistan in the real wages of agricultural workers. For most of the period real wages were below the 1949 level. Only in the early 1960s did it show some improvement, but it declined again in later years (see table 12.12). The combined effect of stagnant wages, a deteriorating employment situation, and a high growth of population was that the number of people below the poverty line was increasing throughout the period. The absolutely poor population was 40 percent in 1963/64 but increased to 76 percent in 1968/69.[46] The same trend was found in the 1950s also.[47] The position of the higher income brackets must have improved, especially in the 1960s, as agricultural income at constant prices increased by 37 percent during the decade as against a population increase of 34 percent.[48]

The exchange control regime had a significant impact on the pattern of agricul-tural growth in West Pakistan. This was particularly evident in the spread of mechanization and tube wells. The credit policy of the government strongly reinforced this effect. The acceleration of agricultural growth in the 1960s was primarily the result of investment in private tube wells and fertilizers, the use of which increased sixteen times and thirteen times, respectively, between 1959/60 and 1968/69.[49] This increased the growth rate of crop output by 5 percent per annum. The investment in tube wells could be largely ascribed to the import policy of the time. However, despite the low import price of tube wells, their access was limited to the larger farmers. Seventy percent of the tube wells were installed by farmers owning more than 25 acres and only 4 percent by the size group owning from 0 to 13 acres.[50] Most of the income resulting from better

45. Government of Pakistan, National Planning Board, *The First Five Year Plan (1955-60)*.

46. Khan, "Poverty and Inequality."

47. S. R. Bose, "Trend of Real Income of the Rural Poor in East Pakistan, 1949-66," *Pakistan Development Review* 8, no. 3 (Autumn 1968): 452-88.

48. Government of East Pakistan, *Economic Survey of East Pakistan, 1970* (Dacca, East Paki-stan, 1970), appendix table I.

49. J. J. Stern and W. P. Falcon, *Growth and Development in Pakistan, 1955-69*, Harvard University Center for International Affairs, Occasional Paper no. 23 (Apr. 1970), p. 46.

50. S. M. Naseem, "Rural Poverty and Landlessness in Pakistan," in K. Griffin and A. R. Khan, eds., *Poverty and Landlessness in Rural Asia* (Geneva: ILO, 1977), p. 224.

Table 12.12.   Index of Real Wage Rates in
Agriculture (East Pakistan)

	Index[a]		Index
1949	100.0	1960	87.3
1950	90.3	1961	96.2
1951	84.7	1962	93.6
1952	83.5	1963	100.0
1953	72.5	1964	112.7
1954	n.a.	1965	94.1
1955	81.4	1966	80.5
1956	n.a.	1967	81.4
1957	84.3	1968	86.4
1958	81.8	1969	94.1
1959	82.2	1970	95.0

Source: A. R. Khan, ''Poverty and Inequality
in Rural Bangladesh,'' International Labor Organization, Working Paper (Geneva, 1976).
[a] 1949 = 100.

irrigation and increased fertilizer use therefore accrued to the higher income groups. The distributional impact stemmed partly from existing resource distributions and partly from biased access to credit and foreign exchange at less than its opportunity cost.

The most detrimental aspect was the process of mechanization. The lower income groups were affected most adversely by it in terms of unemployment, landlessness, and tenancy. The incentive for mechanization originated from the exchange control system, which allowed imports of agricultural machinery at less than its scarcity price.[51] Its average cost was much below world prices.[52] This situation was further aggravated by low interest on borrowed capital.[53] The consequent distortion in relative prices led to the substitution of machinery for labor. While the net effects of the seed–fertilizer–tube well revolution may have been favorable to employment and only moderately unfavorable to income distribution, tractor mechanization affected the poorer sections of the rural population, especially tenants, very adversely. If mechanization was used mainly to reclaim uncultivable land, it would be land augmenting. However, in the form used, tractor mechanization in Pakistan was applied mostly to already cultivable land. The primary function of tractor mechanization was thus to replace animal or manpower by machine power in the cultivation of land. The principal argument in favor of tractor mechanization in Pakistan was that it would bring higher yields

51. For details see chap. 10.

52. In the case of tractors, e.g., it was priced at 25–70% lower than in the United States.

53. Interest rate charges was around 6.5% per annum while the shadow price of capital varied between 10 and 15%.

per acre, but the evidence was not conclusive.[54] In Pakistan there was evidence that mechanization led to the growth or increase in the size of farms of those farmers who used tractors. A survey of farmers who received loans to purchase tractors showed that there was a 142 percent increase in the average size of such farms, from 45 to 109 acres.[55] Only 10 percent of the farms did not add to their acreage.

Estimates of the employment-displacing effects of tractor mechanization in Pakistan have differed widely. It was reported that "interviewing farmers in the Punjab who had mechanised, we received a remarkably consistent response that the labour force per acre had been reduced by 50% over the mechanisation period."[56]

Although the amount of labor used per farm increased for every size group, when one allowed for the growth in farm size the labor use per cultivated acre decreased by about 40 percent. Total paid labor input (including both permanent and casual labor) per cropped acre declined by 23 percent. In addition, unpaid family labor input per cropped acre fell by about 47 percent.[57]

Some corroboration or refutation of these likely trends could be obtained by looking at changes in rural wages. As regards wages, no reliable time series was available in respect to the trend in real wages in rural West Pakistan. All that was obtainable was the periodic wages surveys in one part of West Pakistan, i.e., the Punjab, that contained monthly wage rates in Punjab in December 1960, December 1966, and June 1973.[58] The growth rates were found to have increased by 2.1 percent over the period. However, as in other countries, there were quite sharp short-term fluctuations in rural wage rates. Thus the estimate for December 1960 was probably biased downward because the 1960/61 fiscal year witnessed a 5 percent decline in per capita food output. On the other hand the 1966 figure was possibly biased upward because during 1966/67 a sharp recovery in output and income was achieved compared with the preceding year of drought and crop failures. Khan and Bose estimated that money wages for unskilled workers in rural Punjab increased from Rs 2.00 per day in 1960 to Rs 2.50 per day in 1967.[59] Because the cost of living for such workers increased by at least 25 percent over the same period there was at best no increase in rural wages. In 1971 approximately

54. B. Ahmed, "Field Survey of Large Farmers in Pakistan Punjab," Harvard University, Center for International Affairs, Working Paper no. 7, Project on Rural Development of Pakistan (June 1972).

55. IBRD, "The Consequences of Farm Tractors in Pakistan" (Washington, D.C., Feb. 1975).

56. S. R. Bose and E. H. Clark II, "Some Basic Considerations of Agricultural Mechanisation in West Pakistan," *Pakistan Development Review* 9, no. 3 (Autumn 1969): 273-308.

57. IBRD, "The Consequences of Farm Tractors."

58. This figure was most likely overestimated.

59. T. M. Khan and S. R. Bose, "Report on Income of Agricultural Workers in Pakistan," unpublished report submitted to the ILO, Karachi, 1968.

one-fifth of the money wage rates reported for various types of work were higher in real terms than those paid five years earlier.[60] Of those that reported an increase, the change in money terms was only a little higher than that in the cost of living.

Thus the evidence for Punjab (the most prosperous province) does not provide a firm basis from which to conclude that real wages increased significantly during the period under consideration, at least at a rate at which the per capita agricultural income was increasing. All this suggests that income inequality in rural sectors worsened in West Pakistan also during this period.

Trend in Urban Income Distribution

Although large transfers of resources from agriculture to industry occurred, the workers in the factories experienced no rise in their level of living. The differential exchange rates and the investment licensing system consistently discriminated against small scale in favor of large, despite the former's lower capital intensity.[61] Further, it has been shown how the trade regime within the large-scale manufacturing sector directed the choice of technique toward greater capital intensity. This implied a lower level of employment than would exist in the case of a lower capital intensity.[62] What is clear, therefore, is that the effect of industrial growth on employment was limited. The manpower surveys of the government of Pakistan reported that employment in manufacturing increased from 1.9 million in 1955 to 2.5 million in 1965 and that the share of the manufacturing sector in total employment in fact declined from 15 to 14.3 percent during the period.[63]

The real wages of industrial workers stagnated between 1954 and 1962/63 in both East and West Pakistan and then started rising. But the increase was confined mainly to West Pakistan, as can be seen from table 12.13.

The failure of industrial wages to advance was partly a result of the constancy of rural real wages, which encouraged labor push from the rural to the urban

60. J. Eckert, *Rural Labour in Punjab: A Survey Report,* Planning and Development Department, Government of Punjab (Lahore, July 1972); see also Stephen Guisinger and Mohammad Irfan, "Real Wages of Industrial Workers in Pakistan: 1954–1970," *Pakistan Development Review* 13, no. 4 (Winter 1974): 363–80.

61. Seven times higher capital intensity in large scale over small is associated with only 2½ times higher labor productivity. Thus the capital/output ratio in large scale is three times as high as in small scale. See A. R. Khan, *The Economy of Bangladesh* (London: MacMillan, 1972), p. 60. It has been estimated that only one-quarter of the value added in manufacturing accrued to labor; the rest went to capital. In fact there was a decline in the labor share.

62. Value added in large-scale manufacturing grew in real terms by 72% in 1959/60 to 1967/68 while employment grew by only 41%. (L. J. White, *Industrial Concentration and Economic Power in Pakistan* [Princeton: Princeton University Press, 1974]).

63. I. Hussain, "Employment Aspects of Industrial Growth in West Pakistan," *Pakistan Development Review* 13, no. 2 (Summer 1974): table I, p. 212.

Table 12.13.   Trend of Real Wages in Industry

	East Pakistan	*West Pakistan*
1954	100	100
1955	88.4	94.3
1957	91.4	94.2
1958	93.6	97.5
1954/60	92.8	97.3
1962/63	91.6	90.4
1963/64	n.a.[a]	102.4
1964/65	n.a.	110.9
1965/66	95.2	117.2
1966/67	n.a.	111.4
1967/68	n.a.	104.3
1969/70	99.3	126.3

Sources: East Pakistan: A. R. Khan, ''What Has Been Happening to Real Wages in Pakistan,'' *Pakistan Development Review* 7, no. 3 (Autumn 1967); 317–47 (for date up to 1963/64). West Pakistan: Guisinger and M. I. Irfan, ''Real Wages of Industrial Workers in Pakistan'': 1954–1970, *Pakistan Development Review* 13, no. 4 (Winter 1974): 363–88. (The index has been adjusted from base 1959/60 to 1954.)

Note: Real wages in the second study will be higher because it includes noncash benefits, which rose from 1.5% of wages in 1959/60 to 3% in the later period.

[a] Not applicable.

sector, and partly an inadequate upturn in employment compared to the increase in the labor force. The latter was attributable to the high capital intensity of large-scale manufacturing and the slow growth of the small-scale manufacturing sector.

All these factors led to a fall in the share of wages in the industrial value added, which can be noted from table 12.14. For all manufacturing industries in West Pakistan, where the large-scale industries were mainly located, the wage share in value added fell from 35 percent in 1959/60 to 21 percent in 1969/70, and this trend was shared by most of the industries. The decline was especially acute for the manufacture of textiles, which was a major employer of labor in the industrial sector. This implies that the share of profits increased, which must have accentuated the distribution of urban income during the period. Thus, although there occurred a resource transfer from agriculture to industry and a high growth rate of manufacturing, most of the increase in urban incomes went to industrialists and traders, the upper income groups of the urban sector.

Concentration of Controls

Not only were profits high and increasing throughout the period but also they were enjoyed by a few privileged groups. Various barriers to entry resulting from

Table 12.14.   Share of Wages in Value Added in the Manufacturing Sector of West Pakistan

Industrial groups	1959/60	1963/64	1967/68	1969/70
Food manufacturing	31	16	14	13
Beverage industries	20	13	8	14
Tobacco manufactures	13	10	7	7
Manufacture of textiles	41	32	25	26
Manufacture of footwear	35	37	32	29
Manufacture of wood and cork	—	—	—	—
Furniture and fixtures	48	48	46	68
Paper and paper products	22	17	34	30
Printing and publishing	67	38	32	35
Leather and leather products	37	16	18	11
Manufacture of rubber products	34	28	16	16
Chemical and chemical products	25	15	17	19
Products of petroleum and coal	—	—	—	—
Nonmetallic metal products	20	23	13	19
Basic metal industries	35	31	22	29
Manufacture of metal products	51	46	37	44
Machinery except electrical	39	41	37	42
Electrical machinery	41	31	23	30
Transport equipment	63	30	31	68
All industries	35	25	19	21

Source: Government of Pakistan, *Census of Manufacturing Industries,* 1959/60, 1963/64, 1967/68, 1969/70.

the exchange control system and investment licensing protected the existing industrialists from new entrants to domestic production. This inevitably led to very high degrees of concentration in the control of industry and in income.

Many estimates of overall concentration had previously been made. In the early 1960s, 75 units, or 2.1 percent of the total number of manufacturing units, produced 43.8 percent of all the value added in the large-scale manufacturing sector. Moreover, these 75 units themselves were owned directly or indirectly by a much smaller nucleus of families. A study in 1967 found that, although there were more than 3,000 individual firms in Pakistan in 1959, only 7 individuals, families, or foreign corporations controlled one-quarter of all private industrial assets and one-fifth of all industrial assets. Approximately 15 families owned about three-quarters of all the shares in banks and insurance companies.[64] Another study on the concentration of assets revealed that 43 important families and groups controlled 98 listed nonfinancial companies with total assets of Rs 5.1657 billion. This amounted to 53.1 percent of the total assets of nonfinancial firms listed on the stock exchange. The four largest families controlled one-fifth of the total assets of nonfinancial companies, the 10 largest families controlled

64. Papanek, *Development Policy Theory and Practice,* p. 67.

over one-third of the total assets, and the 30 largest controlled over half. Of the private Pakistani-controlled firms, for example, the four leading families controlled over one-quarter of the assets, the 10 leading families controlled just under half the assets, and all 43 families and groups controlled just under three-quarters of the assets.

For a check on total assets as a measure of control, Papanek also computed the percentages of net worth, fixed assets after depreciation, and sales, which was accounted for by the 43 families and groups. The conclusions were generally comparable. There was no significant change in the degree of concentration over time.[65] An international comparison revealed that the overall concentration in manufacturing was greater in Pakistan than in India, the United States, and Germany and was about the same as in Chile and Japan.

The dominant position of the leading industrial families and groups was related to their control over both investment and the import licensing system. This was true because a family or group could become a big manufacturer only by using imported capital equipment, and it could obtain the imported capital equipment only by getting an investment sanction. As a family or group expanded, it became a more likely recipient of future licenses and the system protected those who were lucky enough to get within it first. The established industrialists had an advantage because once they got licensing and permission to invest, they would get financing from the government financing institution for imports of capital goods at the official exchange rate. By contrast, a firm that could not get a sanction for investment under the system of industrial licensing had to buy its capital equipment secondhand or at a substantial markup (reflecting the scarcity premium of foreign exchange) from a commercial importer. It did not get automatic financing. Because its capacity was not sanctioned, the firm would have a great deal more difficulty receiving an import entitlement. In the absence of an entitlement it had to buy its imported raw materials and spare parts from commercial importers, again paying the scarcity value of foreign exchange.

The relationship between the dominant industrial families and groups and the import licensing system is indicated by the fact that there was a strong and significant relationship between family importance, as measured by assets of the 43 leading families in 1968, and the receipt of foreign exchange licenses for capital goods in the 1960–65 period. These families received 51 percent of the total investments sanctioned during the period 1960–65 and 64 percent of the finances provided by the largest industrial financing institutions for the implementation of investment licensing. One could argue that the pattern of capital

65. The holdings of the 43 industrial families were not equally split between the two wings of Pakistan. Rather, 72.4% of the families' holdings were in West Pakistan and only 27.6% were in East Pakistan. They also controlled a large percentage of the total manufacturing assets in the west wing (48.3%) compared to only 31.2% of the total in the east.

goods imports, even in the absence of licensing, would be related to the relative profitability of firms. Because the efficient and thus more profitable firms would find it worthwhile to expand their operations, the relationship is not a conclusive effect of the trade regime. However, the pattern of capital goods licenses was also related to the importance of a family at the beginning of the licensing period (1961), when the system of industrial investment licensing in its comprehensive form was introduced.

There is one further piece of evidence that could be adduced to support the argument that the wealth and prestige of the large industrial families were influential in their receipt of capital goods import licenses. PICIC was the agency responsible for sanctioning large-scale industrial projects. Between its inception in 1957 and the end of 1968 it sanctioned Rs 1.657 billion in loans and guarantees for industrial projects. During the Second Plan (1960–65) it sanctioned one-third of the private investment projects. The composition of the 21-man board of directors of this agency was revealing. Five of the directors were non-Pakistanis, representing the donor countries and institutions that provided the foreign funds, loans, and credits from abroad, which were to be relent to the domestic investors by the agency. Three were representativesof the Central, West, and East Pakistan governments. The remaining thirteen members were private individuals in Pakistan of whom seven were members of the leading industrial families: Adamjee, Bashir, Dawood, Fancy, Jalil, Rangoonwala, and Valika. These seven families received 21 percent of the investment sanctions distributed by this financing agency during 1960–65.

The exchange control system contributed to the concentration of economic and industrial power in a few hands. The latter in turn influenced the operation of the exchange control system in such a way as to derive maximum benefits from it. The initial recipients of licenses earned high profits because of the high scarcity premium on imports. It was they who subsequently became the new generation of industrialists and secured investment licenses for the establishment of industrial enterprises. The possession of import licenses gave them access to short- and medium-term credit because an import license in effect served as collateral and enhanced their credit worthiness. An investment license, at the same time, was usually combined with long-term borrowing from the investment financing institutions. In a process of cumulative causation, wealth begot wealth through the operation of the licensing system. The traders who turned into industrialists eventually owned and operated financing and banking institutions.

The prevailing structure of controls discouraged a wide diffusion of industrial investment opportunities because access to credit and licenses was restricted to a few. The inefficiencies of a monopolistic economic system were superimposed on the inefficiencies of the exchange control system. Accordingly, together they inhibited the diffusion of wealth and income and contributed to the inequality of income in Pakistan.

The integration of financial and industrial enterprises prevented the growth of capital markets, where small savers would invest and small entrepreneurs could borrow on competitive terms. The rapid development of small-scale industries, with a limited capital base, was one of the principal ways to provide expanding employment opportunities to a growing middle class. The big industrial houses owned and managed large-scale, capital intensive enterprises, with limited effect on the expansion of employment.

The concentration of ownership and control of the industrial and commercial assets inhibited industrial progress in yet another way. Industries were frequently organized as family concerns and noncorporate enterprises that relied upon a managerial cadre drawn from friends and relatives, unlike the corporate enterprises, which depended more upon professional management. The span of control and management that could be exercised by family concerns limited the number and variety of enterprises in which their savings could be invested. The surplus funds in excess of what could thus be managed within this institutional constraint either were spent mostly on extravagant consumption or were transferred abroad. The dominant role of a few big family houses in private investment thus acted as a constraint on the growth of investment.

The concentration of ownership and control of wealth had its consequences for the political system of Pakistan. The authoritarian government that ruled Pakistan from 1958 to 1970 was built upon an alliance between the big trading-cum-industrial families on the one hand and the military establishment on the other. They shared political power with the big landlords, who supplied a large proportion of the members of the upper echelons of the army and of the bureaucracy. This phenomenon was an obstacle in the way of democratization of the political system and institutions in Pakistan. There was no wide sharing of political power, which in turn would have generated pressure for a diffusion of economic power and opportunities as well. A more vigorous democratization of the political system would have led to a demand for the breakup of the industrial families. By the end of the 1960s the glaring disparities in living standards and in economic power were beginning to cause discontent and disaffection, especially among the urban middle and working classes.

13

Regional Development and Economic Policy

Most of the discussion up to this point is related to data for the entire United Pakistan. Yet until 1971 Pakistan consisted of two separate and distinct parts. Between the two regions lay a thousand miles of alien territory. The only effective communication link between the two regions consisted of 1,100 miles by air or 3,000 miles by sea. Both the air and sea fares were way out of the reach of the majority of Pakistanis.[1] This permitted little mobility of labor between the two regions. Mobility of capital was also limited. The two wings had different price structures, industrial structures, and patterns of trade as well as distinctive agricultural bases and cultural milieu.

At independence in 1947 Pakistan had roughly 77.5 million people, more than half[2] of whom lived in East Pakistan. Per capita income in West Pakistan was 17 percent higher than in the East in 1949/50. In 1949/50 nonagricultural output in the East was 34.8 percent of GNP compared to 45.5 percent in the West; nonagricultural employment was 15.3 and 34.7 percent, respectively, of total employment in each wing. The infrastructural facilities such as transport, communications, water, and power were relatively less developed in East Pakistan.[3] West Pakistan in the early 1950s had 47,000 miles of roads, while East Pakistan had about 22,000 miles. Similarly, East Pakistan had a smaller share of urban facilities, including the availability of power. These differences were further accentuated over the two decades of growth primarily because of differential shares of public and private investment resources and foreign exchange allocations.

1. A single round-trip air fare cost about Rs 500, which was approximately the same as the average annual per capita urban income. The interwing transportation by ship for one round-trip journey cost about 40% of the average per capita urban income but then it took 10 days or more.

2. Proportion was 54% of total population.

3. M. Akhlaquir Rahman, *The Private Sector of East Pakistan: An Analysis of Lagged Development* (Karachi: United Bank Ltd., 1970), pp. 26–28.

The acceleration of economic growth in West Pakistan at a rate higher than in the East was associated with a structural change. Annual per capita income in the West rose throughout the 1950s, albeit slowly, and then accelerated in the 1960s. The GNP of West Pakistan increased at a rate of 3.2 percent between 1949/50 and 1954/55 and 3.18 percent between 1955/56 and 1959/60. In the 1960s this rate rose to an average of 6.2 percent.[4] The annual per capita GNP compound growth rates per year were 1.1 percent in the 1950s and 2.7 in the 1960s. The relative share of the nonagricultural sectors in West Pakistan increased from 46 percent of the regional product in 1959/50 to 53 percent in 1959/60, 58 percent in 1964/65, and 60 percent in 1969/70.[5] Manufacturing expanded uniformly, its rate of growth being highest in the first half of the 1960s. The structure within industries underwent significant changes. The importance of agriculturally based industries in the West declined from 61 percent in 1954 to 59 percent in 1960 and 56 percent in 1965 of total manufacturing value added. This was accompanied by a rise in the relative importance of intermediate products and equipment industries: from 21 percent in 1954 to about 31 percent in 1965. Not only did this group grow fast, it also had considerable diversification of output. In 1965 the engineering industries' output was quite diversified, varying from basic metals, metal products, and machinery to electrical equipment and transport equipment, with each subsector producing between 2 and 3 percent of the total manufacturing value added.

On the other hand East Pakistan had a uniformly slower growth than the West. Its GNP grew at a rate of 2.38 percent in the first half of the 1950s and 1.78 percent in the second half. In the 1960s GNP averaged 4.2 percent. Per capita income declined throughout the first decade; by 0.18 percent in the first half and by 0.58 percent in the second. The structural changes were also slow. The nonagricultural sector contributed only 45 percent to GNP by 1969/70, compared to 35 percent in 1949–52. The growth rate of manufacturing was very rapid initially (largely owing to the small initial base) but then tapered off. However, within manufacturing the structural changes were in the direction of agriculturally based industries, which increased their share of value added from 56 percent in 1954 to 73 percent in 1965/66.

Intermediate products manufacture increased slightly from 6 to 10 percent in the same period. Engineering industries contributed a mere 6 percent with concentration on metal products and transport equipment yielding 4.5 percent. On

4. Per capita gross regional product is calculated in constant prices of 1959/60 factor cost. See T. M. Khan and A. Bergan, "Measurement of Structural Change in the Pakistan Economy: A Review of National Income Estimates, 1949–50 to 1963–64," *Pakistan Development Review* 6, no. 2 (Summer 1966): 163–208, and Planning Commission *Report of the Panel of Economists for the Fourth Five Year Plan* (Islamabad, 1970).

5. Ibid.

the whole East Pakistan's pattern and rate of growth were different from and slower than West Pakistan's.

The consequence of these two decades of differential growth in the two wings was an increase in regional disparity. Per capita income in West Pakistan, which was only 17 percent higher than in the East, was 22 percent higher in 1954/55, 32 percent in 1959/60, 45 percent in 1964/65, and 61 percent in 1969/70.[6] Given the lower purchasing power of a rupee in the East vis-à-vis the West as well as evidence of relative overstatement of various components of the East's GNP in the national income estimates, these rates of disparity were underestimates of the real differential between the two wings. To some extent this was perhaps indicated by other indices of relative welfare such as per capita consumption of essentials as well as health, education, and housing facilities.

The implicit model underlying the strategy of regional development was to concentrate investment in West Pakistan, which was better endowed with physical and social infrastructure. It was hoped that returns would be higher and income would grow faster, so that at a later stage as total annual income grew to an adequate size, the growth effects, in terms of income and employment, would trickle down to East Pakistan.[7] On the basis of this strategy West Pakistan was allocated a disproportionately higher share in total development expenditure. In per capita terms this disparity was greater. Centralizing the allocation of crucial foreign exchange in Karachi gave the West's initial edge a further boost. Thus total investments in the West in absolute and per capita terms were substantially higher. In addition, there was a transfer of resources from the poorer East to the richer West via East Pakistan's net export surplus with the rest of the world, and via unfavorable terms of trade. The trade and exchange control policies were the prerogative of the central government of Pakistan.

The problem with the above strategy was the nonexistence of spillover effects on the East from development in the West. The reason lay in the physical separation of the two wings by a thousand miles of foreign territory. Mobility of labor from the overpopulated East to the land abundant West was virtually absent. This distinguished the East-West Pakistan economic disparity from other regional disparities.

Exchange Control System and Regional Development

The exchange control system played a crucial role in determining the pattern and magnititude of growth in the two wings of United Pakistan. The trade regime

---

6. Ibid.
7. M. Haq, *The Strategy of Economic Planning–A Case Study of Pakistan* (Karachi: Oxford University Press, 1963).

consisted of the centralization of foreign exchange earnings of both regions and its allocation, as well as the tariff and quantitative restrictions on imports. Discrepancies in interregional allocation of imports determined the disparity in industrial growth between East and West. Because most of the industrialization was pursued under the protective umbrella of quantitative restrictions (QRs) and tariffs, the differential industrial base of regions determined the volume and composition of interregional trade in manufactured goods. The centralization of earnings and allocations and the resulting discrepancy between the East's export earnings and import allocations led to a transfer of resources from East to West.

Disparity in Foreign Exchange Allocations

There was a remarkable degree of stability in the proportion of foreign exchange resources allocated between the two regions. Throughout the two decades about one-third of the total imports of Pakistan went to the East as a result of the way import licensing along with private and public investment policies were administered. The same proportion was maintained with regard to all the different groups of imports. In the case of public imports the eastern wing was similarly discriminated. The initial advantage accruing to a region from this licensing system could be perpetuated because subsequent allocations were based on earlier performance and the results of utilization of earlier licenses, thus leading to the establishment of industries. The centralized investment licensing authority determined the flow of private investment between regions. Because a domestic capital goods industry was virtually absent, investment licenses were a binding constraint on private investment. In the first five years of Pakistan's existence more than two-thirds (i.e., 70%) of capital imports went to West Pakistan. This share in total capital imports was maintained for the two decades. Because industrial licensing allocations were linked to the quantum of installed capacity, this preponderant share in investment imports preempted future imports of raw materials and spare parts. Regional bias in allocation was also built into the system of commercial licensing. The principle devised in 1952/53 that categories would be fixed for commercial importers on the basis of their actual imports in the 1950–52 period favored the West Pakistani importers.

The argument had often been presented that the lower share of imports for East Pakistan was not a result of lower allocation but of poor demand. This, however, could not be supported by facts. Although East Pakistan did have a weaker industrial base and fewer entrepreneurs than the West, evidence indicates that private investment would have been higher than it was, if foreign exchange allocations were high. An analysis of the applications for private investment screened by the East Pakistan industries department in 1960/61 revealed a large unsatisfied demand for industrial investment in East Pakistan. Eighty-five percent of the total applications were rejected (530 out of 621 applicants) for want of foreign exchange resources although 40 percent of those rejected were considered financially and technically sound. Even for the sanctioned projects, of which there were 29, the required amount of foreign exchange could not be provided, thus slowing down their implementation.[8] Furthermore, a guaranteed allocation of a larger share of foreign exchange to East Pakistan would have persuaded prospective investors from the West to move to East Pakistan; this would have been particularly effective in those industries where the locational advantages of West Pakistan from the point of view of relative costs were not significant, and where the alternative to a private investor not investing in East Pakistan was to forgo opportunities of investment altogether.

The importance of the disparity in the relative share of different categories of imports between East and West Pakistan can also be highlighted in terms of the ratio of imports to gross regional product in different years (see table 13.1).

Not only did West Pakistan have a higher ratio of intermediate and capital goods to regional product because of its greater degree of industrialization and modernization of agriculture,[9] but also its dependence on imported consumer goods was also greater (table 13.2). A greater availability of imported consumer goods as well as more domestic production of consumer goods vis-à-vis regional output and expenditure resulted in a higher level of consumption in West Pakistan.

REGIONAL DISPARITY IN INVESTMENT

Private Investment

The faster growth of private enterprise in West Pakistan was partly due to the stimulating effects of large and growing public investment in creating external economies and infrastructure. Even as late as 1969/70 disparities between East and West Pakistan in certain crucial prerequisites for private investment, especially in the field of industry, have been shown to be wide.[10]

A number of factors were responsible for a higher growth rate of private investment in West Pakistan. The bulk of commercial and industrial entrepreneurs in Pakistan were immigrant Muslim traders from India, the majority of whom moved to West Pakistan. This was partly because of their cultural and linguistic affinity with the West but was also due to the choice of the capital city.

8. Government of East Pakistan, Department of Planning and Development, *Financial Resources and Development Potential of East Pakistan* (Dacca, 1962), pp. 160–70.

9. The East's share of different categories of imports is seen in table 13.2.

10. Government of Pakistan, Planning Commission, "Bench Marks for the Fourth Five Year Plan," unpublished mimeographed paper (May 1970).

Table 13.1. Ratio of Imports to Gross Regional Product (In percent)

Period	Consumer goods		Intermediate goods		Capital goods		Total	
	East	West	East	West	East	West	East	West
1959/60– 1961/62	1.3	3.4	1.9	3.5	2.1	5.1	5.5	1.2
1962/63– 1964/65	1.7	3.3	2.1	3.8	3.0	7.3	6.8	14.4
1965/66– 1968/69	1.2	1.9	1.0	2.4	2.8	5.1	5.1	9.4

Source: Appendix tables in Nurul Islam, *Imports of Pakistan: Growth and Structure: A Statistical Study,* Pakistan Institute of Development Economics, Statistical Papers no. 3 (Sept. 1967), pp. 1–17.

Because the government exercised control over trade and investment through its commercial and investment licensing policy, nearness to the seat of government was crucial for business enterprises.[11] The immigration of traders and industrialists to West Pakistan, combined with the location of the government, conferred substantial initial advantages upon West Pakistan.

The basis for the distribution of import licences, as already explained, was the volume of business of the established importers during the period of the relatively free imports in 1950–52. The established importers in control of most of the import trade of the country were located in West Pakistan, largely owing to the concentration in Karachi of Muslim entrepreneurs and traders from prepartitioned India. The concentration of importers in Karachi also implied that they organized and undertook import for the rest of the country, including East Pakistan, through their agents or branch offices in the East. Therefore, in the early years the import trade in East Pakistan was also under the control of the importers, who were mainly based in West Pakistan. To the extent that they could reexport foreign merchandise to East Pakistan, the importers in Karachi served the market for imported goods there as well. Later on, when the reexport of imports from one region to another region was restricted, their branch offices carried on most of the import trade in East Pakistan. In the case of commodities that were imported in large quantities and for which participation in import trade required command over or access to substantial financial resources, West Pakistani traders were the only entrants.

11. Papanek points out, in his survey of the factors affecting industrial location, proximity to the seat of government as the most important. High profit or ruin hinges on government decision on a firm's application for land or power, for permission to import machinery or float securities, for licenses to import raw materials and spare parts, for protection from import competition and exemption from taxes. At least until the 1960s (time of the survey), industrialists' ability to deal with the government was more important for their success than any other management function.

Table 13.2.   Percentage of East Pakistan's Share in Imports

	Consumer goods	Intermediate goods	Capital goods
1951/52–54/55	20	42	30
1955/58–59/60	27	34	28
1960/61–64/65	31	37	26
1965/66–68/69	35	31	31

Source: See table 13.1.

The profits earned in the import trade provided the majority of the resources for industrial investment. The capital accumulated in preindependence days was a minor, insignificant source of industrial investment. The profits from trading activity in the 1950s provided the bulk of the original investment in industry. Thus a process of cumulative causation in West Pakistan contributed to capital accumulation. This process was further aided by the fact that all commercial banks and government-sponsored financing institutions were located in West Pakistan. The proximity and personal contact with the financing institutions gave them an additional edge over East Pakistanis, who were already handicapped by meager personal capital. Most often the the East Pakistani entrepreneurs, few as they were, could not maintain the debt/equity ratio that was required as a necessary condition for financing by government institutions. Therefore, these entrepreneurs were deprived of the opportunities for very high rates of profit created by the exchange control system. Most of the banks were owned by West Pakistan-based industrial entrepreneurs. Thus they had easier access to financial facilities.

The financial problems and difficulties of the emerging new, private investors in East Pakistan were partly those of the new small entrepreneurs in an underdeveloped region attempting to compete with the large, established entrepreneurs, who often had control of financing institutions. Also, the industrialists based in West Pakistan were naturally less eager to invest in the East, except in industries based mainly on local raw materials. Since these were also the industries that were relatively simple and in which profitability was high, the local entrepreneurs of the East were preempted.

The fiscal concessions to stimulate private enterprise in East Pakistan that were given in small doses in the late 1960s were not strong enough either to stimulate domestic enterprise in the East or to attract enterprise from West Pakistan. The principal measure was the longer tax holidays for new industries in the underdeveloped regions in the East and the West. New industries were in general eligible for longer tax holidays than established industries in East and West Pakistan.[12] What was necessary was to attract private investment from West to East Pakistan

12. Only underdeveloped areas in the East were favored vis-à-vis under developed areas in the West. East Pakistan as a whole was not considered relatively more underdeveloped than West Pakistan.

to compensate for the East's lagging investment. This would mean that even the developed areas of East Pakistan had to have preferential treatment over underdeveloped areas in West Pakistan. In view of the differential advantages enjoyed by West Pakistan in terms of financial institutions and government patronage, fiscal measures failed to offset those advantages and thus to attract investment to East Pakistan.[13]

The second complicating factor acting as an obstacle in the way of growth of private enterprise in East Pakistan was the problem of infant industries in the East facing competitors from the established producers in West. Poor infrastructure and the relative lack of experience of East Pakistani management and labor contributed to high production costs. Because East and West Pakistan constituted one currency and economic union without interregional mobility of labor, there was no way of protecting East Pakistani industries. Even fiscal concessions were inadequate or absent. The alternative was to grant infant industry subsidies to East Pakistani enterprises or temporarily to raise tariffs against West. Neither of these alternatives was pursued.

The technique of industrial planning by means of the industrial investment schedule worked on occasion against the interests of East Pakistan's development. In a situation where private enterprises were inadequate and shy, putting limits on them in specific areas had the effect of thwarting them altogether. Investment that was attracted to a specific line of activity in the East was not sanctioned if it was thought to be duplicating existing capacity in the West. Although the industrial schedule prevented investment in the East in areas in which it would compete with industrial capacity in West, sufficiently effective measures were not undertaken to ensure that in other areas where the schedule permitted investment in East Pakistan investment did in fact materialize. The net result of this licensing policy was a shortfall in total investment in East Pakistan. Ideally economic policy should have promoted an efficient pattern of regional specialization, along with effective measures to overcome the short-run disadvantages of the East in terms of the limited availability of social and economic infrastructure. The cost advantages of many footloose industries, especially those dependent upon imported raw materials, were often a matter of historical accident. Therefore, a policy of specialization with a long-term perspective would have justified industrialization in East Pakistan beyond the point to which it was promoted.

One of the principal means of promoting private investment was the development of financial institutions that were intended to grant loans, to invest in equities, and to float and underwrite the shares and debentures of private enter-

13. IBRD, *Industrialization of Pakistan, The Record, the Problems and the Prospects* (1970), vol. 3, pp. 25–30, and USAID, *An Approach to Accelerating Industrial Growth in East Pakistan* (Dacca, Feb. 1970).

Table 13.3.   East Pakistan's Share in Financial Assistance (Percentage share)

IDBP (1961/62-1967/68)	*PICIC* (1960-67)	*Scheduled banks* (1963-66)	*NIT* (1963-68)	*ICP* (1966/67)	*Total*
47	30	32	23	40	32

Source: A. Rab, *Institutional Finance for Private Sector Industry in Pakistan* (EPIDC) Industrial Development Seminar, Dacca, Oct. 1968.

prises. The role of these financial agencies was highly concentrated in West Pakistan. The share of the East in financial assistance provided to the private sector by the primary financing agencies is given in table 13.3.[14]

The low share of East Pakistan in the financial assistance provided by these agencies was partly due to the fact that some of these organizations were designed for large-scale enterprises whereas East Pakistan's entrepreneurs were mostly small investors, and partly due to the fact that East Pakistan entrepreneurs suffered from the problem of the equity gap. The financing agencies insisted on a certain safe ratio of debt to equity. Because the capital market was virtually absent in East Pakistan there was no way of combining the equity capital of a large number of shareholders and thereby attracting bank financing. The individual entrepreneurs could not amass adequate financial resources of their own.

Total private investment in East Pakistan was in any event grossly deficient. Its share in the sector was smaller than that in public investment. Therefore with a higher population the disparity in per capita total investment was considerably greater.

Public Investment

The most important aspect of government policy with respect to regional development was the pattern of public expenditure. This could have been used to offset the disparity in private investment but it accentuated it. East Pakistan's share in total development expenditure, both public and private, did not exceed 36 percent of total expenditures, public and private, during the entire two decades of Pakistan's development efforts (table 13.4).

Until 1964/65 the East's share did not exceed 31 percent. East Pakistan's growth potential was sacrificed during the 1950s by limiting its share in develop-

14. Industrial Development Bank of Pakistan (IDBP) was catering mainly to medium- and small-scale industries. PICIC was a channel for the inflow of foreign equity capital, partly financed by the International Finance Corporation (IFC) (IBRD), and was engaged primarily in financing by participation in the equities of the larger enterprises. The National Investment Trust (NIT) and the Investment Corporation of Pakistan (ICP) were underwriting and investing in industrial shares and debentures. A. Rab, *Institutional Finance for Private Sector Industry in Pakistan* (EPIDC) Industrial Development Seminar, Dacca, Oct. 1968.

Table 13.4.   East Pakistan's Share in Development Expenditure (In percent)

	Public	*Private*	*Total*
1950/51–1954/55	26	13	20
1955/56–1959/60	33	20	32
1960/61–1964/65	40	22	31
1965/66–1969/70	51	26	36

Sources: Planning Commission, *Report of the Panel of Economists for the Fourth Five Year Plan* (Islamabad, 1970). Also, unpublished estimates from the Planning Commission.

ment expenditures to about 20 percent.[15] That was precisely the period when a big push was necessary to overcome whatever initial disadvantages were suffered by East Pakistan. It was during the 1950s that heavy investments were made in West Pakistan which started to yield results during the 1960s. The fact that the East's share in public development expenditure was no more than one-third of the total during the first decade had particularly adverse consequences for East Pakistan's future growth. First, during this period, total public development expenditure played a predominant role in aggregate development expenditure in view of the limited role of the private sector in the early years. Thus, a low share in public development expenditure meant a low share in total expenditures. In view of the poor performance of private enterprise in East Pakistan, only public expenditure could have offset the disadvantage. A large share of public expenditure in the eastern region could have prevented the widening disparity in per capita incomes between the two regions. Instead, the larger share for the West only aggravated the disparity in water, power, and infrastructural development. During the First Five Year Plan public expenditure constituted about 64 percent of the total development expenditure.

It was during the 1950s that foundations for future growth in terms of building up physical infrastructure were laid. Not only was there inadequate public expenditure in East Pakistan but also no more than 20 percent of East Pakistan's public expenditure was devoted to transport and communications and a mere 8 percent was spent in physical planning and housing.[16]

In the 1960s there was an improvement in the East's share of public development expenditure but this was not enough to redress the imbalance in view of the very slow growth in private investment. This was also the period when the relative role of public expenditure declined. During the Second and Third Five

15. The figures for public sector development expenditures and private investment are derived from the Planning Commission, *Report of the Panel of Economists*.

16. Akhlaqur Rahman, "The Role of the Public Sector in Economic Development of Pakistan," in E. A. G. Robinson and M. Kidion, eds., *Economic Development in South Asia* (New York: MacMillan, 1970), pp. 10–11.

Table 13.5.   West Pakistan's Per Capita
Development Expenditure as a Multiple of East
Pakistan's

1951/52–1954/55	4.90
1955/56–1959/60	3.44
1960/61–1964/65	2.59
1965/66–1969/70	2.18

Source: Planning Commission, *Report of the Panel of Economists.*

Year Plans public and private development expenditures were roughly of equal magnitude (table 13.5). An improvement in the East's share in public expenditure, which itself was of declining importance, was not sufficient to arrest the growth in disparity. In terms of per capita share in development expenditure the inequality was larger.

Not only did the public investment in the East not increase adequately to redress the regional imbalance in income, but also its pattern or sectoral distribution did not meet the requirements of growth in East Pakistan. In spite of a great disparity in the availability of social and physical infrastructure, the pattern of allocation of public expenditure to both regions was roughly similar during the Second and Third Five Year Plans. The West's relative development expenditures in the most crucial areas of transport and communications and water and power were consistently higher than those in the East. During the Third Plan, however, there was some improvement in the education, training, and health sectors in East Pakistan.[17]

In revenue expenditure too the East's share was very small, as seen in table 13.6. The disparity was particularly acute in defense expenditure. There was a heavy concentration of military establishments in West Pakistan from the preindependence days. West Pakistan's inheritance of military establishments was considerably buttressed by Pakistan's policy of speeding up defense expenditures in that wing. Moreover, the social infrastructure, such as roads and railway tracks built for defense purposes in West Pakistan, contributed substantially to economic development. The major cities in West Pakistan developed around the major cantonment centers. The external economic effects of construction of large cantonment towns, in the form of extension of transport and communication facilities as well as the supply of power and water, greatly promoted general economic development. The establishment of such facilities as hospitals and

17. Planning Commission, *Evaluation of the Second Five-Year Plan* (May 1970). See also Planning Commission, "Planned Public Sector Development Expenditure during the Third Plan," unpublished memorandum (1970), annex III, pp. 10–11.

Table 13.6. Revenue (Nondevelopment and noninvestment) Expenditures in West Pakistan as a Multiple of Those in East Pakistan

1951/52–1954/55	5.0
1955/56–1959/60	4.0
1960/61–1960/65	3.5
1965/66–1969/70	5.5

Source: Planning Commission, *Report of the Panel of Economists.*

schools in such areas catered not only to the military establishments but also to the civilian population in the surrounding areas.

The economic benefits of a large army and associated defense expenditures on physical facilities, infrastructure, and industrial output cannot be ignored. Although defense expenditure was not productive as an equivalent expenditure on economic activities, i.e., agriculture and industry, not all of it was pure consumption expenditure. A substantial amount was spent on physical infrastructures useful for general economic development. Participation in the armed forces was predominantly by West Pakistanis (about 90–92%); the benefits of military expenditure thus were heavily concentrated in West Pakistan. Even the additional income generated by the high employment in the defense services in West Pakistan provided an extension of the market for the goods and services of the civilian industry located in West Pakistan near the source of demand. The direct and indirect economic benefits of the location of the predominant share of the administrative expenditures of the government in West Pakistan further strengthened the economic position of that wing in terms of expanded income and employment generation as well as modernization of the economy.

INTERREGIONAL TRADE AND DISPARITY

The central government regulated and controlled international trade but trade between East and West was free of both quantitative restrictions and tariffs. Although interregional trade was free of controls, allocation of resources for investment between regions was largely determined by the government without adequate attention to opportunity cost criteria. Thus East–West Pakistan trade was influenced mostly by the pattern and magnitude of demand because conditions of supply were largely predetermined by the controlled allocation of investment.

At the time of Pakistan's independence its two regions were economically integrated with the adjoining areas of India by means of a well coordinated network of transport and communications, which facilitated not only trade but also the movement of factors, especially labor.[18] West Pakistan supplied wheat and cotton to the industrial areas of northwestern India and provided the market for finished goods, whereas East Pakistan supplied jute and rice and provided the market for the industrial areas of eastern India. The customs union represented by preindependence India was disrupted at the time of partition. A new customs union was formed between East and West Pakistan but without much mobility of labor. Decisions with respect to trade and industrial investment were centralized in the government of Pakistan, whose seat was located in and mostly manned by West Pakistan. The great bulk of public and private investment also took place there. Import substitution proceeded apace under heavy protection mainly in West Pakistan (for reasons already discussed), except in industries such as raw jute, where raw material was a crucial determinant of location. The cumulative effect of the initial decisions to locate most industrial investment, by both the public and private sectors, in West Pakistan was to generate built-in advantages for West Pakistan in the subsequent industrialization process.

It was in the context of this evolving pattern of regional development that interregional trade developed. Interregional trade in agricultural commodities followed the natural and climatic advantages of each region. In manufactures, trade followed the pattern of industrialization that developed in both regions. Each region replaced imports from abroad by imports from the other region. East Pakistan's imports from West Pakistan, as a proportion of its total imports, increased from 40 percent during this period of 1948/49 to 1954/55 to 46 percent during 1965/59 to 1968/69.[19] East Pakistan's exports to West Pakistan, as a proportion of its total exports, increased from 12 percent during the early 1950s to 34 percent during the late 1960s. Similarly, West Pakistan's imports from the East, as a proportion of its total imports, grew from 7 percent in the early 1950s to 19 percent during the late 1960s and its exports to the East, as a proportion of its total exports, increased from 26 to 46 percent. The progress in economic interdependence between the two wings was predominantly in terms of a market for West Pakistan's manufactured exports in the East. There was an absolute decline in many individual imports of East Pakistan from abroad. This was accompanied by a compensating increase in imports of the same commodities or their substitutes from West Pakistan. In the case of some commodities there was no absolute decline in imports from abroad but there was an increase in imports from West Pakistan to meet rising demands. As the restrictions in imports from abroad were tightened, there was a corresponding growth in interregional trade.

The East's imports from the West consisted predominantly of manufactured

18. M. A. Rahman, *Partition, Integration, Economic Growth and Interregional Trade* (Karachi: Pakistan Institute of Development Economics, 1963).

19. N. Islam, "Some Aspects of Interwing Trade and Terms of Trade in Pakistan," *Pakistan Development Review* 3, no. 1 (Spring 1963): 1–36.

goods that were previously imported from abroad. Forty percent of its imports from the West were agricultural commodities such as rice, raw cotton, mustard, rapeseed, and unmanufactured tobacco. Some of these commodities, such as raw cotton, could not be grown in East Pakistan, and the importation of other items, such as rice and seeds, were necessitated by stagnation of agriculture in East Pakistan in the early period. The manufactured imports of East from West were highly diversified and consisted of a large number of items. In 1963/64 about 30 percent of the total imports of East from West consisted of cotton manufactures; another 5 percent was machinery and the rest of the manufactured imports (constituting about 25% of total imports) consisted of many small individual items. West Pakistan's imports from the East, on the other hand, were few and comprised of a small number of commodities. Even though agricultural commodities comprised 40 percent of its imports, tea comprised 35 percent of the total imports. Forty-five percent of the total imports from the East and 80 percent of manufactured imports consisted of four manufactured items: jute manufactures (22%), paper (12%), matches (6%), and leather manufactures (5%).[20]

The relative importance of interregional trade in manufactured goods was greater for the West than for the East. For some manufactured exports the proportion of total exports going to the East was as high as 80–90 percent. These exports were cement, medicine, machinery, paper and pasteboards, and tobacco manufactures. Chemicals, books and stationery, basic metals, rubber manufactures, soap, and cotton manufactures and other textiles accounted for 50–60 percent of West Pakistan's total exports to East Pakistan. In the case of the rest of the manufactured items the proportion of total exports going to the East varied between 20 and 30 percent. Only in two manufactured items, matches and paper manufactures, was East Pakistan's export dependence on West's market high, i.e., 80 percent of its total exports in these items went to West Pakistan. In leather the proportion was about 35 percent and in its most important manufactured export, jute, the proportion was about 25 percent.[21] Furthermore, manufactures as a whole were a greater proportion of West Pakistan's total exports, of which a large share was exported to East Pakistan. Therefore, West Pakistan's dependence on the latter as an export market was substantial.

Interregional Transfer of Resources

The exchange rate policy pursued in Pakistan, which created a wide array of effective exchange rates for different exports and imports, implied that East and West were faced with different exchange rates as a result of a different commod-

20. Ibid.
21. Ibid.

ity composition of exports and imports in the two regions. There was an additional complication in terms of the effective exchange rates of imports insofar as part of East Pakistan's exports abroad were exchanged for imports not from abroad but from West Pakistan. The rupee cost of a dollar's worth of imports was not simply the CIF price of overseas imports in East Pakistan multiplied by the taxes and bonus premium in the case of bonus imports, for example, but also the rupee cost of a dollar's worth of imports from West Pakistan. The weights in determining the effective import exchange rate of East Pakistan should include different categories of imports from West and from abroad, which carried different exchange rates (table 13.7). The exchange rates applicable to imports from West Pakistan would be determined by the differential between prices at which they are available in the East and their world prices. If we assume that the prices of West Pakistani commodity exports to the East were the same as the domestic prices of the competing foreign imports in the West, the effective exchange rates for exports to East Pakistan would be the relevant basis for the estimation of the effective exchange rate for imports from West Pakistan. However, in this case the effective exchange rates would include the scarcity margin on the landed cost of competing imports because the prices of domestically produced goods were equal to the landed cost plus the scarcity margin on competing imported goods (table 13.8).[22]

Throughout the period from 1950 to 1970 East Pakistan had a surplus in the balance of visible foreign trade except for three years. West Pakistan, except in 1950/51, had a deficit in the balance of visible foreign trade. Both East and West Pakistan had a deficit in the balance of invisible trade throughout the period. The deficit of West Pakistan on account of invisible trade was considerably higher than that of East Pakistan.[23] The balance of payments for East and West Pakistan for various periods is shown in table 13.9.

22. The effective exchange rates in table 13.7 are calculated as follows. The exchange rate for foreign imports in East or West Pakistan is equal to the landed cost of foreign imports, i.e., import price plus import duty plus sales tax in the case of imports under normal licensing, and is equal to the landed cost of imports plus bonus premium or premium on bonus vouchers for imports under the Export Bonus Scheme.

The exchange rate for imports of one part of Pakistan from another part is equal to the landed cost of foreign imports into a part of Pakistan (import price plus import duty plus sales tax and bonus premium added to it in the case of bonus imports) plus the scarcity margin on the landed cost of such imports in the domestic market, which compete with commodities produced in one part of Pakistan and exported to the other. The landed costs of imports are the weighted average of the landed costs of two types of imports, i.e., imports under the Export Bonus Scheme and those under normal licensing. In table 13.8 effective exchange rates for foreign imports include scarcity margins in the case of imports under both the bonus scheme and normal licensing. Such rates are higher than those in table 13.7.

23. Separate data on the exports and imports of East and West Pakistan were published by the Central Statistical Office (*Monthly Statistical Bulletins*). However, the data on the invisible receipts

Table 13.7. Effective Exchange Rate (Excluding scarcity margins on landed cost of foreign imports) for Foreign and Domestic Imports from East and West Pakistan (Rs per dollar)

	1955/56–1959/60	*1963/64–1964/65*	*1965/66*	*1968/69*
East Pakistan				
From West Pakistan	13.72	15.99	17.06	18.26
From rest of world	8.20	9.23	10.44	10.55
Bonus	15.47	15.34	16.86	17.76
Normal licensing	7.61	8.73	9.92	9.96
Total	10.73	12.33	13.48	14.09
West Pakistan				
From East Pakistan	10.81	12.30	13.05	13.97
From rest of world	8.89	9.83	11.13	11.19
Bonus	15.69	15.80	17.54	18.42
Normal licensing	8.06	9.10	10.34	10.30
Total	9.20	10.23	11.44	11.64

Export		
	1955/56–1959/60	*1963/64–1964/65*	*1968/69*
East	4.42	4.78	5.30
West	4.61	5.57	5.91

Sources: W. E. Hecox, ''The Export Performance Licensing Scheme,'' *Pakistan Development Review* 10, no. 1 (Spring 1970): 30–31; idem,*The Use of Import Privileges: As Incentive to Exporters in Pakistan,* Pakistan Institute of Development Economics, Research Report no. 30 (Karachi: 1966); Nurul Islam, *Export Incentive and Responsiveness of Exports in Pakistan: A Quantitative Analysis,* Yale Economic Growth Center, Discussion Paper no. 58m (Oct. 1968); Government of Pakistan, Planning Commission, International Economic Section, *A Background Note on Bonus Exports during the Third Plan* (Rawalpindi, Sept. 1969); Government of Pakistan, Ministry of Finance, ''Report of the Working Group on the Export Bonus Scheme,'' unpublished (Rawalpindi, 1964), pp. 20–21: Government of Pakistan, Report of the Working Group on Rupee Resource Projections (Islamabad, 1968), pp. 22–24; and N. Islam, *Nature and Impact of Export Incentives and Effective Export Subsidy,* Pakistan Institute of Development Economics, Research Report no. 86 (1968).

---

and payments were not available separately for each region. They were available for the entire country; regional shares were decided by certain criteria; and alternative criteria of dividing regional shares did not yield very different estimates. The criteria for the regional division of the invisible receipts and payments from 1961/62 onward were those used by the Planning Commission. The criteria used for the earlier years follow roughly the same principles as those used by the Planning Commission for 1960s. (*Report of the Panel of Economists* [Islamabad, May 1970]).

Table 13.8   Effective Exchange Rate (Including scarcity margins on landed cost of foreign imports) for Foreign and Domestic Imports from East and West Pakistan (Rs per dollar)

	1955/56–1959/60	*1963/64–1964/65*	*1965/66*	*1968/69*
East Pakistan				
From West Pakistan	13.72	15.99	17.06	18.26
From rest of world	11.33	12.74	14.15	14.28
Bonus	15.74	16.56	19.30	20.40
Normal licensing	10.97	12.43	13.73	13.78
Total	12.43	14.23	15.49	16.11
West Pakistan				
From East Pakistan	10.81	12.30	13.05	13.97
From rest of world	11.76	13.51	14.66	14.72
Bonus	16.09	17.29	19.97	20.97
Normal licensing	11.23	13.05	14.01	13.96
Total	11.61	13.31	14.40	14.60

Source: See table 13.7.

In the foregoing estimates, foreign balance is evaluated at the official exchange rate. But the domestic prices of both exportables and importables and hence foreign exchange earnings or receipts were worth more in rupees than their equivalents valued at the official exchange. In order to ensure comparability between foreign balance and balance in interwing trade, which was recorded in domestic prices, the foreign balance should be converted into domestic prices by using an estimate of the scarcity price of foreign exchange.[24]

Without any adjustment for the overvaluation of exchange, East Pakistan's balance of payments with the rest of the world including West Pakistan had a consistent surplus from 1948/49 to 1954/55. From the mid-1950s it started to develop a deficit in its overall balance of payments. For the entire period until 1960/61 East Pakistan was still left with a surplus of Rs 592.5 million for the entire period from 1948/49 to 1960/61. If corrected for the underestimate owing to overvaluation of the rupee (as shown in table 13.10), the surplus of the same period amounts to Rs 5.377 billion, ten times the surplus estimated without any adjustment of the exchange rate. During the 1960s East Pakistan's deficit after adjustment was about Rs 9.386 billion, i.e., 50 percent higher than what it was without adjustment, whereas West Pakistan's deficit was 2.2 times larger than what it was without adjustment.

The relative importance of the interregional resource flow can be evaluated in

24. Aminul Islam, "An Estimation of the Extent of Overvaluation of the Domestic Currency in Pakistan at the Official Rate of Exchange, 1948/49–1964/65," *Pakistan Development Review* 10, no. 1 (Spring 1970): 50–67. The extent of overvaluation is assumed to have remained unchanged between 1964/65 and 1968/69.

Table 13.9.   Balance of Payments of East and West Pakistan (Rs million)

	Balance of visible foreign trade		*Balance of invisible foreign trade*		*Balance of visible and invisible foreign trade*		*Balance of interregional trade*	*Net balance of payment*	
	East	*West*	*East*	*West*	*East*	*West*	*East*	*East*	*West*
1948/49-1949/50	+1,123	−806	−195	−412	+928	−1,218	−306	+622	−912
1950/51-1954/55	+2,122	−1,002	−587	−1,400	+1,537	−2,402	−809	+726	−1,593
1955/56-1960/61	+2,019	−5,175	−907	−2,304	+1,112	−7,479	−1,868	−756	−5,612
1948/49-1960/61	+5,364	−6,983	−1,690	−4,116	+3,577	−11,099	−2,983	+593	−8,116
1961/62-1968/69	+69	−14,645	−2,829	−4,300	−2,760	−21,946	−3,766	−6,526	−1,818

Sources: Government of Pakistan, Central Statistical Office, *Monthly Statistical Bulletins*; idem, Planning Commission, *Report of the Panel of Economists* (Islamabad, May 1970); Aminul Islam, "An Estimation of the Extent of Overvaluation of the Domestic Currency in Pakistan at the Official Rate of Exchange, 1948/49-1964/65," *Pakistan Development Review* 10, no. 1 (Spring 1970); 50- 67; IBRD, *Industrialization of Pakistan, The Record, the Problems and the Prospects* (1970), vol. 3, pp. 25-30; and U.S. Agency for International Development, *An Approach to Accelerating Industrial Growth in East Pakistan* (Dacca, Feb. 1970).

relation to (a) the regional domestic product and (b) the gross fixed investment or development expenditure in each of the regions.[25]

During the early 1950s the transfer of resources from the East in nominal prices constituted 1.24 percent of its regional income whereas, in terms of scarcity prices, it was as high as 6.48 percent during the same period. This transfer took place during a time when East Pakistan registered a decline in per capita income. During the second half of 1950s, even though East's balance of payments registered a deficit in nominal price, amounting to 0.7 percent of regional income, in terms of scarcity price it transferred about one-half of 1 percent of its regional income to the West.[26] West Pakistan, on the other hand, consistently enjoyed an inflow of resources from the East and abroad; in nominal

25. The data on the gross regional domestic product were available in constant prices of 1959/60 starting in 1948/49. Their conversion into current prices was only possible for the years starting 1950/51. Because the balance of payments and resource flows are expressed in current prices, the relationship of resource flow to gross regional product could be traced only for the years 1950/51 onward. The constant price regional income from 1950/51 to 1959/60 was taken from T. M. Khan and A. Bergan. It was converted into current price on the basis of regional prices indices for East and West Pakistan. See also S. R. Lewis, "Effects of Trade Policy on Domestic Relative Prices: Pakistan, 1951-64," *American Economic Review* 58, no. 1 (Mar. 1968): 60-78.

26. Khan and Bergan, "Measurement of Structural Change," and Lewis, "Effects of Trade Policy."

Table 13.10.   Balance Payments of East and West Pakistan (In scarcity price of foreign exchange)

	Balance of visible and invisible foreign trade		Interregional trade	Net balance of payments	
	East	West	East	East	West
1948/49–1949/50	+2,102	−2,919	−306	+1,796	−2,614
1950/51–1954/55	+4,135	−6,407	−809	+3,325	−5,597
1955/56–1960/61	+21,135	−14,554	−1,868	+247	−12,686
1948/49–1960/61	+8,350	−13,881	−2,983	+5,377	−20,898
1961/62–1968/69	−5,620	−43,841	−3,766	−9,386	−40,075

Sources: See table 13.9.

price the inflow of resources increased from 2.7 percent of its regional income within the early 1950s to 9.2 percent in the first half of the 1960s and went down to 5.8 percent toward the end of the 1960s. In terms of the scarcity price of foreign exchange, the inflow of external resources to the West increased from 10 percent in the early 1950s to 20 percent of regional income in the early 1960s; it dropped to 13.3 percent toward the end of the 1960s (as shown in table 13.11).

It is apparent from the above that West Pakistan's dependence on resource inflow was considerable. It was highest in the late 1950s during the First Five Year Plan. The external resource inflow constituted 50 percent of development expenditure and 68 percent of the fixed investment in West Pakistan during the period (as shown in tables 13.12 and 13.13). During the early 1960s the ratio of external resources to both development expenditure and fixed investment declined to 45 percent and in the late 1960s to 33 percent. In East Pakistan the dependence on external resources, when resource flow was evaluated in nominal prices, did not exceed one-third of either development expenditure or fixed investment. The highest dependence reached was 33.5 percent of fixed investment in the early 1960s.

The above analysis of total resource flow into each region from outside the regions[27] does include the effect of the flow of foreign aid to both regions. Each region's imports were partly financed by foreign assistance but the figures of interregional flows given do not take this into account.

The total amount of foreign economic assistance between 1948/49 and 1960/61 was estimated to be Rs 15.610 billion, valued at the scarcity price of foreign exchange. East Pakistan's share was estimated to be Rs 4.840 billion. During the

27. The other wing of Pakistan and foreign countries.

Table 13.11.   Interregional Resource Inflow (Ratio of resource flow to GDP in percent or balance of payments deficit as a percentage of GDP)

	Unadjusted for overvaluation		*With adjustment for overvaluation*	
	East	*West*	*East*	*West*
1950/51– 1954/55	+1.2	−2.7	+6.5	−10.1
1955/56– 1959/60	−0.8	−5.8	+0.5	−13.4
1960/61– 1964/65	−3.4	−9.2	−4.6	−20.1
1965/66– 1969/70	−3.6	−5.8	−5.2	−13.3

Sources: Aminul Islam, "An Estimation of the Extent of Overvaluation of the Domestic Currency in Pakistan at the Official Rate of Exchange, 1948/49-1964/65," *Pakistan Development Review* 10, no. 1 (Spring 1970) 50-67; T. M. Khan and A. Bergan, "Measurement of Structural Change in the Pakistan Economy: A Review of National Income Estimates, 1949/50 to 1963/64," *Pakistan Development Review* 6, no. 2 (Summer 1966): 163-208; S. R. Lewis, "Effects of Trade Policy on Domestic Relative Prices: Pakistan, 1951-64," *American Economic Review* 58, no. 1 (Mar. 1968): 60-78; IBRD, *Industrialization of Pakistan, The Record, the Problems and the Prospects* (1970), vol. 3, pp. 25-30; and U.S. Agency for International Development, *An Approach to Accelerating Industrial Growth in East Pakistan* (Dacca, Feb. 1970).

same period East Pakistan had a surplus on balance of payments of Rs 5.370 billion. If the imports financed by foreign aid were deducted from the East's balance of payments, it had a surplus of Rs 10.210 billion rather than of Rs 5.370 billion. East Pakistan, therefore, had transferred to West Pakistan Rs 10.210 billion during the period, which worked out at about Rs 800 million annually. The transfer constituted about 6.5 percent of its regional income and 6.1 percent of West Pakistan's regional income. During the 1960s (1961/62-1968/69) the magnitude of the transfer was much less, amounting to about Rs 640 million annually. The East's deficit was Rs 9.390 billion for the period (1961/62-1969/69) and its share of foreign aid was Rs 14.490 billion for the same period. The excess of aid over the estimated deficit in balance of payments constituted the transfer to West Pakistan, which on average constituted 2.9 percent of East's regional income and 2.4 percent of the West's regional income.[28] In both periods East Pakistan exchanged its own earned foreign exchange for a share in foreign aid.

It could be argued that a transfer of resources of this magnitude to the West

28. The average population of East Pakistan during the 1950s was about 50 million, which increased to about 64 million during the 1960s. East Pakistan transferred Rs 16 and 10 per head in the earlier and later periods, respectively.

Table 13.12.   Ratio of Resource Inflow to Development Expenditure in Percent (Without adjustment for exchange rate)

	East	West
1950/51– 1954/55	outflow	39.5
1955/56 1959/60	20.0	56.0
1960/61 1964/65	31.5	45.0
1965/66– 1967/70	28.8	33.0

Sources: The data on development expenditures and fixed investment are from *Report of the Panel of Economists,* p. 6, table 2, and investment figures are from (a) M. Akhlaqur Rahman, *The Private Sector of East Pakistan: An Analysis of Lagged Development* (Karachi: United Bank Limited, 1970), p. 73, for 1954/55–1958/59; (b) J. J. Stern, "Growth Development and Regional Equity," in *Development Policy II: The Pakistan Experience,* Harvard University, Center for International Affairs (1970), tables 1–3, p. 1.48 (mimeographed copy) for 1961/62 and 1962/63; (c) Planning Commission, *Final Evaluation of the Second Five Year Plan (1960–65),* Dec. 1966, p. 181, and IBRD, *Current Economic Position and Prospects, 1970,* vol. 2, tables 2.1.1, and 2.1.2.

Note: Development expenditure is distinguished from fixed investment in that the former includes noninvestment expenditure such as subsidies on fertilizers, current expenditure during the period of construction of an investment project, and subsidies on water charges or irrigation projects and subsidies on seeds or pesticides.

was in fact a payment for invisible services that the East had received from the West. The most important components of these services were (1) defense and administrative services of the central government located in the West and (2) services of the West Pakistan entrepreneurs working in the East. These factors were not quantifiable but it was doubtful that the entire transfer could be explained by them. East Pakistan's representatives in central services, both defense and nondefense, had been meager and a source of constant friction and complaint between East and West Pakistan. Not only was East Pakistan's representation in the services low but also the armed services were located in West Pakistan, providing indirect beneficial effects to the West.

Even assuming that the transfer was necessary, it was not obvious that the form in which this transfer was made was either efficient or equitable from the point of view of East Pakistan. A more equitable method would be for it to surrender foreign aid to an equivalent amount and keep for its own use the corresponding foreign exchange out of its own earnings. To surrender East Pakistan's own foreign exchange earnings for foreign aid was disadvantageous for East Pakistan for several reasons. One was the high cost of imported goods obtained under tied aid against the opportunity of buying imported goods in the cheapest market with its own foreign exchange earnings. The cost of com-

Table 13.13.   Ratio of Resource Flow to Fixed
Investment in Percent (Without adjustment for
exchange rate)

	East	*West*
1950/55–1959/60	20.0	68.2
1960/61–1964/65	33.5	45.0
1965/66 1969/70	31.3	31.5

Sources and *Note:* See table 13.12.

modities under tied aid was at least one-third higher so that the foreign exchange it received under tied aid was worth at least one-third less than the foreign exchange it surrendered. Second, aid was available only for the purchase of imported intermediate goods or capital goods. Such aid did not finance the purchase of wage goods from abroad so that the development projects or economic activities that required expenditure on domestic inputs and wage goods and that had a low import component had to suffer. The domestic resources component of development projects was in short supply in East Pakistan, which increasingly needed wage goods to undertake projects that had a low foreign exchange component. With its free exchange it could purchase wage goods wherever necessary from abroad to mount a larger development program. Third, surrender of foreign exchange in return for foreign aid not only involved high cost and built-in inflexibility but also involved a repayment and interest burden. West Pakistan received a free gift whereas East Pakistan undertook an obligation to repay and pay debt service charges until the external debt was repaid. Thus it was quite conceivable that East Pakistan should have surrendered foreign aid or reduced its import surplus from West Pakistan rather than surrender its free foreign exchange. Of course if Pakistan established an equilibrium rate of exchange in some sense and if there was perfect substitutability between imports (from the West and from abroad), there was nothing to choose between an import surplus from West Pakistan and free foreign exchange resources to be imported from abroad.

CONCLUSION

There were other countries in the world where regional disparity in income and development existed. The situation in Pakistan, however, had some distinctive features and characteristics that set it apart from the rest. Because mobility of labor and other factors of production are severely limited by distance and costs of transportation, as well as by language and culture, the growing disparities in development and income could not be arrested by the equilibrating role of factor movements. The absolute level of per capita income of East Pakistan was one of the lowest in the world. If growth in income in the East was considerably accelerated, the unfavorable social and political implications of regional disparity would have been less. But during most of the period the East Pakistan economy stagnated and could feel the pinch of regional disparity.

The poorer region not only stagnated but consistently transferred resources for the development of the richer West Pakistan, which was facilitated by the Pakistan trade policy. Although the inflow of foreign aid accelerated, East Pakistan's share in it remained small relative to any criterion (e.g., per head of population or as a proportion of regional income).

East Pakistan accounted for the majority of Pakistan's population. This was unique. In most situations of regional disparity the poorer region also formed a smaller part of the country in terms of population.

It was not until the Third Five Year Plan that the reduction in disparity became one of the objectives of the planning process. However, as it took many years for the principle or the objective to be recognized, so also there was always a lag between recognition of a principle and its implementation. By this time the disparity issue had become highly political. It was inevitably linked with the inadequate representation of East Pakistan in the administrative and political decision-making process in the country. The introduction of army rule in 1958 effectively ruled out the participation of East Pakistan in economic decisions. The political dominance of the West became closely interlinked with economic domination, which was both cause and consequence of the former. The tide of Bengali nationalism gathered momentum in the late 1960s on the twin grievances of economic stagnation and political deprivation. Pakistan lay in shambles in March 1971 as an armed attempt was made to crush Bengali aspirations. Out of this emerged an independent Bangladesh.

14

Conclusions

Pakistan had an impressive achievement to its credit in terms of industrial growth, especially the growth rate of large-scale manufacturing industry. Its record of achievement in the field of agriculture was not comparable. In fact, except for a brief period of five years (between 1960 and 1965) agriculture had been a lagging sector, resulting in an increasing volume of food imports during the late 1960s, especially for East Pakistan.

The country's performance in respect to attainment of an equitable distribution of income, expansion of employment, and interregional equity was far from satisfactory. The government introduced a wide range of economic controls and directly intervened in economic activities not only by public investment and ownership of economic enterprises but also by means of licensing of private investments and allocation of the use of foreign exchange resources, control over prices, distribution and allocation of selected domestic inputs and outputs, and rationing of credit and financing resources through public financing institutions. Economic controls, including trade and foreign exchange controls, were introduced, often on an ad hoc basis, over a number of years in response to the needs of specific sectors and special circumstances such as a changing balance of payments, but they were not coordinated in a systematic manner. As controls proliferated, their consistency was not always ensured and their interrelationships were not closely evaluated. There was no system for overall monitoring of the complex system of controls administered by diverse agencies, each with its limited set of objectives.

The effects of controls in terms of delays, administrative costs, and inflexibility and uncertainty in decision-making processes have been described and analyzed in detail in the preceding chapters. There were social costs of the administration of controls insofar as traders and investors had to maintain contacts with the bureaucratic machinery administering the system of licensing and controls in order to respond to the requirements of controls or to circumvent them or to bend them in their favor. The very nature of the system of controls disallowed frequent and smooth adjustment to the changes in conditions of demand

and supply and had, therefore, a built-in inflexibility. In the administration of the import licensing system there were instances of unutilized licenses for particular commodities on the one hand, and excessive demand for other commodities on the other. The inflexibility in the composition of imports eligible for licensing, despite occasional attempts to introduce adjustments and changes, coupled with the restriction on the transferability of licenses, created rigidities and inefficiencies in the working of the import regime. Changes in the import control system and in the multiple rates of exchange associated with it generated as a consequence an uncertainty about the volume and composition of imports, on the one hand, and about the prices of imports and earnings from exports on the other. This hampered any attempt at a systematic planning of production and investment, especially in the private sector in import intensive industries.

The allocative effects of this system of controls have been documented in the earlier chapters. The exchange control system favored import substitution over export expansion. Moreover, it undertook to make detailed differentiation among individual industries or commodities in terms of both import restriction and export expansion.

Import restrictions, given the limited domestic market in relation to the size and number of potential enterprises in a particular field, constrained the extent of competition in the domestic economy. In view of the risks and uncertainties of export markets, especially in the early years of Pakistan's export promotion drive, including the additional costs of information gathering and selling efforts in the export market, there was a case for a higher exchange rate for exports than for imports. In fact the reverse was the case. In the absence of quantification or lack of evidence to justify the differential infancy or external economies originating in different industries and products, a detailed differentiation of effective exchange rates by commodity was unwarranted and led to inefficiencies and misallocation of resources. The wide dispersion of the domestic resource costs of import substitution or export promotion in various economic activities, resulting from a highly differentiated exchange control system, indicated egregious inefficiencies in the allocation of resources.

Much has been said about the intrasectoral allocation of resources. No less important was the impact of the system of controls, especially exchange controls, on the intersectoral allocation of resources between industry and agriculture. Agriculture was the predominant export sector in Pakistan and hence the discrimination against the export sector inherent in the exchange control system worked against an efficient and fast growth in the agricultural sector. The inputs into the agricultural sector were derived from imports as well as from the outputs of the domestic manufacturing industries. Both these components were available to the farmers only at high scarcity prices in the domestic market created by import restrictions, whereas the receipts from agricultural exports were depressed by the continuation of an overvalued exchange rate. The net returns from the export sector were, therefore, depressed below what would otherwise have been the case under the system of a uniform exchange rate. It is true that over the years, especially in the 1960s, authorities sought to reduce the degree of discrimination against exports substantially but not completely through the introduction of various export incentives. The terms of trade of agriculture deteriorated from the 1950s to the early 1960s because of the combined impact of the exchange control system on the one hand and controls over prices and distribution on the other.

While the returns from the production of export crops were kept depressed through the continuation of overvalued exchange rates throughout the 1950s and 1960s, the prices of import competing crops, mainly food crops or cereals, were also kept low through the government procurement of cereals from domestic producers often at less than free market prices and through the imports of food grains, often financed by aid. Both domestically procured and imported food grains were distributed through the public rationing system at subsidized prices to selected consumers, mainly in the urban areas. However, the depressing effects of low output prices on agricultural development were partly offset by the new, high yielding variety of seeds, used primarily in wheat production in West Pakistan, and by generous subsidies for the use of modern inputs such as irrigation, fertilizers, and pesticides, with a view to increasing the profitability of food production. A substantial increase in food grain production took place in West Pakistan in the early 1960s, contributing to a reduction of foreign exchange constraint and a liberalization of imports, although the bias in the exchange rate system against exports was not completely eliminated.

Subsequently there was an improvement in the terms of trade of agriculture, partly as a result of exchange rate adjustment and partly as a result of domestic pricing policy, which, however, demonstrated that the higher terms of trade of the agricultural sector did not necessarily bring a corresponding improvement in the conditions of the rural poor. There was considerable inequality of ownership of the rural assets, principally land, especially in West Pakistan, which led to an unequal incidence of the benefits of new technology. There was substantial inequality in the distribution of available marketable surplus among the farming households, and consequently the distribution of the benefits of an improvement in terms of trade, which occurred for a brief period, was skewed. Moreover, the pricing policy for imports, including tractors and mechanical implements, brought in at overvalued exchange rates encouraged the use of capital and energy intensive rather than labor intensive technology. The pattern of domestic prices in agriculture that resulted from import controls, export taxes, subsidies, price controls, and rationing, including the control and regulation of acreage under different crops (as in the case of sugar cane and jute), diverged widely from the pattern of world prices. This disparity led to a composition of agricultural output or a cropping pattern that did not truly reflect comparative resource costs, which were conceived in a dynamic and long-run prespective and in the context of the trading opportunities that were open to Pakistan.

The state of progress in agriculture played a crucial role in the changing pattern and intensity of the exchange control system in Pakistan. Progress toward liberalization of the exchange control system in the early 1960s was aided by an improvement in agricultural performance, which brought both an expansion of exports and a reduction of imports of food grains. This situation led to an improved balance of payments and hence to the relaxation of controls over imports. Improvement in agricultural performance also dampened inflation, helped industrial growth by lowering input prices, and increased both private savings and public revenues. By expanding the domestic market for the manufacturing sector, the agricultural sector contributed to an increase in the rate of utilization of capacity and hence to the competitive ability of the manufacturing sector in the export markets through a reduction in costs.

In Pakistan the liberalization of controls and the move toward a greater use of the price mechanism were associated with an improvement in the supply of foreign exchange resources. There was great resistance against relying upon the price mechanism for adjusting demand to supply when the supply shortage was considered acute, despite the demonstrated deficiencies of heavy reliance on numerous, complex, and cumbersome controls. Relaxation of controls was also associated with a larger capital inflow in Pakistan. As was the case with better agricultural performance, foreign capital inflow augmented the supply of foreign exchange resources and relieved the shortage of essential commodities. Hence it gave a fillip to the relaxation of direct controls. With an increase in the total volume of imports there was a tendency to reduce direct controls over the composition, size, use, and destination of imports in the domestic economy. Foreign aid, especially commodity assistance or direct balance of payment support, could act as a catalytic agent in strengthening a trend toward liberalization of the exchange control system when the climate was ripe for a reexamination of the pros and cons of the price and market mechanism. The availability of foreign assistance allays or moderates the apprehension that a relaxation of exchange controls during excess demand may cause a change in price and evoke a response in forces of supply and demand which would be greatly out of line with long-run equilibrium while in the short run it imposes undue distress. Availability of foreign exchange resources, augmented by an inflow of foreign control, provides a cushion to moderate the effects of substantial and abrupt changes in prices. When market forces remain suppressed for a long time under a regime of controls, the policymakers question their ability to predict how prices, supply, and demand would respond to a relaxation of controls. Foreign aid may ease the process of transition.

Pakistan was unable to sustain the process of import liberalization and relaxation of exchange controls introduced in the early 1960s partly because the belief of the policymakers in the effectiveness of the price and market mechanism was weak. Second, the short period of attempted liberalization was not combined with determined efforts to improve the efficiency of the economic system. In this connection failure on three interrelated aspects of economic policymaking was crucial. First, there was the failure to sustain the momentum of agricultural growth initiated in West Pakistan and to extend it to East Pakistan in the face of mounting population pressure. No less important were the shortcomings and inadequacies in the pricing and distribution policy in agriculture. Second, there was the inability to mobilize public and private savings at an accelerated rate—including the failure to constrain an increase in nondevelopment and defense expenditures during and after the 1965 war with India. In respect to public saving, what was especially disturbing were the persistent deficiencies in the management of public enterprises, including an inadequate incentives structure and a faulty pricing and marketing policy, which resulted in either a small surplus or outright losses. Third, economic progress in East Pakistan lagged behind that in West Pakistan, creating economic and political tension within East Pakistan as well as between the two wings of Pakistan. This situation was inimical to political and economic stability and progress in the country as a whole.

At every stage in the history of the exchange control regime, often too little was done too late. It was true that irrespective of Pakistan's exchange rate policy in 1949 and in view of the strained overall political relationship with Pakistan, India would have pursued its policy of promoting self-sufficiency in raw jute production, thus depriving Pakistan of an export market. But at the same time it was clear by 1955 that the prevailing exchange rate could not be sustained and that the degree of devaluation actually undertaken was far from adequate, as was soon demonstrated by subsequent events. Again, when in 1958 another round of effective devaluation was undertaken through the Export Bonus Scheme, it fell short of what was required. Moreover, there was no need and very little economic rationale for the excessive multiplicity of exchange rates that were introduced. By then the dominant political influence was exercised by the new urban industrial class in search of a protected domestic market and cheap subsidized inputs, and by the class of prosperous large farmers who resisted any effort toward a reduction of subsidies on agricultural inputs despite the very substantial profitability of new technology. The deficit farmers and the poorer urban consumers (who were the net purchasers of food) were disadvantaged, except to the extent that they benefited from the public distribution system of food grains.

In the early 1950s it would have not been politically feasible to direct an ample portion of the domestically produced consumption goods (e.g., textiles, sugar, and edible oils) to export markets because of the low level of overall per capita consumption. But there was no reason why in the 1960s substantial increases in income and consumption taxes on the rich and middle income classes could not have been imposed, with a favorable impact on both savings and export performance. The pattern of import substitution followed in Pakistan in the early years was for the most part consistent with comparative cost considerations. The extent of inefficiencies was in many cases significant and there were cases of excessive protection against import competition as well. Most of the inefficiencies were also due to managerial and organizational deficiencies, compounded by taxation and import control policies, including inappropriate incentive structures and pricing policies. It was not readily recognized that public enterprises must generate surplus, should follow the principles of the market mechanism, and above all, have to meet the test of market profitability. This would have necessitated that the public enterprises have the freedom or autonomy to pursue output, wage, employment, and pricing policy in response to supply and demand. The principles governing the behavior of managers of public enterprises could not be very different from those relating to private enterprises in terms of autonomy in decision making and in terms of rewards and penalties for success and failure in management and organization. In view of the large public sector these considerations were crucially important and relevant in the context of the impact of controls on economic growth.

The lesson of Pakistan's experience, as in many other developing countries, demonstrates that given unequal ownership of assets and hence an unequal distribution of economic and political power, the benefits of economic progress, increased output, and productivity are likely to accrue predominantly to those who have higher initial income and assets. This would be true in a system of controls as well as in a system of prices and markets or in a system combining both, unless the policymakers are sufficiently detached from the sources of economic and political power or unless, even if they originate from the dominant class, they have "declassed" themselves sufficiently to pull the levers of power to benefit not the special interest groups but the poor masses and the disadvantaged groups. Economic controls by themselves can not redress poverty or inequality because one cannot be sure how and in whose interests the economic controls were being exercised. How to control the controllers or to plan the planners was the crucial question.

Direct controls in a private enterprise system tend to strengthen disequalizing tendencies operating in the market economy, given (a) the initial unequal distribution of ownership of assets and income and (b) imperfections in the working of the pricing system. The result might be greater inequities in a market economy subject to direct controls than in one in which controls are scarcely used. What is important is to recognize who operates the controls and in whose interests they are operated.

Because of the way in which the licensing system and controls worked in Pakistan, they did restrict competition and encourage monopolistic forces by concentrating access to foreign exchange and investment resources in a few hands. The privileged few with a greater access to scarce resources and to the levers of power added to their economic strength. This aspect of the system retarded a wide diffusion of economic opportunities and brought adverse income distributional effects.

The authoritarian political system was dominated by an alliance between the bureaucratic and military establishments on the one hand and the big landed interests on the other and was supported by an emerging trader-cum-industrial class, which was drawn principally from the former groups. These conditions did not encourage a wide diffusion or sharing of political power or the growth of a political opposition. This situation, combined with a lack of organization among the urban working classes and among the small farmers or landless laborers, discouraged the emergence of a countervailing power that would have substantially mitigated the adverse consequences of the concentration of economic power.

For the poor to take advantage of the price mechanism and the free market forces in the allocation of resources, inputs, and services, including foreign exchange, they need more access to credit and financial facilities than the rich. How can we ensure that disadvantaged groups or regions secure access to credit, inputs, and services provided by the government or by the private market mechanism? The political pressures of special interest groups in Pakistan were operative in the market system as well as in a system of controls. The provision of basic physical and social infrastructures, including education and training and credit facilities, for the poorer groups and for the underdeveloped region of East Pakistan was crucial if they were to take advantage of market opportunities, including access to foreign exchange, even when controls were relatively relaxed. Another factor that aggravated inequality and facilitated the concentration of control of industrial and commercial enterprises was the absence of organized financial intermediaries to mobilize household savings. This could have helped promote investment in noncorporate enterprises by individual private entrepreneurs and diffused ownership of industrial assets. The process of capital accumulation by means of reinvestment of profits in the same or related enterprises led to a concentration of ownership and control of capital assets. It encouraged a vertical and horizontal integration of trading and industrial enterprises. Profits of corporate or noncorporate enterprises were not available for mobilization by financial intermediaries so that those with little or no capital resources of their own but with initiative and enterprise for risk taking could gain access.

The exchange rate system in Pakistan, because of the differential economic structure of East and West Pakistan (the East being predominantly an agricultural exporter), discriminated against East Pakistan. The centralized foreign exchange allocation policy, combined with the inadequate political leverage of East Pakistan, effected a transfer of resources from the poor majority province of East Pakistan to the richer minority province of the West. The exchange rate policy in Pakistan suffered from elasticity pessimism vis-à-vis jute in the export market, which was only slightly eroded in the 1960s by the threat of synthetics. Similarly, there was no systematic attempt over the long run, given the exchange rate policy, to formulate and implement an internal jute-cum-rice pricing policy that would have encouraged an optimum cropping pattern consistent with their comparative costs and world trading opportunities.

In conclusion, experience in Pakistan and in the similarly placed, predominantly private enterprise countries confirms that either unhindered price mechanisms or an all embracing system of controls would rarely prevail in practice. In most mixed economies there will be various combinations and permutations of the market mechanism and controls. An appropriate combination depends upon a number of factors. Foremost among them are the adequacy and quality as well as the honesty and integrity of the bureaucratic machinery. The greater the need for the exercise of discretion and personal judgment in the dispensation of licenses or claims over resources, the greater the risk or the temptation for corruption or the abuse of power for self-advancement. Democratic political institutions and eternal public vigilance in respect to the conduct and public accountability of the administrators are crucial in ensuring an honest and efficient administration of economic policies and controls. At the same time, institutions for the proper functioning of markets must be developed; in this context the role of financial institutions, the encouragement of competitive forces, and easy access to market information regarding the prices and availabilities can hardly be exaggerated.

Moreover, for a system of controls to succeed, it is desirable that they do not operate in a way contrary to what is warranted by the forces of supply and demand. In a situation of excess demand, either of aggregate demand in relation to aggregate supply or in a particular commodity and foreign exchange market, controls are likely to be more effective the greater the extent to which supplementary measures of fiscal and monetary policy or price changes help to restrain demand and increase supply. If other policy measures accentuate rather than reduce imbalance between supply and demand, the measures of direct control either would be less effective or would encourage a misallocation of resources.

For example, in a situation of excess demand, economic controls that keep prices persistently below the long-run supply price would tend to reduce supply and increase demand and thus tend to defeat the very purpose for which they were designed. Under these circumstances the gains from, and hence incentives for, the violation of controls are high.

It must also be noted that overall macroeconomic policy measures such as fiscal and monetary policies do not work very well in a subsistence economy. Their effectiveness presupposes a large monetized sector. In Pakistan direct taxes were relatively unimportant, and indirect taxes, predominantly import taxes and excise duties on domestic production, coupled with public expenditures were the most important fiscal instruments. The banking and monetary policy was ineffective because credit institutions and financial intermediaries covered a relatively small sector of the economy. The rural areas were not well integrated with the urban monetary and financial mechanisms. The same was true about the lack of sufficient integration between the subsistence and monetized sectors of the economy. Economic policy in Pakistan did not succeed in adequately developing institutions as well as physical infrastructure that would have permitted a greater role for indirect macroeconomic policy measures rather than direct controls. In a way their absence inhibited the working of direct controls as well and restricted the range of choice between various policy instruments and detracted from the possibility of their mutual reinforcement.

Index

Adamjee family: investment sanctions, 232
agriculture: Five Year Plan strategies, 11;
  growth rate accelerated, 42; green revolution,
  46n29, 48, 189, 190, 208; performance sum-
  marized, 107–08; Export Bonus Scheme,
  122–23; domestic resource cost, 174–76, 179;
  exchange rate policy's effect, 186; mechanization's private and social costs, 187–89;
  polarization of farmers, 188–89; unemployment in, 189–90; exchange rates, 200–01; intersectoral resource transfer, 200–05; terms of
  trade, 203–05; East and West Pakistan compared, 235; policy summed up, 258–60
aid consortium for Pakistan: foreign aid increases, 42–43
Amjad, R., 216
Aus rice: domestic resource cost, 174–75
Ayub government: "basic democracy" introduced, 15–16; reasons for downfall, 16; political agitation's effect, 222

balance of payments: post-devaluation, 37; uncertainty's effect on imports, 160; East and
  West Pakistan, 248, 250–51, 252
Bangladesh: emergence of, 256
banking: State Bank's use of credit control,
  44–45, 47; bill rediscounting scheme, 81–82
barter agreements, 76–77, 136–37
Bashir family: investment sanctions, 232
basic democracy: introduction, 15–16
bill rediscounting scheme, 81–82
bonus vouchers. See vouchers
Boro. See rice
Bose, S. R., 227

capacity utilization: import controls related,
  190–92

capital goods: contribution to manufacturing
  growth, 62–63; cost ratios, 164–67; imports
  of, 180; capacity utilization, 192
capital intensities: United States, Japan, and
  Pakistan compared, 181–82; small- and
  large-scale industry, 194–97, 228
cash-cum-bonus scheme, 54, 55 and n, 126–27
Central Investment Promotion and Coordination
  Committee, 139–40
civil service's role, 14–15
consumer goods: contribution to manufacturing
  growth, 62–63; cost ratios, 164–67; capacity
  utilization, 192
Controller of Exports and Imports: compulsory
  registration of traders, 29–30
corporate sector: savings rates, 208–11;
  shareholder dividends, 212. See also agriculture; industrial sector; manufacturing sector;
  private sector; public sector
cost ratios: infant industries, 164–65; consumer,
  intermediate, and capital goods, 164–67
cotton: performance as primary export, 89; direct controls on, 151–52; domestic resource
  cost, 175
Cotton Textile Association: export targets enforced, 83
credit: State Bank's control of, 44–45, 47; small-
  and large-scale industry, 196
customs union, 246

Dawood family: investment sanctions, 232
decontrol. See economic controls
deficit financing: post-devaluation, 36–37
devaluation: justifications against, 28–29; India,
  29; justifications for, 33; effect, 32–38. See
  also exchange rates
dividend income: household savings, 211–12

267

Economic Growth Center Book Publications

Werner Baer, *Industrialization and Economic Development in Brazil* (1965).

Werner Baer and Isaac Kerstenetzky, eds., *Inflation and Growth in Latin America* (1964). Out of print.

Bela A. Balassa, *Trade Prospects for Developing Countries* (1964). Out of print.

Albert Berry and Miguel Urrutia, *Income Distribution in Colombia* (1976).

Thomas B. Birnberg and Stephen A. Resnick, *Colonial Development: An Econometric Study* (1975).

Benjamin I. Cohen, *Multinational Firms and Asian Exports* (1975).

Carlos F. Díaz Alejandro, *Essays on the Economic History of the Argentine Republic* (1970).

Robert Evenson and Yoav Kislev, *Agricultural Research and Productivity* (1975).

John C. H. Fei and Gustav Ranis, *Development of Labor Surplus Economy: Theory and Policy* (1964).

Gerald K. Helleiner, *Peasant Agriculture, Government, and Economic Growth in Nigeria* (1966). Out of print.

Samuel P. S. Ho, *Economic Development of Taiwan, 1860–1970* (1978).

Nurul Islam, *Foreign Trade and Economic Controls in Development: The Case of United Pakistan* (1981).

Lawrence R. Klein and Kazushi Ohkawa, eds., *Economic Growth: The Japanese Experience since the Meiji Era* (1968). Out of print.

Paul W. Kuznets, *Economic Growth and Structure in the Republic of Korea* (1977).

A. Lamfalussy, *The United Kingdom and the Six* (1963). Out of print.

Markos J. Mamalakis, *The Growth and Structure of the Chilean Economy: From Independence to Allende* (1976).

Markos J. Mamalakis and Clark W. Reynolds, *Essays on the Chilean Economy* (1965). Out of print.

Donald C. Mead, *Growth and Structural Change in the Egyptian Economy* (1967). Out of print.

Richard Moorsteen and Raymond P. Powell, *The Soviet Capital Stock* (1966). Out of print.

Kazushi Ohkawa and Miyohei Shinohara, eds. (with Larry Meissner), *Patterns of Japanese Economic Development: A Quantitative Appraisal* (1979).

Douglas S. Paauw and John C. H. Fei, *The Transition in Open Dualistic Economies: Theory and Southeast Asian Experience* (1973).

Howard Pack, *Structural Change and Economic Policy in Israel* (1971).

Frederick L. Pryor, *Public Expenditures in Communist and Capitalist Nations* (1968). Out of print.

Gustav Ranis, ed., *Government and Economic Development* (1971).

Clark W. Reynolds, *The Mexican Economy: Twentieth-Century Structure and Growth* (1970). Out of print.

Lloyd G. Reynolds, *Image and Reality in Economic Development* (1977).

Lloyd G. Reynolds, ed., *Agriculture in Development Theory* (1975).

Lloyd G. Reynolds and Peter Gregory, *Wages, Productivity, and Industrialization in Puerto Rico* (1965).

Donald R. Snodgrass, *Ceylon: An Export Economy in Transition* (1966). Out of print.